THE REFERENCE SHELF

Vol. 20   No. 1

REPRESENTATIVE AMERICAN
SPEECHES: 1946-1947

Selected by
A. CRAIG BAIRD
Department of Speech, State University of Iowa

THE H. W. WILSON COMPANY
NEW YORK   1947

PS
668
R4
1946-
47

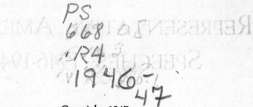

Copyright 1947
By The H. W. Wilson Company

All Rights Reserved

Published October 1947

Printed in the United States of America

3320

287 p.

PREFATORY NOTE

REPRESENTATIVE AMERICAN SPEECHES: 1946-1947 is the tenth in this annual series. Each volume includes some thirty speeches of "representative" orators speaking in the United States. Together these ten volumes include some two hundred speakers and almost three hundred addresses.

The speeches are grouped according to content, such as International Policies, Atomic Energy, Labor Relations. An alternative classification according to speech types can easily be made, such as Congressional Speeches, Eulogies, Professional Lectures, Sermons, Radio Commentaries.

This volume, like the earlier ones, may be used as a reference text for the study of contemporary American problems; as a record of recent history; as subject matter for courses in debate or extempore speaking; as a series of speeches to be included in the systematic study of contemporary American public speaking. The book, then, in addition to its general value for reference workers is especially serviceable to students of extempore speaking, debate, communication, social sciences, history, and general public speaking.

The Introduction to this volume interprets this editor's concepts, standards of good speaking, and his suggestions for a method of criticizing speeches. The brief introduction to each address is a further help in the analysis of the oration as the product of the speaker, audience, occasion, and the address itself.

The Introductions to each of the ten volumes together summarize this editor's philosophy of speechmaking and provide suggestions by which students can make progress as public speakers.

The biographical notes in the Appendix may well be supplemented by the more detailed treatment in *Current Biography* and similar sources.

The Table of Contents of each annual edition and the Cumulative Author Index at the end of this volume serve as a further

key for review of the individual speakers of the period of 1937-1947.

The editor of this collection is heavily indebted to the various authors of these speeches for permission to reprint their productions, and to the publishers and organizations that have graciously cooperated. Specific acknowledgment is made in the footnotes accompanying each speech.

June 1, 1947

A. CRAIG BAIRD

CONTENTS

LABOR RELATIONS

EDUCATION

RELIGION

INTRODUCTION

WHAT CONSTITUTES AN EFFECTIVE SPEECH?

What are the marks of a superior speaker and a superior speech? Why do we single out one platform orator over another for special recognition and for commendation to posterity?

1. *The effective speaker has uncommon weight and originality of ideas.* On a given occasion he may falter and echo shopworn thoughts. By and large, however, in season and out, he reveals on the platform distinctive traits of thinking and unusual intellectual penetration. He is a Webster, at the laying of the Bunker Hill monument cornerstone, who sums up his country's history and predicts with vast wisdom its future. He is a Calhoun who, however mistaken he may be in the practical bearings of his nullification position, nevertheless conceives with maturity certain robust postulates of government. He is a Burke, Fox, Pitt the Younger, or Churchill of the British parliament. He is a Jonathan Edwards, Alexander Hamilton, Wendell Phillips, Charles W. Eliot, Woodrow Wilson of America. These speakers had intellectual vigor and independence.

What are these traits of intellect? The effective speaker has mental range and consistency of principles. In the light of such principles, he measures the economic, social, political, or other problems of his day. He interprets, defends, and modifies these premises in the light of his growing wisdom and the turns of events. To understand him we must be able to single out these fundamental ideas. We may thus segregate his tenets, scrutinize them as they are implicit or explicit in a given address, and so evaluate the orator as thinker.

This integrity of the speaker's ideas implies also his ability to analyze a topic, that is, to break it down into its subdivisions so that the essentials of the controversy are highlighted. Through selection and formulation of these fundamental ideas, he can say with confidence, "This is the basic issue."

In addition to this breadth of thinking and this ability to analyze, the superior speaker as thinker is an economic and social philosopher. He is not content to present merely the surface themes. He steps outside the immediate problem to view it in its larger setting. He is a historian and a logician. He generalizes from specific instances; he observes comparison and analogy. Chiefly he traces causes and results. He states with calm decisiveness the more general assumptions and conclusions. He is thus a genuine philosopher. But he is no armchair speculator, but rather, like Burke, is a "philosopher in action." His speculations are tied to the living, changing world.

In this philosophical grasp of contemporary perplexities American speakers are chiefly deficient. Either because of lack of educational discipline or the national preoccupation with material concerns, the speechmakers of this country are limited in their philosophic imagination. Hundreds of speechmakers as recorded in the *Congressional Record* or elsewhere move almost entirely among economic and other details. These orators are apparently unconscious of the broad currents on which their minutiae are swept along. David Lilienthal, in his testimony before a Senate committee, reflected the rare philosophical judgment of which I speak.[1] Not many of our contemporaries on the platform can thus generalize and hark back to "basic causes."

2. *The effective speaker enriches his general ideas by specific and varied details.* According to his particular topic, interests, and background, he cites figures, specific cases, historical analogies, circumstantial details, hypothetical or authentic illustrations, authorities, or quotations, to amplify, prove, or clarify his point. He calls upon his broad experiences, his ample memory, his wide reading, his continual contacts with many phases of human nature. He does not engulf any one speech in such plethora of supporting details. But he does select, sharpen the outline, and so impresses with the aptness of his concrete applications. If a lawyer, he moves judge or jury by his research and his wealth of counter-evidence. If a preacher, he continually astonishes his listeners by his illustrative richness. If a Senator, he commands

[1] See p. 150.

respect by his authoritative treatment of facts and inference in his hour-by-hour debating.

3. *The effective speaker is superior in organizational ability.* He is an artist in design. No matter how complicated the details he fuses them together in sequence and relevancy. He composes a pertinent introduction, evolves a main body of ideas, and concludes with distinction. He inserts transitions, summaries, and controls his extempore adaptations.

His architecture need not be apparent. Dr. Sockman, among the preachers, is evidently more orderly than is Dr. Fosdick. Each is a master of sermon structure. Dr. Norwood Brigance molds his discourse after a definite plan. Herbert Hoover is given to a speech that sometimes appears like a debater's brief. Franklin Roosevelt's pattern was not so obvious. His campaign speeches especially seemed loosely developed. His veteran skill, however, shaped each paragraph to suit the mood of his audience and the theme. His was a structure that employed a high degree of organic movement and illustrated the "natural procedure" in persuasion.

American speechmakers, although routine in thought, usually rate well in organization. Perhaps our national interest in professional, legal, and occupational procedures inclines us to incorporate method in our speech composition.

4. *The speaker is effective in his language.* No subtle or incidental factor in speaking are the words and phrases. The superior speaker is at home with word meanings. He has absorbed much of the richness of the English vocabulary. He achieves accuracy of statement and connotative liveliness. His style, furthermore, is oral rather than "literary." He is no essayist. As his speaking is for the moment, so is his language of and for auditors. He avoids floridity. His style may be repetitious and broken, as becomes the speaking style. But his phrasing is simple and uncomplicated. Trite phrases are few. The texture of the whole is fresh and distinctive. An emotional-imaginative quality usually pervades the composition. If the occasion calls for it, he is naturally eloquent. (I still refer to language.) If the report is of factual and scientific validity, he has stylistic restraint. The style suits the subject, the speaker,

and the occasion. Each situation invokes an individualistic pattern of words and collocations.

What of the speakers of the day concerning language? Commonplaceness, mediocrity, triteness are too often unrelieved. Occasional smartness, especially in radio speaking scripts, is equally inappropriate. Eric Johnston, former president of the United States Chamber of Commerce, has alertness and interestingness. Other speakers often move more heavily through their sentences.

Here and there a speaker illuminates his language with genuine originality. Woodrow Wilson, we think, has come alive again.

5. *The effective speaker adapts his discourse to his audience.* The group may be a small town service club meeting, or it may be a nation-wide radio audience. The seasoned orator, in any case, has a "kind of genius for understanding human nature." [2] Whether or not he is graduated from a university, whether or not he is deeply schooled in proper voice and gesture, he does unfold his ideas so that auditors respond. He governs his subject and its details, his language, organization, and delivery so as to effect maximum response. At every turn he reacts to the attitudes, beliefs, stereotypes, and drives of his audience. He usually makes no formal pre-inventory of age, occupation, education and other items of audience analysis, but he does have constant awareness of these factors and manipulates every detail of his speaking art in relation to them. Thus he effects audience homogeneity, interest, and approval of his presentation. His is the art of supplementing dry logic and mere information with emotional and personal proofs. His is the art of persuasion.

6. *The effective speaker is superior in delivery.* His voice has range and flexibility. Perhaps it has the depth and resonance of Bryan's. His pronunciation may be that of Aroostook, Maine, or Atlanta, Georgia. His enunciation may be imperfect. But he invariably projects his voice to his group. He is active physically and mentally. He has fluency; he calls forth "circular" response. He uses pauses effectively.

[2] See *Representative American Speeches: 1939-1940.* Prefatory Note. p. 10.

His personality, moreover, is essential to his speaking effectiveness. He is intellectually and emotionally stable and controlled. He has self-confidence, humor, good taste, tact, generosity, good will, modesty, and above all, sincerity. These qualities of personality strongly enforce his appeals and dominate his bodily action and tones.

The superior speaker is free from bombast and declamation. He is at comparative ease in almost any audience situation. Furthermore, his repeated experiences before listeners give him extempore ability. The speakers in the present volume, without exception, have on scores of occasions demonstrated their extempore freedom. They have ability to prepare and read from a prepared manuscript. But their added virtue is their skill in talking off-hand and at length before committees or formal audiences. This extempore asset is one crucial test of one's right to recognition as a "representative" speaker.

7. *The superior speaker rates high in total speaking effectiveness.* Our estimate of "superior speaking," then, is determined not by focusing on language, or ideas, or even on voice and other externals of delivery, but rather by taking account of the combination of these separate skills. We isolate them for description and observation. But the speaker, as is obvious, utilizes these functions as a single process. So further are we to judge him. Seldom does any one orator excel in all the categories listed above. Henry Wallace relies chiefly on "progressive" ideas; Harry Truman, on Presidential prestige and a personal likability; Arthur Vandenberg, on some compositional distinction and energy of platform manner; Claude Pepper, on all-round debating and formal eloquence; Robert Taft, on close and extended analysis and defense of a specific motion; George Marshall, on direct, unadorned statement, often with extempore forthrightness; Walter Lippmann, on philosophical insight and uncommonly sound interpretation of current problems; Philip Murray, on rough and tumble extempore platform leadership with unionists and others; Fulton Sheen, on strong moral diagnosis combined with a dignity of voice and language that produces high persuasion. In the total interplay of these elements the speakers we include in any exclusive category rank high.

How Shall We Criticize A Speech and Speaker?

On the basis of the suggestions listed above you will criticize a speech or speeches. (1) You will reconstruct the social and political background of the address or addresses. (2) You will analyze the speaker's audience. (3) You will reconstruct the speaking situation itself. (4) You will determine the speaking type—whether sermon or congressional debate. (5) You will review the biographical facts concerning the speaker that may help in your appraisal of his performance. (6) You will examine the text itself to be sure that the speaker himself composed it and that the report as it comes to you closely reproduces what the orator actually said. (7) You will single out and weigh the ideas of the speaker. (8) You will examine and judge the worth of the concrete details (forms of proof) by which he establishes his ideas. (9) You will outline the discourse and pronounce judgment on the speaker's organizational skill. (10) You will judge the effectiveness of the language. (11) You will view the speaker's methods of audience adaptation, including his modes of "appeal." (12) You will study and evaluate the speaker's delivery—his voice, enunciation, pronunciation, and bodily action. Especially will you attempt to understand his platform personality, including his sincerity, tact, humor, and other traits of character. (13) You will view these elements separately and in combination so that your judgment is a balanced one. (14) Finally, you will appraise the speech in view of its immediate and long-range impressiveness. Your pursuit of this final inquiry does not assume that your successful speaker must always command the most votes. He may be hopelessly in the minority. But he should demonstrate platform leadership and should stir at least a small ripple on history. He should be a social force through his speechmaking.[3]

June 1, 1947

A. Craig Baird

[3] For more detailed analysis of the method of speech criticism, see *Representative American Speeches: 1944-1945.* p. 9-17.

INTERNATIONAL POLICIES

POLICIES OF THE UNITED NATIONS [1]

WARREN R. AUSTIN [2]

Warren R. Austin, chief United States delegate to the United Nations General Assembly, gave this address before the General Assembly at Flushing Meadow, New York, on October 30, 1946.

The Assembly had convened on October 24 for its first meeting in the United States. President Truman welcomed the delegates; Vyacheslav Molotov congratulated him. The atmosphere suggested optimism.

On October 29, Mr. Molotov addressed the delegates for more than an hour in Russian, "in an expressionless monotone." The translation quickly made it evident that the speech was a vigorous criticism of the general American policy concerning disarmament, the atomic bomb, mandated territories (including Palestine), the solution of India's unrest, and other matters.

Mr. Austin, speaking the next day, revised the first part of his prepared address and replied directly to the Russian charges. To interpret the Austin argument, the student should read carefully Molotov's part of the debate.

Mr. Austin was speaking as a lawyer, as a firm friend and sponsor of the United Nations, and as a cautious interpreter of official American diplomacy toward Russia. His preliminary reply to Molotov was firm but unbelligerent. His detailed analysis of the principles underlying the United Nations charter was exceptionally strong, though uninspired.

Critics of the United Nations should review carefully this Austin defense, and will probably weigh the recent accomplishments of the organization as evidence to support or condemn this defense. This session of the United Nations disposed of seventy-five items, some of them serious questions.

Austin, a graduate of the University of Vermont, was a successful Vermont lawyer of "dignity, solidity, and dependability." He engaged in politics; had experience in China in 1916, as representative of the American International Corporation; became a Republican United States Senator; was an early Senate leader in American preparedness; and supported Roosevelt in Lend Lease and similar pre-Pearl Harbor legislation.

---

[1] The text is from the *New York Times*, October 31, 1946. By permission of the *New York Times*. Text also furnished and permission for reprinting through the courtesy of the United States Delegation to the General Assembly.

[2] For biographical note see Appendix.

He was one of the American delegation to the Chapultepec Conference. President Truman's appointment of him as head of the American delegation to the United Nations was thus a logical outcome of earlier Austin activities and abilities.

As a speaker Mr. Austin is somewhat slow and restrained. He uses little emotionalism in his discourse. He does exhaust his subject. His method in preparing law cases was to gather material, index and study it in detail. He prepared the case of his opponent practically as carefully as he did his own side. Such was the technique he carried over into his preparation and presentation of problems before the United Nations.

In the beginning of what I have to say to you tonight I must refer briefly to the address made yesterday by the distinguished representative of the Union of Soviet Socialist Republics.

Mr. Molotov's speech indicated distrust and misunderstanding of the motives of the United States and of other members of the United Nations. I do not believe that recriminations among nations allied in war and in peace promote that unity which Mr. Molotov so rightly points out is essential to the success of the United Nations.

In war we gave to our Allies all the help and cooperation a great nation could. In peace the "United States will support the United Nations with all the resources we possess."

Our motives in war and peace we leave to the judgment of history. We fought for *freedom* side by side without recrimination. Can't we fight for *peace* side by side without recrimination? That closes the sad chapter, so far as we are concerned.

I shall not participate in any exchange of recriminations.

We welcome the confidence expressed by Mr. Molotov that unanimous agreement among all the nations both large and small can be achieved on such vital matters as the control of atomic energy, and on steps to lighten the burden of armaments and military expenditures which still rests so heavily upon the peoples of the world.

The United States urges disarmament.

The United States believes that Mr. Molotov's proposal should be placed in our agenda and fully considered and discussed.

The initiative of the Soviet Union in this matter is appropriate, because of its mighty armies; just as the initiative of the United States was appropriate in proposing measures to prevent the manufacture and use of atomic weapons.

In November 1945, the United States took the initiative for outlawing the atomic bomb in the conversations at Washington among President Truman, Prime Minister Attlee, and Prime Minister Mackenzie King. At Moscow in December 1945, that is, the following month, conversations were held between Mr. Byrnes, Mr. Molotov and Mr. Bevin on this same subject. In this Assembly last January the resolution creating the Atomic Energy Commission and establishing its terms of reference was unanimously adopted. Since then in the commission itself the distinguished United States representative, Mr. Bernard M. Baruch, presented proposals expressing the policy of the President of the United States.

The United States goes further. As President Truman emphasized again last week, it attaches the greatest importance to reaching agreements that will remove the deadly fear of other weapons of mass destruction in accordance with the same resolution passed by this Assembly.

So far as Mr. Molotov's resolution concerns the regulation and reduction of other armaments, the whole world knows where the United States stands and has always stood. For twenty years before the war and in the fifteen months since the fighting stopped the United States has consistently been in the forefront of those striving to reduce the burden of armaments upon the peoples of the world. Since the end of the war in Europe and the Pacific, the United States has progressively and rapidly reduced its own military establishment.

After the last war we made the mistake of disarming unilaterally. We shall not repeat that mistake.

The United States is prepared to cooperate fully with all other members of the United Nations in disarmament. It advocates effective safeguards by way of inspection and other means to protect complying states against the hazards of violation and evasion.

We cannot reduce armaments merely by talking about the "regulation of armament and possible disarmament," or the "heavy economic burden caused by excessive expenditures for armaments." We cannot achieve it without positive acts which will establish the "peaceful postwar conditions" to which Mr. Molotov also referred.

Nor can a system for the regulation of armaments and possible disarmaments as contemplated in Articles 11, 26 and 47 of the Charter be effectively planned except in relation to progress in the negotiation of the armed forces agreements called for by Article 43. At the beginning of April, four of the five members of the Military Staff Committee made specific proposals concerning the principles which should govern the negotiation of these agreements. In September the Soviet Union submitted for the first time a statement of its views on the problem.

I am happy to note that Mr. Molotov referred to the work of the Military Staff Committee. I hope that it will now be possible for the committee to make rapid progress. The conclusion of these agreements, providing the Security Council with peace forces adequate to prevent acts of aggression, is essential to carrying out the objectives of Mr. Molotov's resolution for the reduction of armaments.

Mr. Molotov also referred to Article 43 in connection with the Soviet proposal concerning the presence of armed forces of the United Nations on foreign territories. He said, and I quote: "In this connection it is natural that the Security Council should know the actual situation, namely, where and what armed forces of the United Nations are situated at present outside the confines of the countries. . . . For its part the Soviet Union is prepared to submit this information to the Security Council," end quote.

The Government of the United States understands Mr. Molotov's statement to mean that the Soviet Union is fully prepared to report on its armed forces in ex-enemy states as well as in other foreign territories. Therefore, the United States urges prompt fulfillment of this policy. The United States has nothing to hide with respect to our armed forces either at home or abroad. The United States will promptly fulfill that policy.

In no case are the United States forces in friendly countries except with the consent of those countries.

It is our opinion that the proposed inquiry should include
all mobilized armed forces, whether at home or abroad.

The President of the United States in his address to the
General Assembly at its opening meeting defined the policies of
the United States toward the United Nations and the work of
the Assembly.

As the general debate has progressed, I have been increasingly moved by the potentialities that I perceive in this Assembly
for advancing toward a real and lasting peace.

Its members have pointed to the vision of President Truman
of a—I am quoting the President's address—"peace with justice
for all—justice for small nations and for large nations and justice for individuals without distinction as to race, creed or color
—a peace that will advance, not retard, the attainment of the
four freedoms," end of quote.

United in this aspiration as we appear to be, we are united
in our service. From disagreement we forge agreement. From
free and frank discussion of differing points of view we extract
the degree of unity necessary for constructive action. It would
help us if we should make always our chief concern what is right
not who is right.

There is an injunction contained in the Constitution of Vermont—my native state. It calls for "a frequent recurrence to
fundamental principles."

It seems to me that before this general debate comes to an
end it would be helpful for us all to recur to the fundamental
principles of the United Nations.

The reports that we have before us from the Secretary General, the Security Council, and the Economic and Social Council
refer to some discouraging things and many difficulties in the
record of the United Nations during the past year. Some of
the speakers have referred at length to these disappointments and
difficulties.

To me the real story related by these reports seems to be the
immense sum of accomplishment and agreement that the United
Nations has achieved in one year under all the handicaps of a

world in turmoil and just emerging from the disasters and desolation of war.

In one year we have advanced toward a rule of world law and have created institutions for international action far beyond the dreams of any one of us as recently as September 1, 1939; June 22, 1941, and December 7, 1941.

So I say—let us review the theory and practice of the Security Council and the Economic and Social Council, their powers and their work, without evasion, but let us review them in perspective and as a whole in relation to the powers and work of all the other agencies and institutions of the United Nations.

Australia and Cuba have proposed discussion of Article 27, relating to voting procedures in the Security Council. Let us consider Article 27, but let us consider it in relation to the other 110 articles of the Charter of the United Nations. We cannot tear Article 27 from its context.

A recurrence to first principles of the United Nations starts with the necessity for unity of the large nations on matters essential to the maintenance of peace among the nations both great and small.

I recall to the Assembly that the spirit of unity of the nations which became permanent members of the Security Council animated the nativity of the United Nations. The united and coordinated action of the great powers in winning the war and in generating the principle of an international organization for security and peace based on the sovereign equality of all peace-loving nations both great and small, was the very travail of the United Nations.

The remedy for the labor pains at Moscow, at Dumbarton Oaks, at Yalta and at San Francisco was the unanimity of the great powers. The principle of unanimity in essential matters also reflects the realities of the world as it is today. At the same time it provides the basis for a lasting peace during which all nations can, we hope, work together toward transforming the kind of world we have today into a true world society for tomorrow. Certainty—certainty of abolition of war depends upon cooperation by all countries competent to wage war.

The United Nations was created with the purpose of making it unnecessary for the civilized world to resort again to the ultimate sanction of war against an aggressor, with all its bloody sacrifices and terrible costs to humanity. Toward the fulfillment of this purpose the Security Council has been assigned a limited part of the responsibilities placed upon the Untied Nations by the Charter.

Let me remind you that Article 1 of Chapter I of the Charter lists four purposes of the United Nations and of these the primary responsibility for only the first—to maintain international peace and security—rests with the Security Council—just one of four.

The other purposes as stated by the Charter are—I am quoting:

"To develop friendly relations among nations based on respect for the principle of equal rights and self-determination of peoples, and to take other appropriate measures to strengthen universal peace;

"To achieve international cooperation in solving international problems of an economic, social, cultural or humanitarian character, and in promoting and encouraging respect for human rights and for fundamental freedoms for all without distinction as to race, sex, language or religion; and

"To be a center for harmonizing the actions of nations in the attainment of these common ends."

The primary responsibility for the fulfillment of these other purposes—three out of four—rests with the other organs of the United Nations, the General Assembly, the Economic and Social Council, the Trusteeship Council, the secretariat and the specialized agencies related to the central organization. The International Court of Justice has the responsibility of applying international law established by the United Nations Charter and in other ways and as it is progressively extended by the nations in the new agreements they will reach through the continuing use of all the other organs of the United Nations.

These are the tasks of building the basis for a peaceful world society—these three bases: the political basis, the economic basis, the social and cultural basis, the basis of knowledge and understanding and the basis of law.

Of all the institutions of the United Nations, the General Assembly is by its constitutional functions and its potentialities the most important. It has responsibilities for carrying out *all* the purposes of the United Nations.

The General Assembly is the supreme deliberative body of the world community. Although it is not a legislative body enacting laws which must be obeyed by the member states, it exercises great responsibilities and wields great power.

The Assembly is responsible for forming the organization of the United Nations as laid down by the Charter. It has already accomplished at the first part of this session many of these organizational tasks.

The Assembly also has the power of the purse. This is a vital power in any governmental entity. Its control of the budget will become more significant as the activities of the United Nations are increased by the addition of new functions and the expansion of existing programs.

The General Assembly wields power primarily as the voice of the conscience of the world. Its recommendations have behind them the intangible force of the international community. The peace-loving states which are members of the United Nations will not lightly disregard or flout recommendations of the General Assembly which express the will of an alert and aroused world public opinion.

Even when it makes no recommendations, its mere power of discussion under Articles 10, 11 and 14 of any matter within the scope of the Charter and of any situation, regardless of origin, which may impair the general welfare, is one of the most constructive functions in the whole organization. By discussion it can clarify the issues and promote mutual understanding among the nations and peoples of the world.

Under the broad and flexible construction of the Charter which the United States wishes to develop, we foresee a great and expanding area of operations for the General Assembly. I need not quote in detail the broad range of the Assembly's competence as it is established in Chapter IV of the Charter in questions involving the maintenance of peace and security, international political and legal cooperation, the coordination of international activities in economic, social, educational and health matters, and in the domain of the realization of human rights and fundamental freedoms for all.

In all these fields the General Assembly speaks as the voice of all the United Nations, and establishes the general goals or objectives toward which the organization and all its component parts will move.

The General Assembly must also exercise definitive powers, such as the determination of the location of the headquarters, and the approval of agreements relating to the powers of the organs and special agencies of the United Nations.

The General Assembly will, we believe, explore new fields of activity as time goes on, and as functions which may not be specifically provided for in the Charter, but which are not precluded by the Charter, are entrusted to it by the members of the United Nations. The General Assembly has only just begun its career as the most broadly representative organ of the United Nations. The final extent of its development cannot even be foreseen; but there can be no doubt that it has a vast and increasingly important position to fill in the international community.

These possibilities will be realized to the extent that the Assembly exercises its very broad competence in strict accordance with the fundamental purpose of the United Nations set forth in Article 1, Paragraph 4—"to be a center for harmonizing the actions of nations in the attainment of these common ends." The Assembly's recommendations, particularly under Articles 10, 11, 13 and 14, can greatly extend and develop the rule of law among nations, provided its recommendations are such that they are generally accepted and carried out by the member states.

All the actions of the Assembly in these broad fields are taken in accordance with Article 18 of the Charter, which provides that, on important matters, a two-thirds majority of the members present and voting shall be required, while other questions are settled by a simple majority of the members present and voting.

It is obvious that recommendations of the Assembly will be effective in proportion to the size of the majority by which they are adopted.

As in the case of other organs of the United Nations, it is better for the Assembly to go to great lengths to attain, or at least approach, unanimity than it is to enact resolutions over the opposition of a large dissenting group.

The United Nations Charter recognizes the transcending importance to world peace of close cooperation in the economic and social field. In the Economic and Social Council, its subsidiary bodies and the specialized agencies being brought into relationship with the Council, the United Nations has already created a far more effective and comprehensive institutional structure for these purposes than the world has ever seen before.

In a recent address the Honorable John G. Winant, United States representative on the Economic and Social Council, said:

"Peace, if it is to be real and lasting, means more than resolving conflicts between nations. It means positive action to lift the levels of human welfare. . . . Now, in our age peace cannot be secured by political action unaccompanied by economic cooperation. If we are not to drift backward to catastrophe, we must go forward together toward a fuller life for all peoples everywhere."

We Americans represent many races and came from many countries. We could not have built one nation out of many peoples and have learned to live as good neighbors and members of one community without the opportunities for a decent life and rising standards of living that nature and the course of history have given us, or without the spirit of the Golden Rule to guide our conduct toward each other.

We, the representatives of the United Nations, can never forget that wars find their breeding ground in poverty, ignorance and hunger. That is what gives aggressors their chance. Strong men gain power by contrasting a new order with the old. We cannot build a peaceful world without higher standards of living and greater opportunities for all peoples.

Decisions in the Economic and Social Council are taken by a simple majority vote, but here, as in the Assembly, the constant effort has and should continue to be to achieve the greatest possible degree of unanimity, rather than to achieve victories based on narrow majority votes. It is not votes that count, but agreements that are or will become universally acceptable, because they are necessary and because they are right for the peoples of the world.

Considering that the Council has been at work for less than one year, it has made a remarkable record. Like the other organs, its organizational work has been a necessary preliminary toward making it possible for the United Nations to move ahead toward the realization of the purpose set forth in Article 55 of the Charter—that is, "higher standards of living, full employment and conditions of economic and social progress and development."

At this session of the Assembly we are called upon to examine and approve agreements which bring four important specialized agencies into relationships with the United Nations— the International Labor Organization, the Food and Agriculture Organization, the United Nations Educational Scientific and Cultural Organization, and the International Civil Aviation Organization.

In the constructive work of the specialized agencies, the decisions of their policy-making bodies are for the most part taken by a simple or two-thirds majority.

The great flexibility of the constitutional structure of the United Nations will facilitate the development of other special agencies for international action as their creation becomes wise and feasible. Each of these agencies can be endowed by its own charter with powers in its own field as great as the community of nations is willing to give and as necessity compels it to give.

The proposal of the United States with respect to the establishment of an International Atomic Development Authority is an example of what can be done in this way. We propose that the charter of this Authority will endow it with power sufficient to ensure that atomic energy will be developed and used for peaceful purposes only and that complying states will be protected against the hazards of violations and evasions. This is in accordance with the Assembly's resolution of last January.

I wish to make clear at this point that the position which I am taking today in regard to the unanimity of the permanent members of the Security Council is entirely consistent with the position taken by the United States representative on the Atomic Energy Commission, Mr. Bernard M. Baruch, who repeatedly has made clear that the United States proposals regarding control of atomic energy do not attack the general requirements for unanimity of the permanent members in the Security Council.

The International Court of Justice is now established as one of the principal organs of the United Nations and is potentially one of the greatest of international institutions. It is given a clearly defined role in the process of pacific settlement, namely, that of deciding disputes of a legal character which states submit to it. The Court has a second and even greater function. It stands as the institutional symbol of the rule of law in international relations.

Progress is being made through multiplying acceptance of the Court's jurisdiction under Paragraph 2 of Article 36 of the Statute of the Court. By accepting compulsory jurisdiction over justiciable disputes the nations give practical recognition to the principle of the supremacy of law. I am proud that the United States has been among the first to accept the compulsory jurisdiction of the present court.

Progress is also being made by widening the scope of matters which may be deemed legal and limiting the questions regarded as political and non-justiciable. This is being accomplished through the willingness of states to accept solutions based on law and to cooperate in the development of peaceful judicial procedures which can assure that the law will be based on justice and equity.

The Charter of the United Nations and the constitutions of the specialized agencies form a network of legal obligations which guide and regulate the dealings of states with each other and the actions of the international community.

By Article 13 the General Assembly is specifically charged with the task of initiating studies and making recommendations for the further development of international law. But the establishment of standards of justice and equity for the international community is the concern of all the organs and related agencies of the United Nations. Every recommendation that is ratified by the member governments as a convention, agreement or treaty becomes part of the law of nations.

There is another provision of the Charter to which I wish to call the Assembly's attention. That is Article 99, which gives to the Secretary General, in addition to his wide administrative powers, unprecedented political responsibilities. Under Article 99, the Secretary General may bring to the attention of the Security Council any matter which, in his opinion, may threaten the maintenance of international peace.

While the ultimate significance of this grant of political authority remains in large part to be determined by future events and by the good judgment of the Secretary General, I believe that the less patient critics of the United Nations might do well to consider the full implications of this authority.

We need not await its full implementation to recognize that the power of the Secretary General to study conditions which in his opinion threaten the peaceful relations of the members of the United Nations and to make recommendations based on his findings, represents a significant departure from the usual concepts of international organization and national sovereignty.

The Secretary General's right of access to the forces of public opinion—even if we adopt such a restricted interpretation of this authority—is a vital responsibility which distinguishes the United Nations from its predecessor international organization.

Less obvious, but perhaps equally important, is the function of the Secretary General and his staff to serve as a cohesive and coordinating force in the preparation of studies and proposals for the several organs, by suggesting compromises or techniques for dealing with matters under discussion and by acting as an intermediary or conciliator. Many of these activities will never be a part of the official record, but the ability of the Secretary General and his staff to function effectively in this manner will have an important bearing on the development of the United Nations.

Members of the United Nations are pledged under the Charter to accept as a sacred trust the obligation to promote the interests and well-being of the inhabitants of all non-self-governing territories. In addition, the Charter provides for a trusteeship system for such territories as may be placed under it by agreement. The human rights and fundamental freedoms of the Charter apply equally to all peoples—to peoples who do not yet govern themselves, as well as to those who do.

Draft trusteeship agreements have been submitted to this Assembly by nations administering League of Nations mandates. The United States hopes that a sufficient number of these agreements will be approved by the Assembly to make possible the immediate establishment of the Trusteeship Council and the trusteeship system. This structure of the United Nations cannot be completed until this is done.

The fullest possible implementation of the Charter provisions that deal with all non-self-governing peoples is just as important as implementation of the trusteeship system itself. In its first years, at least, the trusteeship system will probably apply to only a small percentage of the non-self-governing territories.

The provisions of the Charter recognize that the economic, social and political development of dependent peoples toward their full participation in the family of nations must be advanced if peace is to be made secure. The Charter and the institutions of the United Nations provide greater opportunities to that end than dependent peoples have ever had before.

In considering both the Australian proposal and the Cuban proposal in this Assembly we bear in mind the whole constitutional and institutional structure of the United Nations to which I have alluded and their relationship to the political realities of today and the political necessities of tomorrow.

These proposals are directed against Paragraph 3 of Article 27 of the Charter. This provides that on all except procedural matters, decisions of the Security Council shall be made by an affirmative vote of seven members, including the concurring votes of the permanent members, with one important exception—that a party to a dispute shall abstain from voting in decisions relating to the pacific settlement of disputes. In decisions under

Chapter VII relating to enforcement action with respect to threats to the peace, breaches of the peace and acts of aggression, the rule of unanimity of the permanent members is absolute. There is no exception in matters of enforcement.

The principle of unanimity of the great powers has from the first—and by general agreement—been limited in its application as a voting procedure to matters essential to the maintenace of international peace and security. The Charter requires unanimity of the major powers only in substantive decisions by the Security Council. There is no requirement for unanimity in the Assembly, in the Economic and Social Council, and in the Trusteeship Council. Similarly, the Statute of the International Court of Justice specifically provides for decisions by majority vote. The United Nations specialized agencies do not require unanimity of the major powers.

This does not mean that unanimity or the closest possible approximation to it is not to be desired and striven for in all these agencies. It means only that it was not deemed essential to apply the principle to those voting procedures. The greatest possible degree of agreement in all these organs and agencies is most important, for through them laws and customs of the international community are made.

These organs and agencies do not have the power to enforce the law. That power rests with the Security Council, and that is the reason why the members of the United Nations applied the principle of unanimity to the voting procedures of the Security Council and not to the voting procedures in any of the other institutions of the United Nations.

The large nations that are permanent members of the Council possess the power to keep peace in the world—to enforce observance of the law. The Charter does not give them that power. It merely recognizes that power and places obligations upon these nations to use that power in accordance with the law.

The unanimity requirement in the Security Council does not relieve the permanent members from any of the responsibilities and obligations they have assumed under the Charter. I have heard it said by critics of the unanimity formula that it legalizes aggression by a permanent member because that member can prevent enforcement action against itself. Of course this formula does no such thing.

The permanent members are bound legally and morally in the same degree as all other members of the United Nations, to quote from the Charter: "to settle their international disputes by peaceful means in such a manner that international peace and security, and justice are not endangered," end quote.

In the same degree as all the other members, they are bound to—I am quoting again from the Charter—"refrain in their international relations from the threat or use of force against the territorial integrity or political independence of any state, or in any other manner inconsistent with the purposes of the United Nations," end quote. These sweeping and binding commitments are not limited by the power of veto in the Security Council. The veto does not legalize any violations of the law. That is the law.

No member of the United Nations can be permitted to ignore the fact that, as Secretary Byrnes said on February 28, 1946, quote: "the mere legal veto by one of the permanent members of the Council does not in fact relieve any state, large or small, of its moral obligations to act in accordance with the purposes and principles of the Charter." We say: nor does the failure of any organ of the United Nations to take a decision relieve any member of that obligation.

Besides being bound by the law of the United Nations Charter, twenty-three nations, members of this Assembly, including the United States, Soviet Russia, the United Kingdom and France, are also bound by the law of the charter of the Nuremberg Tribunal. That makes planning or waging a war of aggression a crime against humanity for which individuals as well as nations can be brought before the bar of international justice, tried and punished.

It is true—and our facing this fact helps bind us together more closely in the unity we seek—it is true that if one of the great powers violates the law of the charter and the law of Nuremberg against aggression there is, ultimately, only one way to enforce the law—and that is by a major war. However, just remember this: that would be equally as true if the Charter did not require unanimity in the Security Council. A decision involving military measures against one or more of the permanent members by other permanent members would not be a decision for police action as the Charter contemplates it—it would be a decision for war.

I believe I have made clear the reasons why the United States considers that unanimity of the permanent members of the Security Council in action by the Council concerned with the enforcement of peace is wise and necessary at this stage in the development of the international community.

Criticism of Article 27 is directed particularly at the fact that the requirement of unanimity of the permanent members extends to decisions concerning peaceful settlement as well as to enforcement action.

It is true that the requirement of unanimity tends to reduce the speed of action of the Security Council and increases the difficulties in the way of adopting a clear-cut decision. It may even prevent action which might peacefully settle a dispute.

It is our view that the unanimity requirement tends to discourage the taking of intransigent positions and to encourage the achievement of agreement through compromise. Certainty is better than speed. In the long run, important decisions unanimously accepted by the permanent members are likely to produce better results than decisions which find the permanent members divided; also that the unanimity requirement—properly applied—prevents the Security Council from being progressively committed to a course of action inconsistent with the vital interests of some permanent member

It was these latter considerations that prevailed at San Francisco. In the four-power statement of June 7, 1945, to which France later agreed, the permanent members took the position that substantive decisions on peaceful settlement require the concurrence of the permanent members of the Council because of the possible consequences of those decisions. Here's where that very significant theory about a chain of events came into play. It was believed they might have major political repercussions and might initiate a chain of events which in the end would require the Security Council to invoke measures of enforcement under Chapter VII.

It was held that, since the Council cannot take enforcement action without the concurrence of all the permanent members, it might endanger the effectiveness of the Council's work if decisions under Chapter VI that might lead to the necessity for enforcement action under Chapter VII were taken by a vote which found the permanent members divided.

But now what is our present position—the position of the United States?

Despite the attitude of the five powers and the decisions made at San Francisco, which I have described, the United States *hopes* that the five permanent members may find it desirable at some time in the future in full agreement among themselves and with other members to support modification of the unanimity requirement in its application to matters arising under Chapter VI.

I want it distinctly understood that we are persuaded that a case for amendment of the Charter ought not be made on the basis of so brief an experience. The United States is opposed to the amendment of Article 27 of the Charter at this time.

We must recognize that during its first nine months the Security Council has labored under unusually difficult circumstances. In its infancy, before it had established its rules and its precedents, the Council was forced to consider substantial differences among the permanent members about problems arising directly from the war.

We must remember that the Security Council—and the United Nations as a whole—was not intended to deal with the peace settlements that must be made as a result of the war. These settlements, both with the ex-enemy states and among the major allies themselves, were left to separate negotiation. Until they have been made, differences among the major allies about the terms of settlement inevitably will handicap the work of the Security Council. As these settlements are made, we can expect that the areas of present disagreement among the permanent members will be greatly reduced.

But now here is our long-range policy—speaking for the United States.

The United States does recognize that there is room for improvement in the operations of the Security Council. There is room for improvement in the application of Article 27 and of the four-power statement in the Security Council. There can be little doubt that a number of the difficulties which have arisen could have been avoided if the voting formula adopted at San Francisco had been more fully and clearly defined.

There have been confusion and misunderstanding both within and without the Security Council.

Necessary action by the Council for the peaceful settlement of a dispute should never be prevented by the votes of any one or any number of its members, permanent or non-permanent. In this connection, we should not forget that the non-permanent members possess six votes in the Council and that at least two of these votes are always necessary to action by the Council.

Restraint and self-discipline to avoid doing anything contrary to the letter or spirit of the Charter are essential in the application of the voting formula. This is one of the greatest challenges to conduct if we are to give strength to the United Nations for peace.

A program for interpretation and application of the voting principles which will facilitate and not hinder peaceful settlements ought to be pursued. Here is where clarification through discussions, definition, regulation and practice are necessary to carry out the spirit as well as the letter of the Charter. Let me say to you that this is a United States policy.

We would not have today the laws and the institutions of the United Nations without the unanimous agreement of the great powers and the general agreement of all nations. We must continue that unity.

As they stand, these laws and institutions offer in their entirety far greater possibilities for the establishment of a just and lasting peace than humanity has ever known before.

We have hardly begun to explore and to exploit these possibilities. That they are virtually limitless can be perceived the moment we stand back far enough to get perspective.

The Charter and the institutions of the United Nations reflect the greatest common denominator of agreement now realizable in a world of sovereign states, with different ideology, political and economic systems and cultural and social traditions.

Science and technology are uniting the world as it has never been united before. Fears and suspicions must not continue to divide the peoples of the world. We must use the institutions and laws of the United Nations to banish these fears and suspicions. So far as we succeed in doing this we shall succeed in creating a world society and a world rule of law in which the veto will just wither away.

This may take a long time. Probably it will. But there is no short-cut, no magic formula, by which we can escape the price of peace.

Only by a frequent recurrence to fundamental principles will we give to the Charter a living spirit in the moral sense of nations and of the human race.

IS AMERICAN FOREIGN POLICY
LEADING TO WAR? [3]

HENRY A WALLACE [4]

Henry A. Wallace, then Secretary of Commerce, gave this address on American foreign policy, in Madison Square Garden, New York, on Thursday evening, September 12, 1946, at an anti-Republican, anti-Dewey rally sponsored by the National Citizens Political Action Committee and the Independent Citizens Committee of Arts, Sciences and Professions.

His audience of fifteen thousand repeatedly applauded. Senator Claude Pepper, on the program, was also received with great enthusiasm.

Wallace's argument was a striking event in American diplomatic history. The speaker's vigorous indictment of those who followed the "get tough with Russia" policy, his endorsement of a kind of "Monroe Doctrine" for Eastern Europe in which Russia would be sponsor for the region, his condemnation of any American policy that supported the British "balance of power manipulations" aroused instantaneous world-wide reaction—much of it unfavorable.

Correspondents, with advance copies of the speech, had secured from President Truman at a press conference in Washington that day an admission that he had gone over the address, that he had approved it, and that the Wallace position was also that of Secretary of State Byrnes, at that time negotiating with Russia in Paris. [5]

Immediately after Wallace had finished appealing to his "leftist" audience, the storm broke. His critics pointed out that the address differed sharply from the policy of the State Department and constituted, whether or not so intended, a direct criticism of Mr. Byrnes. Senator Vandenberg, then in Paris with Byrnes, stated that "We can cooperate with only one Secretary of State at a time." Diplomats everywhere asked whether our policy was now to be modified. On September 14 the President explained to the press that "there had been no change in the established foreign policy of our government," that there had been "a natural misunderstanding" of his previous remarks, and that he had aimed merely to approve "the right of the Secretary of Commerce to deliver the speech."

On September 16 Wallace stated, "I stand on my New York speech." The next day he released the text of a four-thousand-word letter on

[3] From Henry A. Wallace, *The Fight for Peace*. A Pamphlet Press Book. Reynal and Hitchcock. New York. 1946. Through the courtesy of the publishers.

[4] For biographical note see Appendix.

[5] Compare James F. Byrnes' addresses at Stuttgart, Germany, September 6, 1946, and at Paris. October 3, 1946.

foreign policy that he had sent to the President on July 23. The letter stated the essentials contained in the Madison Square Garden speech. Students should examine this letter as interpretation of the later public argument. On September 18, Wallace interviewed the President and announced that he would remain in the Cabinet. On Friday, September 20, after consultation with Paris and presumably after firm words from Secretary Byrnes and the diplomatic delegation there, the President called for and received Mr. Wallace's resignation.

The official policy at Washington was thus vindicated. This government was apparently committed, as against the Wallace philosophy and argument, to (1) a strong stand against Russia throughout the globe; (2) specific resistance to Russian domination in the Balkans and in the threats to Greece and Turkey; (3) close cooperation with Great Britain to protect mutual interests; (4) strong American military defenses unless there should be corresponding disarmament by Russia; (5) solid support of the Baruch plan for control of atomic energy as contrasted with the Russian plan set forth by Gromyko.

Because the Wallace address involved an analysis of fundamental principles of our international policy and program, discussion of it and of Wallace continued during the following months. Moscow praised Wallace's position, British sources on the whole condemned it bitterly, and American sentiment in Washington and out veered more and more to the Byrnes (and later to the Marshall) attitudes and commitments. In the New York gubernatorial election the Wallace case became a prime issue. Dewey's re-election in November by a decisive majority was attributed partly to the defection of many "conservative" Democrats, and to the loss by the Democrats of some labor voters and independents who followed Wallace.

Mr. Wallace became editor of the *New Republic*. In April 1947, he visited Great Britain, Sweden, and France and continued to denounce the administration's policy toward Russia. Few American public speakers in the past decade had aroused such world-wide controversy. The critics of the former cabinet member especially condemned him for indicting American foreign policy at the time our Secretary of State Marshall and the American delegations were in Moscow attempting to seek a settlement with Russia concerning the peace policy for Germany.

This speaker gained wide attention, more from his challenging ideas than from his public speaking skill. He is hardly a first-rate orator.

First off, I want to give my own personal endorsement to the candidates chosen by the Democratic Party and the American Labor Party in New York. James Mead long has been one of the ablest public servants in Washington—a constant, faithful and intelligent proponent of the New Deal of Franklin Roosevelt. The Senate will miss him—but Albany needs him.

He will make a great governor—worthy of the tradition of Smith and Roosevelt and Lehman.

Herbert Lehman knows full well the problems and the opportunities facing the State of New York, the United States, and the United Nations. His great heart and great mind will be increasingly useful when he is a member of the United States Senate.

Victory for Mead and Lehman in November will mean a long stride in the people's progress.

Tonight I want to talk about peace—and how to get peace. Never have the common people of all lands so longed for peace. Yet, never in a time of comparative peace have they feared war so much.

Up till now peace has been negative and unexciting. War has been positive and exciting. Far too often, hatred and fear, intolerance and deceit have had the upper hand over love and confidence, trust and joy. Far too often, the law of nations has been the law of the jungle; and the constructive spiritual forces of the Lord have bowed to the destructive forces of Satan.

During the past year or so, the significance of peace has been increased immeasurably by the atom bomb, guided missiles and airplanes which soon will travel as fast as sound. Make no mistake about it—another war would hurt the United States many times as much as the last war. We cannot rest in the assurance that we invented the atom bomb—and therefore that this agent of destruction will work best for us. He who trusts in the atom bomb will sooner or later perish by the atom bomb—or something worse.

I say this as one who steadfastly backed preparedness throughout the Thirties. We have no use for namby-pamby pacifism. But we must realize that modern inventions have now made peace the most exciting thing in the world—and we should be willing to pay a just price for peace. If modern war can cost us $400 billion, we should be willing and happy to pay much more for peace. But certainly, the cost of peace is to be measured not in dollars but in the hearts and minds of men.

The price of peace—for us and for every nation in the world—is the price of giving up prejudice, hatred, fear, and ignorance.

Let's get down to cases here at home.

First we have prejudice, hatred, fear and ignorance of certain races. The recent mass lynching in Georgia was not merely the most unwarranted, brutal act of mob violence in the United States in recent years; it was also an illustration of the kind of prejudice that makes war inevitable.

Hatred breeds hatred. The doctrine of racial superiority produces a desire to get even on the part of its victims. If we are to work for peace in the rest of the world, we here in the United States must eliminate racism from our unions, our business organizations, our educational institutions, and our employment practices. Merit alone must be the measure of man.

Second, in payment for peace, we must give up prejudice, hatred, fear and ignorance in the economic world. This means working earnestly, day after day, for a larger volume of world trade. It means helping undeveloped areas of the world to industrialize themselves with the help of American technical assistance and loans.

We should welcome the opportunity to help along the most rapid possible industrialization in Latin America, China, India, and the Near East. For as the productivity of these peoples increases, our exports will increase.

We all remember the time, not so long ago, when the high tariff protectionists blindly opposed any aid to the industrialization of Canada. But look at our exports to Canada today. On a per capita basis our Canadian exports are seven times greater than our exports to Mexico.

I supported the British loan of almost $4 billion because I knew that without this aid in the rehabilitation of its economy, the British government would have been forced to adopt totalitarian trade methods and economic warfare of a sort which would have closed the markets of much of the world to American exports.

For the welfare of the American people and the world it is even more important to invest $4 billion in the industrialization of undeveloped areas in the so-called backward nations, thereby promoting the long-term stability that comes from an ever-increasing standard of living. This would not only be good politics and good morals. It would be good business.

The United States is the world's great creditor nation. And low tariffs by creditor nations are a part of the price of peace. For when a great creditor demands payment, and at the same time adopts policies which make it impossible for the debtors to pay in goods—the first result is the intensification of depression over large areas of the world; and the final result is the triumph of demagogues who speak only the language of violence and hate.

There are those who have expressed themselves as favoring an alliance of mutual defense with Great Britain as the key to our foreign policy. This may sound attractive because we both speak the same language and many of our customs and traditions have the same historical background. Moreover, to the military men, the British Isles are our advanced air base against Europe.

Certainly we like the British people as individuals. But to make Britain the key to our foreign policy would be, in my opinion, the height of folly. We must not let reactionary leadership force us into that position. We must not let British balance-of-power manipulations determine whether and when the United States gets into war.

Make no mistake about it—the British imperialistic policy in the Near East alone, combined with Russian retaliation, would lead the United States straight to war unless we have a clearly defined and realistic policy of our own.

Neither of these two great powers wants war now, but the danger is that whatever their intentions may be, their current policies may eventually lead to war. To prevent war and insure our survival in a stable world, it is essential that we look abroad through our own American eyes and not through the eyes of either the British Foreign Office or a pro-British or anti-Russian press.

In this connection, I want one thing clearly understood. I am neither anti-British nor pro-British—neither anti-Russian nor pro-Russian. And just two days ago, when President Truman read these words, he said that they represented the policy of his Administration.

I plead for an America vigorously dedicated to peace—just as I plead for opportunities for the next generation throughout the world to enjoy the abundance which now, more than ever before, is the birthright of man.

To achieve lasting peace, we must study in detail just how the Russian character was formed—by invasions of Tartars, Mongols, Germans, Poles, Swedes and French; by the czarist rule based on ignorance, fear and force; by the intervention of the British, French and Americans in Russian affairs from 1919 to 1921; by the geography of the huge Russian land mass situated strategically between Europe and Asia; and by the vitality derived from the rich Russian soil and the strenuous Russian climate. Add to all this the tremendous emotional power which Marxism and Leninism gives to the Russian leaders—and then we can realize that we are reckoning with a force which cannot be handled successfully by a "get tough with Russia" policy.

"Getting tough" never bought anything real and lasting—whether for schoolyard bullies or businessmen or world powers. The tougher we get, the tougher the Russians will get.

Throughout the world there are numerous reactionary elements which had hoped for Axis victory—and now profess great friendship for the United States. Yet, these enemies of yesterday and false friends of today continually try to provoke war between the United States and Russia. They have no real love of the United States. They only long for the day when the United States and Russia will destroy each other.

We must not let our Russian policy be guided or influenced by those inside or outside the United States who want war with Russia. This does not mean appeasement.

We most earnestly want peace with Russia—but we want to be met halfway. We want cooperation. And I believe that we can get cooperation once Russia understands that our

primary objective is neither saving the British Empire nor purchasing oil in the Near East with the lives of American soldiers.
We cannot allow national oil rivalries to force us into war.
All of the nations producing oil, whether inside or outside of
their own boundaries, must fulfill the provisions of the United
Nations Charter and encourage the development of world
petroleum reserves so as to make the maximum amount of oil
available to all nations of the world on an equitable peaceful
basis—and not on the basis of fighting the next war.

For her part, Russia can retain our respect by co-operating
with the United Nations in a spirit of open-minded and flexible
give-and-take.

The real peace treaty we now need is between the United
States and Russia. On our part, we should recognize that we
have no more business in the political affairs of Eastern Europe
than Russia has in the political affairs of Latin America, Western Europe and the United States. We may not like what Russia
does in Eastern Europe. Her type of land reform, industrial
expropriation, and suppression of basic liberties offends the
great majority of the people of the United States. But whether
we like it or not the Russians will try to socialize their sphere
of influence just as we try to democratize our sphere of influence. This applies also to Germany and Japan. We are striving to democratize Japan and our area of control in Germany,
while Russia strives to socialize eastern Germany.

As for Germany, we all must recognize that an equitable
settlement, based on a unified German nation, is absolutely
essential to any lasting European settlement. This means that
Russia must be assured that never again can German industry
be converted into military might to be used against her—and
Britain, Western Europe and the United States must be certain
that Russia's German policy will not become a tool of Russian
design against Western Europe.

The Russians have no more business in stirring up native
communists to political activity in Western Europe, Latin America and the United States than we have in interfering in the
politics of Eastern Europe and Russia. We know what Russia
is up to in Eastern Europe, for example, and Russia knows what

we are up to. We cannot permit the door to be closed against our trade in Eastern Europe any more than we can in China. But at the same time we have to recognize that the Balkans are closer to Russia than to us—and that Russia cannot permit either England or the United States to dominate the politics of that area.

China is a special case and although she holds the longest frontier in the world with Russia, the interests of world peace demand that China remain free from any sphere of influence, either politically or economically. We insist that the door to trade and economic development opportunities be left wide open in China as in all the world. However, the open door to trade and opportunities for economic development in China are meaningless unless there is a unified and peaceful China—built on the cooperation of the various groups in that country and based on a hands-off policy of the outside powers.

We are still arming to the hilt. Our excessive expenses for military purposes are the chief cause for our unbalanced budget. If taxes are to be lightened we must have the basis of a real peace with Russia—a peace that cannot be broken by extremist propagandists. We do not want our course determined for us by master minds operating out of London, Moscow or Nanking.

Russian ideas of social-economic justice are going to govern nearly a third of the world. Our ideas of free enterprise democracy will govern much of the rest. The two ideas will endeavor to prove which can deliver the most satisfaction to the common man in their respective areas of political dominance. But by mutual agreement, this competition should be put on a friendly basis and the Russians should stop conniving against us in certain areas of the world just as we should stop scheming against them in other parts of the world. Let the results of the two systems speak for themselves.

Meanwhile, the Russians should stop teaching that their form of communism must, by force if necessary, ultimately triumph over democratic capitalism—while we should close our ears to those among us who would have us believe that Russian communism and our free enterprise system cannot live, one with another, in a profitable and productive peace.

Under friendly peaceful competition the Russian world and the American world will gradually become more alike. The Russians will be forced to grant more and more of the personal freedoms; and we shall become more and more absorbed with the problems of social-economic justice.

Russia must be convinced that we are not planning for war against her and we must be certain that Russia is not carrying on territorial expansion or world domination through native Communists faithfully following every twist and turn in the Moscow party line. But in this competition, we must insist on an open door for trade throughout the world. There will always be an ideological conflict—but that is no reason why diplomats cannot work out a basis for both systems to live safely in the world side by side.

Once the fears of Russia and the United States Senate have been allayed by practical regional political reservations, I am sure that concern over the veto power would be greatly diminished. Then the United Nations would have a really great power in those areas which are truly international and not regional. In the world-wide, as distinguished from the regional field, the armed might of the United Nations should be so great as to make opposition useless. Only the United Nations should have atomic bombs and its military establishment should give special emphasis to air power. It should have control of the strategically located air bases with which the United States and Britain have encircled the world. And not only should individual nations be prohibited from manufacturing atomic bombs, guided missiles and military aircraft for bombing purposes, but no nation should be allowed to spend on its military establishment more than perhaps 15 per cent of its budget.

Practically and immediately, we must recognize that we are not yet ready for World Federation. Realistically, the most we can hope for now is a safe reduction in military expense and a long period of peace based on mutual trust between the Big Three.

During this period, every effort should be made to develop as rapidly as possible a body of international law based on moral principles and not on the Machiavellian principles of deceit, force and distrust—which, if continued, will lead the modern world to rapid disintegration.

In brief, as I see it today, the World Order is bankrupt—and the United States, Russia and England are the receivers. These are the hard facts of power politics on which we have to build a functioning, powerful United Nations and a body of international law. And as we build, we must develop fully the doctrine of the rights of small peoples as contained in the United Nations Charter. This law should ideally apply as much to Indonesians and Greeks as to Bulgarians and Poles—but practically, the application may be delayed until both British and Russians discover the futility of their methods.

In the full development of the rights of small nations, the British and Russians can learn a lesson from the Good Neighbor policy of Franklin Roosevelt. For under Roosevelt, we in the Western Hemisphere built a workable system of regional internationalism that fully protected the sovereign rights of every nation—a system of multilateral action that immeasurably strengthened the whole of world order.

In the United States an informed public opinion will be all-powerful. Our people are peace-minded. But they often express themselves too late—for events today move much faster than public opinion. The people here, as everywhere in the world, must be convinced that another war is not inevitable. And through mass meetings such as this, and through persistent pamphleteering, the people can be organized for peace—even though a large segment of our press is propagandizing our people for war in the hope of scaring Russia. And we who look on this war-with-Russia talk as criminal foolishness must carry our message direct to the people—even though we may be called Communists because we dare to speak out.

I believe that peace—the kind of peace I have outlined tonight—is the basic issue, both in the Congressional campaign this fall and right on through the Presidential election in 1948. How we meet this issue will determine whether we live not in "one world" or "two worlds"—but whether we live at all.

AID TO GREECE AND TURKEY [6]

HARRY S. TRUMAN [7]

President Harry S. Truman gave this message to Congress before a joint session of the two houses, in the House of Representatives, on March 12, 1947.

The immediate cause for this extraordinary proposal and for the enunciation of the "Truman Doctrine" was the statement by Great Britain that at the end of March she would withdraw her economic support from Greece. Behind that decision was the obvious economic plight of Britain. That Empire was apparently unable longer to live up to her commitments. If British-American cooperation were to be effective in the relief and restoration of Europe, in the re-establishment of a self-supporting Germany which could supply economic help to her neighbors, in the determination of proper boundaries for eastern Germany and other European regions, in the solution of peace problems concerning Austria, in the settlement of the Palestine question, and in the restriction of Russian influence to the zones already under Communist control, then the United States must adopt an affirmative policy in accepting some of the British Empire's responsibilities, as well as her own.

The Truman speech on aid to Greece was the answer of our State Department to the Greek-Turkish issue. The assumption was that the expansion of Soviet influence in that region was a major threat to our security, and that we were willing to take the chance of a third World War in our moving into the eastern Mediterranean to block such expansion.

The President's delivery was marked by "flat, undramatic reading," with a Middle Western accent in a monotone. His unemotional reading was probably what the occasion demanded. Observed Bert Andrews,[8] "The reason there were only three interruptions by applause—and not very loud applause at that—was that the address simply was not the kind intended to evoke demonstrations." In Andrews' opinion even Mr. Roosevelt would have paced the speech "with the deliberate view toward averting any such outbursts." Certainly the audience arose at the end and applauded heartily.

This message, broadcast throughout the world, immediately evoked wide comment. Characteristic headlines announced: "Europe is amazed by the blunt warning"; "Diplomats in Paris declare 'new Monroe Doctrine' must force Soviet showdown"; "London gratified by the new U. S.

[6] Text as recorded and transcribed by the *New York Times*, March 14, 1947.
[7] For biographical note, see Appendix.
[8] *New York Herald Tribune*. Section II. p. 1. March 16, 1947.

stand"; "Concern voiced over Soviet stand"; "Washington likens Truman's speech to the 1923 and 1941 warnings"; "Truman's speech hailed by Greece."

Debate in Congress began at once. By June 1, 1947, Congress had enacted legislation giving $300,000,000 to Greece and $100,000,000 to Turkey for financial and military support. The chief questions raised in the debate were the following: (1) Would the policy help to promote peace, or would it increase the danger of war? (2) Would it weaken the cause of the United Nations? (3) Would the financial cost to the United States ultimately be so great as to bankrupt this nation?

What of the preparation of the Truman message? Presumably Secretary of State Marshall knew the outline of the address, but not the details before he departed for the Moscow conference. Truman deliberately sidestepped mention of the Soviet Union and avoided other belligerent elements. The address was presumably timed to affect the Moscow Conference, or at least to make clear to Russia that the United States was squarely behind Marshall in his stand on the issues which remained unsolved as the Four Power Conference adjourned at the end of April 1947.

Mr. President, Mr. Speaker, members of the Congress of the United States:

The gravity of the situation which confronts the world today necessitates my appearance before a joint session of the Congress. The foreign policy and the national security of this country are involved.

One aspect of the present situation, which I wish to present to you at this time for your consideration and decision, concerns Greece and Turkey.

The United States has received from the Greek Government an urgent appeal for financial and economic assistance. Preliminary reports from the American Economic Mission now in Greece and reports from the American Ambassador in Greece corroborate the statement of the Greek Government that assistance is imperative if Greece is to survive as a free nation.

I do not believe that the American people and the Congress wish to turn a deaf ear to the appeal of the Greek Government.

Greece is not a rich country. Lack of sufficient natural resources has always forced the Greek people to work hard to make both ends meet. Since 1940, this industrious, peace loving country has suffered invasion, four years of cruel enemy occupation, and bitter internal strife.

When forces of liberation entered Greece they found that the retreating Germans had destroyed virtually all the railways, roads, port facilities, communications, and merchant marine. More than a thousand villages had been burned. Eighty-five per cent of the children were tubercular. Livestock, poultry, and draft animals had almost disappeared. Inflation had wiped out practically all savings.

As a result of these tragic conditions, a militant minority, exploiting human want and misery, was able to create political chaos which, until now, has made economic recovery impossible.

Greece is today without funds to finance the importation of those goods which are essential to bare subsistence. Under these circumstances the peoples of Greece cannot make progress in solving their problems of reconstruction. Greece is in desperate need of financial and economic assistance to enable it to resume purchases of food, clothing, fuel and seeds. These are indispensable for the subsistence of its people and are obtainable only from abroad. Greece must have help to import the goods necessary to restore internal order and security so essential for economic and political recovery.

The Greek Government has also asked for the assistance of experienced American administrators, economists and technicians to insure that the financial and other aid given to Greece shall be used effectively in creating a stable and self-sustaining economy and in improving its public administration.

The very existence of the Greek state is today threatened by the terrorist activities of several thousand armed men, led by Communists, who defy the Government's authority at a number of points, particularly along the northern boundaries. A commission appointed by the United Nations Security Council is at present investigating disturbed conditions in Northern Greece and alleged border violations along the frontiers between Greece on the one hand and Albania, Bulgaria and Yugoslavia on the other.

Meanwhile, the Greek Government is unable to cope with the situation. The Greek army is small and poorly equipped. It needs supplies and equipment if it is to restore the authority to the Government throughout Greek territory.

Greece must have assistance if it is to become a self-supporting and self-respecting democracy. The United States must supply that assistance. We have already extended to Greece certain types of relief and economic aid but these are inadequate. There is no other country to which democratic Greece can turn. No other nation is willing and able to provide the necessary support for a democratic Greek Government.

The British Government, which has been helping Greece, can give no further financial or economic aid after March 31. Great Britain finds itself under the necessity of reducing or liquidating its commitments in several parts of the world, including Greece.

We have considered how the United Nations might assist in this crisis. But the situation is an urgent one requiring immediate action, and the United Nations and its related organizations are not in a position to extend help of the kind that is required.

It is important to note that the Greek Government has asked for our aid in utilizing effectively the financial and other assistance we may give to Greece, and in improving its public administration. It is of the utmost importance that we supervise the use of any funds made available to Greece, in such a manner that each dollar spent will count toward making Greece self-supporting, and will help to build an economy in which a healthy democracy can flourish.

No government is perfect. One of the chief virtues of a democracy, however, is that its defects are always visible and under democratic processes can be pointed out and corrected. The Government of Greece is not perfect. Nevertheless, it represents 85 per cent of the members of the Greek Parliament who were chosen in an election last year. Foreign observers, including 692 Americans, considered this election to be a fair expression of the views of the Greek people.

The Greek Government has been operating in an atmosphere of chaos and extremism. It has made mistakes. The extension of aid by this country does not mean that the United States condones everything that the Greek Government has done or will do. We have condemned in the past, and we condemn now, extremist measures of the right or the left. We have in the past advised tolerance, and we advise tolerance now.

Greece's neighbor, Turkey, also deserves our attention. The future of Turkey as an independent and economically sound state is clearly no less important to the freedom-loving peoples of the world than the future of Greece. The circumstances in which Turkey finds itself today are considerably different from those of Greece. Turkey has been spared the disasters that have beset Greece. And during the war, the United States and Great Britain furnished Turkey with material aid. Nevertheless, Turkey now needs our support.

Since the war Turkey has sought financial assistance from Great Britain and the United States for the purpose of effecting that modernization necessary for the maintenance of its national integrity. That integrity is essential to the preservation of order in the Middle East.

The British Government has informed us that, owing to its own difficulties, it can no longer extend financial or economic aid to Turkey. As in the case of Greece, if Turkey is to have the assistance it needs, the United States must supply it. We are the only country able to provide that help.

I am fully aware of the broad implications involved if the United States extends assistance to Greece and Turkey, and I shall discuss these implications with you at this time.

One of the primary objectives of the foreign policy of the United States is the creation of conditions in which we and other nations will be able to work out a way of life free from coercion. This was a fundamental issue in the war with Germany and Japan. Our victory was won over countries which sought to impose their will, and their way of life, upon other nations.

To ensure the peaceful development of nations, free from coercion, the United States has taken a leading part in establishing the United Nations. The United Nations is designed to make possible lasting freedom and independence for all its members. We shall not realize our objectives, however, unless we are willing to help free people to maintain their free institutions and their national integrity against aggressive movements that seek to impose upon them totalitarian regimes. This is no more than a frank recognition that totalitarian regimes imposed on free peoples, by direct or indirect aggression, undermine the foundations of international peace and hence the security of the United States.

The peoples of a number of countries of the world have recently had totalitarian regimes forced upon them against their will. The Government of the United States has made frequent protests against coercion and intimidation, in violation of the Yalta Agreement, in Poland, Rumania and Bulgaria. I must also state that in a number of other countries there have been similar developments.

At the present moment in world history nearly every nation must choose between alternative ways of life. The choice is too often not a free one.

One way of life is based upon the will of the majority, and is distinguished by free institutions, representative government, free elections, guarantees of individual liberty, freedom of speech and religion, and freedom from political oppression.

The second way of life is based upon the will of a minority forcibly imposed upon the majority. It relies upon terror and oppression, a controlled press and radio, fixed elections, and the suppression of personal freedoms.

I believe that it must be the policy of the United States to support free peoples who are resisting attempted subjugation by armed minorities or by outside pressures.

I believe that we must assist free peoples to work out their own destinies in their own way.

I believe that our help should be primarily through economic and financial aid which is essential to economic stability and orderly political processes.

The world is not static, and the status quo is not sacred. But we cannot allow changes in the status quo in violation of the charter of the United Nations by such methods as coercion, or by such subterfuges as political infiltration. In helping free and independent nations to maintain their freedom, the United States will be giving effect to the principles of the charter of the United Nations.

It is necessary only to glance at a map to realize that the survival and integrity of the Greek nation are of grave importance in a much wider situation. If Greece should fall under the control of an armed minority, the effect upon its neighbor, Turkey, would be immediate and serious. Confusion and disorder might well spread throughout the entire Middle East.

Morover, the disappearance of Greece as an independent state would have a profound effect upon those countries in Europe whose peoples are struggling against great difficulties to maintain their freedoms and their independence while they repair the damages of war.

It would be an unspeakable tragedy if these countries, which have struggled so long against overwhelming odds, should lose that victory for which they sacrificed so much. Collapse of free institutions and loss of independence would be disastrous not only for them but for the world. Discouragement and possibly failure would quickly be the lot of neighboring peoples striving to maintain their freedom and independence.

Should we fail to aid Greece and Turkey in this fateful hour, the effect will be far reaching to the west as well as to the east. We must take immedate and resolute action.

I therefore ask the Congress to provide authority for assistance to Greece and Turkey in the amount of $400,000,000 for the period ending June 30, 1948. In requesting these funds, I have taken into consideration the maximum amount of relief assistance which would be furnished to Greece out of the $350,000,000 which I recently requested that the Congress authorize for the prevention of starvation and suffering in countries devastated by the war.

In addition to funds, I ask the Congress to authorize the detail of American civilian and military personnel to Greece and Turkey, at the request of those countries, to assist in the tasks of reconstruction, and for the purpose of supervising the use of such financial and material assistance as may be furnished. I recommend that authority also be provided for the instruction and training of selected Greek and Turkish personnel.

Finally, I ask that the Congress provide authority which will permit the speediest and most effective use, in terms of needed commodities, supplies, and equipment, of such funds as may be authorized.

If further funds, or further authority, should be needed for purposes indicated in this message, I shall not hesitate to bring the situation before the Congress. On this subject the executive and legislative branches of the Government must work together.

This is a serious course upon which we embark. I would not recommend it except that the alternative is much more serious.

The United States contributed $341,000,000,000 toward winning World War II. This is an investment in world freedom and world peace.

The assistance that I am recommending for Greece and Turkey amounts to little more than one tenth of one per cent of this investment. It is only common sense that we should safeguard this investment and make sure that it was not in vain.

The seeds of totalitarian regimes are nurtured by misery and want. They spread and grow in the evil soil of poverty and strife. They reach their full growth when the hope of a people for a better life has died. We must keep that hope alive. The free peoples of the world look to us for support in maintaining their freedoms.

If we falter in our leadership, we may endanger the peace of the world—and we shall surely endanger the welfare of our own nation.

Great responsibilities have been placed upon us by the swift movement of events. I am confident that the Congress will face these responsibilities squarely.

FOR AID TO GREECE AND TURKEY [9]

Arthur H. Vandenberg [10]

Senator Arthur Vandenberg, chairman of the Senate Committee on Foreign Relations, delivered this speech in the Senate on April 8, 1947, in support of President Truman's message advocating American aid to Greece and Turkey.

When the President announced his new "doctrine" or "plan" the critics immediately charged him with by-passing the United Nations. He replied that he was attempting to strengthen that organization, because at this time it was too weak for this major task and not legally equipped to deal with problems of the magnitude of the Greek crisis. Warren Austin, America's representative on the Security Council, explained fully the relation of our Greek policy to the United Nations. Senator Vandenberg, to meet further the criticisms, introduced an amendment to the Greek aid bill, by which the U. N. by a majority vote (and without American veto) could modify or end the prepared American program.

On April 7, Andrei Gromyko, Soviet Representative on the Security Council, replied to Mr. Austin. Before a large audience at Lake Success he developed many arguments that duplicated much of the domestic criticism of the Truman proposals. The plan, he contended, would weaken the authority of the United Nations; the independence of Greece and Turkey was thus jeopardized, and the American proposal constituted interference in the internal affairs of those countries.

Mr. Vandenberg's Senate debate on the following day was thus a refutation of the Gromyko argument. The Senator defined his proposition carefully: (1) It was not a "doctrine," but rather a "plan," the specific application of a "pattern." (2) From such interpretation the speaker argued that there were many American precedents for this procedure—precedents in our "open door" in China, in Pan American activities, and in our foreign relief efforts. (3) The plan was "not imperialistic." (4) Greece needed this help and asked for it. (5) Great Britain was unable to do the major job. (6) The situation called for immediate action—if communism was to be blocked. (7) The plan coordinated with the work of the United Nations, but the organization at this time was unable to shoulder the financial and other obligations in Greece. (8) To reject the President's proposal would mean disaster for Greece, Turkey, and perhaps for the world.

[9] Reprinted from *Congressional Record*. 80th Congress, 1st session. 93:3296-9. April 8, 1947 (daily edition). By permission of Senator Vandenberg.

[10] For biographical note see Appendix.

The Senator was blunt in his handling of Russian relations. The style was uncomplicated, brisk, always clear. The speaker, conscious of his task of replying to the propagandistic but cogent attacks by Gromyko, engaged in less rhetoric or colorful phrasing than was his usual practice. His personal appeals were closely knit with his logical pattern. His delivery, as usual, was vehement, earnest, somewhat oratorical. His vocal emphasis was constantly accompanied by bodily animation. Vandenberg ranks among the three or four leading Senate speakers.[11]

In response to the urgent recommendations of the President of the United States, the Senate Foreign Relations Committee has unanimously reported S. 938, the bill entitled "To provide for assistance to Greece and Turkey." It could be alternatively titled "A bill to support the purposes of the United Nations to maintain international peace and security," or it could be titled "A bill to serve America's self-interest in the maintenance of independent governments."

The committee makes this report primarily in response to direct appeals to our government from heroic Greece, which, by her sacrificial World War loyalties has richly earned the right to perpetuate her proud, historic independence. It does so in response to direct appeals from Turkey, which is the only truly independent nation left on the borders of Soviet Russia from the Baltic to the Black Sea. It also does so in the presence of the over-riding strategic fact that the fall of Greece, followed by the collapse of Turkey, could precipitate a chain reaction which would threaten peace and security around the globe. It does so in the profound belief that we Americans have an unescapable stake in all human rights and fundamental freedoms, and that they were better saved—for us as well as others—by adequate and timely support than by waiting for cumulative hazard to magnify the risk. It does so not only in the name of the liberties for which the Allies said they fought two world wars, but also in the name of the intelligent American self-interest which prefers an ounce of precaution to a pound of cure and which believes that "a stitch in time saves nine."

[11] For further comment on Vandenberg as a speaker, see *Representative American Speeches: 1937-1938*, p. 39; *1944-1945*, p. 43-4; *1945-1946*, p. 45-6.

I am not one of those, Mr. President, who conceive that we are launching what has been called, by some, a new "doctrine" in any such unique sense as did James Monroe a century and a quarter ago. Rather, in my opinion, we are launching a plan which has numerous precedents—although we must frankly and honestly assess the fact that it has new and "broad implications," as President Truman himself declared in his message of March 12.

There is no new "doctrine" in American aid to distressed nations. There is no new "doctrine" in striving for "the creation of conditions in which we and other nations will be able to work out a life free from coercion" or in "supporting free peoples who are resisting attempted subjugation"—again quoting the Presidential message. The pending plan unquestionably broadens our precedents when it enters the Mediterranean—although the marines were there in the earliest days of the Republic and in the finest American tradition. The plan broadens geographically—although we long since pronounced the "open door" for China. It broadens when peacetime military missions, heretofore largely confined to Pan America, enter the Near East. But it is not new in concept. Certainly there is nothing new in our opposition to communism outside of areas where it is officially embraced. We have always done these things. It would be "new" only if we now were to desert these ideals. In any event, in whatever degree it is "new," it is necessary.

But it is much more than a plan for "relief" of human suffering in Greece and Turkey. Let's be plain about it. It is a plan to forestall aggression which, once rolling, could snowball into global danger of vast design. It is a plan for peace. It is a plan to sterilize the seeds of war. We do not escape war by running away from it. No one ran away from war at Munich. We avoid war by facing facts. This plan faces facts. But of course there are other facts to face. No "plan" can guarantee peace. The most it can do is to take the better "calculated risk." That, I believe, is what this plan does. It is a plan, I repeat, for peace. It is a plan to strengthen the United Nations by supporting its objectives in respect to immediate necessities, pending the time when the United Nations can take over.

The Senate, in turn, faces an additional fact. If we were to reject the plan in its basic purpose we would give the "green light" to aggression everywhere. Our moral authority and leadership would die on the spot. We would multiply our own hazards. We would weaken the United Nations by multiplying its subsequent responsibilities.

This is not an imperialistic plan. It covets nothing for America but honorable peace in a free world of free men. That is not imperialism. I like what Elihu Root once said of our Monroe Doctrine: "It rests upon the right of every sovereign state to protect itself by preventing a condition of affairs in which it will be too late to protect itself." That is not imperialism. That is intelligent self-interest. That is what we here propose.

I recall President Monroe himself declared that the impulse of his "doctrine" was to prevent aggressive extension of alien systems "dangerous to our peace and safety." This is not imperialism. It is prudent common sense. It is the pattern of this plan. Curiously enough, one of the things contributing to the birth of the "Monroe Doctrine" was old Russia seeking to fish in North American waters. Communism thrives on "fishing in troubled waters" today. It is not imperialism to calm the waters. Our purposes are the exact opposite of imperialism. So is this plan. This truth shines through every word of the statement made on March 28 to the Security Council of the United Nations by our American ambassador. I quote:

"The United States does not desire to dominate, intimidate or threaten the security of any nation, large or small. The United States will support collective security for all nations—large as well as small. The United States respects the rights of all members of the United Nations to follow whatever way of life or system of government they choose, so long as the choice is freely made without intimidation and so long as such nations do not interfere with the rights of other countries or the liberties of other peoples."

I say once more, Mr. President, that we here confront a plan —a special and particular plan. I do not view it as a universal pattern but rather as a selective pattern to fit a given circumstance. We are not suddenly resolved to underwrite the earth. That would be fantastic, improvident and impossible. What we do is to underscore once more a principle long ingrained in the American character—namely, to "support free peoples who are resisting attempted subjugation," again quoting the Presidential message. We point the general direction we propose to go. We do not, we cannot chart the total course.

This plan fits a key strategic need. Undoubtedly there will be other problems facing other and different needs. For example, our occupational responsibilities in Korea unquestionably will soon demand positive support. It is part of World War II— unless we are to lose the peace. It would be a fraud upon our people to pretend that this plan ends all need for aid. Our people prefer the truth. We do face the fact that Greece and Turkey are not isolated phenomena—even though they involve a unique and emphasized importance. We must face the fact that other situations may arise which clearly involve our own national welfare in their lengthened shadows. Let us harbor no soft illusions. But I emphatically repeat that we do not here set a universal precedent, except in basic self-defensive purpose. We shall always react; but we shall react as any given situation seems to require. Meanwhile, it is to be fervently hoped and prayed that we may have enough foresight so that we do not always have to act on a "crisis basis."

This plan requires complete candor with ourselves and with the world. It requires prudence lest we over extend ourselves or over promise others. Equally it requires courage and tenacity of democratic purpose. But I cannot believe it would be intelligent self-interest to deny the plan and thus invite the earth to think that our divided government is impotent. I believe that "standing up" is a better risk than "lying down." I believe that we either take or surrender leadership—and I can find no intelligent, American self-interest in any such surrender.

But the situation, Mr. President, requires something more than is in this bill. It calls for two collateral efforts on our part: (1) to strive for the honorable removal of underlying frictions, if mutually possible, between the two greatest powers on earth; (2) to strive for the closest possible integration of all our plans with the collective responsibilities of a strengthened and matured United Nations which is the world's prime hope for peace.

I shall return to both of these propositions before I have concluded. At the moment I now address myself to the specific plan for which the approval of the Senate is now sought.

Aid for Greece is aid for a brave war ally which suffered war invasion, then four years of cruel enemy occupation, then bitter internal terrorism which the President identifies as of Communist origin, then Communist-inspired violaton of its hard-pressed borders. I have no doubt there also has been terrorism on the right. In any event, Greece is prostrate. British support, assigned to Britain by the Allies as a postwar responsibility, is being withdrawn because Britain herself is in economc straits. In this dire emergency Greece appeals to us to save her political and economic independence. This bill is our response. We are not "bailing out the British Empire." We are not "perpetuating Greek monarchy." We are making it possible for the Greek people to survive in stability and self-determination. We are doing the same thing for the world.

It is highly important at this point to note that financial and other outside aid for Greece is recommended in a powerful contemporary report of the Food and Agriculture Organization of the United Nations itself—with an appeal to the United States for special aid. The report frankly recognizes this need for special aid. Then, praising the Grecian tradition of self-reliance, this international report says that "democratic and voluntary methods of future development, rather than compulsory dictation or direction, are in keeping with the century-old characteristics of the Hellenic temperament." Remember, this is the United Nations speaking! From no other possible source could Greece be quite so sure of "democratic" aid looking toward "self-reliance" as from the United States. It is a precise prescription for the thing we here propose to do.

We need not condone the present Greek regime, though clearly chosen in a free election, in order to come to the aid of the Greeks themselves. We are entitled to expect that the Greeks themselves, responding to the advice they voluntarily have sought from us, will build a more efficient and equitable democracy when relieved of the pressures which have driven them to any sanctuary that has been presently available. But such precious objectives are impossible so long as Greece is torn by externally and internally stimulated civil war. Therefore, aid to Greece must include means to develop adequate Greek defense in behalf of lawful peace. In the absence of lawful peace, our aid would be no more than a transient bounty—as has been the case for the last two years.

Peace is prerequisite. So is helpful guidance in the establishment of a sound national economy. Greece turns to the United States as the only source of these imminently necessary helps. These comprehensive purposes are the program of this pending bill. Lest there be overemphasis in the wrong place, I hasten to add that our contemplated military mission involves only from ten to forty officers and no combat troops. The naval mission contemplates non-belligerent craft like mine sweepers, in the main. The military effort, though accounting for $150,-000,000 of this grant, is to help Greece to help herself to be self-reliant in defense of her self-chosen government, whatever that may be.

The sum of $130,000,000 is for basic reconstruction; $20,-000,000 for agricultural rehabilitation, plus $50,000,000 for relief in the general relief bill now pending in the House.

But that is not all. The plain fact seems to be that if the Greeks in their extremity, are not successfully helped to help themselves to maintain their own healthy right of self-determination, another Communist dictatorship will rise at this key point in world geography. Then Turkey, long mobilized against a Communist "war of nerves," faces neighboring jeopardy. The two situations are inseparable. Turkey confronts no such internal extremity as Greece; but it requires assistance to bulwark its national security. The President says that the maintenance of its national integrity "is essential to the preservation of order in the Middle East." If the Middle East falls within the orbit of aggressive Communist expansion, the repercussions will echo from the Dardanelles to the China Sea and westward to the rims of the Atlantic. Indeed, the Middle East, in this fore-shortened world, is not far enough for safety from our own New York or Detroit or Chicago or San Francisco.

That's where we come in. Do we face it now or later? Which is the wiser course? Which holds the better promise of honorable peace? Which is recommended by intelligent American self-interest? The President's answer is this: "If we falter in our leadership we may endanger the peace of the world —and we shall surely endanger the welfare of our own nation." He adds: "Great responsibilities have been placed upon us by the swift movement of events." God knows these responsibilities are great, no matter what our course. God knows that this would be an infinitely happier land if it were physically possible for us to close our tired eyes, retire within what were our bastions of yesterday and shut out the external menace of shapes and forms which we abhor. God knows that we painfully search our hearts for wisdom. May His way be the way we choose.

This plan is for fifteen months. Can this job be done in fifteen months? I do not know. I doubt it—although in fifteen months both the United Nations and the World Bank should be able substantially to take over.

But I ask neither Congress nor the country to ignore the nature of this obligation. I say again that I trust them to prefer the truth.

In a sense we are a tragic generation, despite our blessings and our place in the sun. We have been drawn into two world wars. Something has been wrong. We finally won two world wars; and yet still confront a restless and precarious peace. It is our supreme task to face these present realities, no matter how we hate them, and to mend the broken pattern if such be within human power.

Therefore, Mr. President, I say again let us all face facts. The problem involved in this bill—like the problem involved in every other phase of languishing peace—is the persistent con-troversy between what we loosely call Eastern Communism and

Western Democracy. From it inevitably stems persistent difficulties between the Soviet Union and its satellites upon the one hand, and the United States and the like-minded non-Communist states upon the other.

Still more explicitly, it involves hostility to Communist expansionism and infiltration. This expansionism, in turn, arises, we constantly are told, from Soviet fears of resurgent aggression by her neighbors and from fears of encirclement looking toward her destruction. If Moscow really has those fears, she is entitled to have them dependably removed. She cannot be expected to react any differently than we do under like circumstances. Given a fair chance, on a two-way street, we should be able to mitigate those fears because we believe in self-determination for Russians precisely as we insist upon it for Americans and others. We plot no offense against the Soviet Union. We are not hunting world dominion. We are not seeking dictation anywhere. But what we deny to ourselves as a matter of morality we also must deny to others as a matter of conquest.

It may be remembered that as long ago as January 10, 1945, I discussed this same, identical theme in the Senate. I said then that if Russia pursues expansionism through fear of a reborn Axis, we should offer her a hard and fast alliance against a reborn Axis. We have made that offer. It still stands. It has not been accepted. We can expand that offer. We can sign anything at Moscow which guarantees the independence of the Soviet Union within its own legitimate domain. But there must be two signatures—and they must both be good—better, I regret to say, than signatures at Yalta and at Potsdam. We, in turn, have the reciprocal right to demand effective proof that Moscow is not plotting to encircle us in a Communist-dominated world; that Communist assaults upon us, within and without the United States, shall cease; and that our mutual pledges to the Atlantic Charter and to the principles and purposes of the United Nations shall be reliably honored in behalf of all concerned. I do not mean in words alone. I mean in deeds. I mean the rebirth of international integrity.

It still seems to me, Mr. President, that the great need is comprehensively candid discussions between us, if possible, with all the cards face up upon the table. Let us not again drift into misunderstanding of what America means when it speaks. The crises will largely disappear if the mutual will exists between Washington and Moscow. If it cannot exist, even that ominous knowledge is worth having. While we cannot avoid the eternal rivalry of these incompatible ideologies, there ought to be an honorable way to "live and let live" within the rules of the United Nations. We should mutually strive to search it out on the basis not only of salvaging the ideals of World War I and World War II, but also and particularly on the basis of the self-interest of the two greatest nations on earth—neither one of whom wants any part of another war. But we, for our part, will never find it through equivocation which will be misread as timidity. We shall never find it except as we succeed in convincing Moscow (1) that we have absolutely no ulterior designs, and (2) that we shall not compromise or whittle away the basic human rights and fundamental freedoms which we both have pledged in the most solemn peacetime commitments of which honorable nations are capable.

But we shall never again be able to convince anybody of this latter, vital fact, if, at the instant moment, we refuse our solid backing to the President of the United States when he speaks in this behalf. It is the task of statesmanship to stop these present trends or lay bare the alternative. It is time to agree, or to agree to disagree. It is our own task to say what we mean and mean what we say in a friendly but incorrigible firmness regarding the only way to establish the realities of peace.

At this point, Mr. President, I want to say a final word about "aggression"—the major sin against a peaceful world. We did not write a definition of "aggression" in the San Francisco Charter because we feared our own inability to find adequate words. Yet it needs definition. One of the best attempts was the "Convention for the Definition of Aggression," signed at London, July 3, 1933, by the Soviet Union and, among others, ironically, the Balkan states. By this definition, an "aggressor" is one who commits acts including the following:

"Provision of support to armed bands formed in its territory which have invaded the territory of another state, or refusal, notwithstanding the request of the invaded state, to take, in its own territory, all the measures in its power to deprive those bands of all assistance or protection."

I content myself with the observation that, in the case at hand, somebody is an "aggressor" on these violated Greek frontiers, according to the Soviet's own specifications.

This brings me, Mr. President, to the most important of all considerations that have been raised by the pending plan. The United Nations, the voice of collective security, must always be our first reliance and our prime concern as far as possible in every problem of this nature. It must be used to the maximum of practical possibilities. In no available aspect should we by-pass its functions. But in no unavailable aspect should we ruin its potential by assigning to it functions which it does not possess. Such an assignment would destroy it for keeps. Meanwhile, under such circumstances as in the present instance, Greece would sink into the Communist orbit and the fateful chain reaction would set in both East and West.

Under the amended bill, now pending in the Senate, this whole situation is honestly and faithfully assessed. The Foreign Relations Committee has added a preamble which recites the facts. It asserts our belief and purpose that this bill "will contribute to the freedom and independence of all members of the United Nations in conformity with the prinicples and purposes of the Charter." The committee has added an amendment which stops the functions of this bill whenever the Security Council, without counting "vetoes," or the General Assembly finds that "action taken or assistance furnished by the United Nations makes the continuance of assistance (under the bill) unnecessary or undesirable."

Mr. President, far from by-passing the United Nations, this amended bill is the greatest act of voluntary allegiance to it in the whole story of the United Nations. It even goes to the heart and core of the "veto" controversy. In the first great test which the Security Council ever faced, Britain and France demonstrated their good faith by accepting a council verdict regardless of "vetoes" in the case of little Lebanon and Syria. We now do so in advance in the case of Greece and Turkey. We accept the untrammeled judgment of the organized conscience of the world on what we do, and we invite it to intervene at its own will. A technical error in the wording of the committee amendment was discovered by us as soon as the printed text was available and will be corrected by an amendment from the floor. This is not a weasel-worded gesture. This is an act of total faith.

Now let us examine the facts. I speak first of what the United Nations cannot do and what no wise well-wisher will ask it to do. It is not and was never intended to be a relief organization. It has no such funds and was never intended to have such funds. It could get the funds only by an assessment in which we would carry the heavy share and thus face, all over again, the vicious dissatisfactions which we suffered through U.N.R.R.A., despite its notable humanities when we put up our money for others too frequently to maladminister to suit themselves. It has no sustaining military force because the Soviet representatives thus far have declined to permit these plans to materialize. If it had either the funds or the force, their use would depend upon the Security Council. In the Security Council this would face a "veto." Any frank assessment of realities, in the light of experience to date, must concede that the "veto" would be used by the Soviet Union in any phase of conflict between communism and democracy.

These are the facts. There is no way to by-pass these facts. Greek independence cannot be saved, at least for the time being, in any such fashion, no matter how adroit the scheme of reference. The "implications" to which the president refers cannot be met by any attempts, no matter how nobly mediated, to misuse the United Nations as of today. The United Nations itself cannot be sustained by any such misuse. The most we can do at the moment is to leave certain special phases of the problem in United Nations jurisdiction, and to leave an over-all authority in the Council and Assembly to hold us to strict accountability for what we do.

Mr. Sumner Welles recently pointed out what he said will be "the line that Soviet propaganda will follow in its efforts to combat the Administration's present foreign policy." He cited "Izvestia" and "Pravda"—both official Moscow publications—which charge us with "destroying the United Nations."

This argument has met with much popular and often innocent support in the United States. On the one hand, this support is a precious tribute to the faithful hopes of humankind. On the other, it is a cunning backfire to becloud the issue. I know of no better way "to destroy the United Nations" than to give it a specific job which it is neither intended nor prepared to do. Indeed, it is a significant thing that this plan is opposed by two totally opposite and incompatible groups in the United States. As has been well said, it is opposed (1) by those who hope it won't work but are afraid it will, and (2) by those who hope it will work but are afraid it won't.

It is no depreciation of the United Nations to frankly recognize the fact that the Greek petition to us seeks primary relief which the United Nations cannot provide. It is of no small significance, in this connection, that Greece and Turkey, both members of the United Nations, did not themselves apply to the United Nations but applied direct to the United States.

But, Mr. President, the United Nations does have its important place in this prospectus even as things are today. It is already rendering important aid. Its Security Council has had a commission on the Greek border investigating disturbances between Greece, Yugoslavia, Bulgaria and Albania. This commission will report within a few weeks. It will establish truth and responsibility at this point of major friction. If a "veto" does not subsequently intervene, the Security Council may well establish a permanent border commission whose moral authority and whose sanctions may well minimize this phase of the Greek hazard. If the Security Council is permitted to function in this regard it will greatly simplify the Greco-Turkish problem and greatly hasten success for our own peaceful adventure. Surely, it does not "destroy" or remotely hamper the United Nations, in this phase, if the United States simultaneously is helping Greece to rebuild her own competent independence and helping Turkey to preserve hers. On the contrary, it is what would be called, in American idiom, "team ball."

Nor is that all. The United Nations Food and Agricultural Organization has submitted a twenty-five-year long-range program for Greek economic rehabilitation. And mark this! I repeat that this important instrumentality of the United Nations has specifically recommended that Greece should apply to the United States, among others, for temporary aid in launching this rehabilitation. It frankly recognizes the present limitations within which the United Nations operates.

Nor is this all. It is definitely anticipated that the World Bank will step into this situation and carry the major rehabilitation load just as soon as the imminent crisis is surmounted; just as soon as peace and preliminary stability are restored; just as soon as there is any basis whatever for banking credit.

So, Mr. President, the United Nations does have its important place in this historic prospectus. It can do things to help as of today even though its larger availability is a matter for tomorrow. We must use it to the maximum of its possibilities. We must use all of its functions which are available. We must take no unilateral or bilateral action without full and constant notice to this world fraternity, and with full and constant eagerness to have it succeed to our separably assumed responsibilities whenever and wherever this can be done.

I frankly regret that when the President spoke to Congress on March 12, he did not simultaneously advise the Secretary-General at New York of our intentions, instead of waiting to present indirect notice through our representative on the Security Council sixteen days later. It might have allayed needless misunderstanding. Any such misunderstanding is needless because the President himself clearly indicates that he is wedded to the United Nations. Nothing could be clearer than our message delivered to the Security Council by Ambassador Austin on March 28:

"The program of economic assistance contemplated by the United States is of an emergency character. The United States believes that the United Nations and its related agencies should assume the principal responsibility, within their capabilites, for the longe-range tasks of assistance required for the reconstruction of Greece. . . . The United States is giving momentum to the

United Nations by its present policy. . . . We look forward to the time when such burdens may be carried through the United Nations."

If that is not clear and adequate, Mr. President, certainly nothing remains unsaid in the preamble and amendment which the Senate Foreign Relations Committee has added to the pending bill. Certainly I would be the last man in America to sanction any blow at the prestige and authority of the United Nations. But I also hope I would be the last man in America to drain off that prestige and authority by assigning them a total task which, in point of time and resources, would be foredoomed to sinister failure.

I am unable to understand how we could undermine an institution dedicated to human rights and fundamental freedoms, to independent governments of free men in a free world, when we supplement these dedications with our own direct succor to those who are imminently threatened with their loss, and when we ask the United Nations to hold us to strict accountability for what we do. No, Mr. President, we are not by-passing the United Nations. We are sustaining them. We are serving peace—emphatically including peace for ourselves—when we strive, in prudent time, to arrest those frictions and disintegrations which otherwise could culminate in an atomic war which must not happen.

Now, Mr. President, as I conclude, let me say that your Foreign Relations Committee unanimously recommends the passage of this amended measure. It is regrettable that policies of such magnitude could not have more time for consideration. I knew nothing of the matter until we were called to the White House on February 27. It is unfortunate when such important decisions have to be made on a crisis basis. But we confront a condition and not a theory. We have made extraordinary efforts to let in the light. We held public hearings. We heard every citizen who asked to be heard. We resorted to the novel technique of inviting all Senators to contribute to a questionnaire, and we have made public the State Department's categorical replies. We are suggesting some amendments to the bill aimed generally at tighter controls and specific liaison with the United Nations. But, sir, the truth of the matter is that, even though we had months of study at our command, Congress does not have an unprejudiced chance to exercise truly independent and objective judgments in such circumstances as we here confront. This statement leads to the final consideration which no Senator can ignore in respect to his decision.

Congress does not enjoy original jurisdiction in foreign relations. That is the prerogative of the Chief Executive. We come in, usually only at the eleventh hour when our choice is the lesser of two evils—as in this instance when we must decide which is the wiser "calculated risk" for us. To be or not to be? To do or not to do? As when we have been asked, upon other occasions, to declare war, the fact is that by the time these issues reach us for ultimate conclusions we are heavily precommitted by the fact of the Presidential request.

I do not for an instant mean to say we cannot act on our own independent judgments. I do not mean to say that it is not still our solemn duty to act in keeping with our own estimate of the national welfare and security. I do not mean to say that we can either shift or dodge our share of responsibility, and I would not do so. But I do mean to say that among the paramount factors to which we dare not deny due weight is this: To repudiate the President of the United States at such an hour could display a divisive weakness which might involve far greater jeopardy than a sturdy display of united strength. We are not free to ignore the price of non-compliance.

In my view, Mr. President, the price of non-compliance in the instant case—in addition to all other reasons for prompt passage of this bill—would be the forfeiture of all hope to effectively influence the attitudes of other nations in our peaceful pursuit of international righteousness. It would stunt our moral authority and mute our voice. It would encourage dangerous contempts. It would invite provocative misunderstandings of the tenacity with which we are prepared to defend our fundamental ideals.

AGAINST AID TO GREECE AND TURKEY [12]

CLAUDE D. PEPPER [13]

Senator Pepper gave this speech before the United States Senate on April 10, 1947, in general opposition to Senate bill S. 938, to provide assistance to Greece and Turkey.

The bill was introduced in the Senate on March 19, and was approved by the Senate Foreign Relations Committee on April 3. Debate continued with much vigor for two weeks. The chief defenders of the bill were Senators Connally, Eastland, Flanders, Hatch, Fulbright, Lucas, Lodge, and Vandenberg. Extended arguments in opposition included those of Bricker, Brooks, Bushfield, Byrd, Johnson (of Colorado), Kem, Pepper, and Taylor. Particularly impassioned were the arguments in the final debate on April 22. The Senators voted 67 to 23 for the bill.

On May 9 the House also acted favorably (287 to 107).

The bill provided (1) expenditures by July, 1948, of $400,000,000 in aid to Greece and Turkey ($300,000,000 to Greece, one half of which was for economic aid and one half for military purposes; $100,000,000 for military aid to Turkey). The bill also included commitment by the United States to halt the program at any time the United Nations found it "unnecessary and/or undesirable." The legislation was interpreted as a direct notice to Russia that its expansion in the Mediterranean and Middle East would meet with military resistance, if necessary, by the United States.

Senator Pepper, identified with the Henry Wallace "left wing," continued as an outstanding Senate debater. His arguments, expressed at times with rhetorical fervor, were nevertheless substantial in content and logic. He was the outstanding negative speaker in this debate, as he was on the labor relations issue.[14]

Mr. President, for a few moments I shall address myself in general terms to the proposal which is now before the Senate, and thereafter I shall address myself to the specific amendments, or substitutes, as they may come severally to the attention of the Senate.

[12] *Congressional Record.* 80th Congress, 1st session. 93:3381-93. April 10, 1947 (daily edition). By permission of Senator Pepper.

[13] For biographical note see Appendix.

[14] For further comment on Senator Pepper as a speaker, and for an address by him, see *Representative American Speeches: 1940-1941.* p. 49-56.

Like millions of other Americans and millions of nationals of other nations over the world, I keep asking myself what President Roosevelt, as the one principally responsible for the United Nations, would have done, faced with the same situation which faces our Government now in Greece and Turkey. And the reply which keeps coming back to me is the statement of the *Manchester Guardian,* a world-honored English newspaper, which said, as quoted on March 21 by the *New York Herald Tribune:*

> One feels that, faced with the same situation, President Roosevelt would first have tried to do the same things through the United Nations by enlisting the support of other nations, including Russia if possible. Peace, the status quo, the integrity of nations—these are not exclusively American interests, but the interest of us all.

What is this proposal we now have to approve or reject? It is not a relief bill—because no relief is asked for Turkey, and half of what is asked for Greece is for equipping, training and maintaining a Greek army of 125,000.

Some say it is a momentous new doctrine and they compare it to the Monroe Doctrine except that it extends to the whole world and not merely to the Western Hemisphere. Some say it is a showdown with Russia and that we have determined to join issue with the Russians at every point of their circumference.

Others say that we have determined to stop communism and now accept its challenge in every continent and country and clime.

Others say it divides the world into two spheres, the East and the West. For example, the *Stockholm Expressen* says:

> In the long run, the speech [referring to the President's address] has merely increased the difficulties and deepened the disagreements between the East and the West, which are shaking the postwar world.

From many parts of the world come the rising murmurs that it is the expression of a new and expanding American imperialism, while a French newspaper adds that the President's "concern is not for democracy but for the interest of American big businessmen who are in full action in the Near East."

Mr. President, surely a doctrine subject to so many different interpretations—and I am giving them to the Senate only for what they are worth—which has aroused such sincere concerns and fears from noncommunistic sources in so many parts of the world, which has illimitable and incalculable implications, as admitted by its own proponents, should not be adopted without the American people taking ample time to debate and to weigh the solemn judgment they shall cast upon it.

The Congress and the country debated lend-lease, another momentous American policy which had my hearty support, for many months before we enacted it. The Senate Foreign Relations Committee conducted hearings before it recommended it. Those of us who are deeply disturbed by this momentous proposal now before us protest against the effort to secure its hasty passage by the Senate without adequate opportunity for debate in the Senate and in the country.

Especially is it regrettable that the Senate, where the privilege of debate can be unlimited according to the rules, has chosen to act first upon this measure instead of following the practice we used in connection with lend-lease and letting the measure first pass the House and then come to the Senate after the nation has been more fully advised of its significance and implications.

Let me hasten to assert that in these observations in no sense of the word do I cast any disparagement upon or direct any criticism to the able chairman of the Foreign Relations Committee [Mr. Vandenberg] or to the distinguished members of that committee. On the contrary the chairman has been characteristically distinguished in the fairness with which he has approached every aspect of this question. He has already told the Senate that the committee heard every witness who asked to be heard. Yet it is a fact—and I am sure it was a necessity on the part of the committee—that in many cases the witnesses were limited in the time they were allowed before the committee. I feel that, if the hearings are considered by the committee to have been adequate, surely here in the Senate, Senators should search their souls and minds upon this momentous proposal and give the American people an opportunity to express their sentiments to their Congress before we launch America upon a course, the implications of which no honest man can foretell.

From church people, from those whose faith in the future is pinned to the United Nations, from those who both love America and love peace, there is a rising tide of opposition to this measure as it is now before the Senate, in spite of the generous gesture which the Foreign Relations Committee, in the utmost of good faith, has extended to the Untied Nations. I believe Senators will have to go no further than their own mail to affirm the growing opposition to the proposal, the end of which no one can honestly foretell.

Robbed of the military aspects, this measure would have had no opposition in Congress, for we all favor Greek relief to the utmost. In 1945 I had the privilege of spending a few days in Athens. I saw the horror which those people had experienced as the Germans sought to wreak their vengeance upon them for knocking out of order Hitler's timetable to invade the Soviet Union. I heard this at Nuremberg in 1945 from the mouth of General von Brauchitsch, who had been commander in chief of the German Army. The timetable called for an attack upon Russia by the Germans on the 8th of May 1941. Then they determined to occupy Greece and Yugoslavia. Hitler gave the order for General von Brauchitsch for execution. He occupied those two countries. But Von Brauchitsch was a good enough general and an able enough commander to anticipate the difficulty of this assignment. Perhaps he sensed ahead of time the glorious and heroic defense which would be made by the peoples of Greece and Yugoslavia. He called upon Hitler, he said, to allow him to withhold the attack upon Russia until the job in Greece and Yugoslavia was completed. He testified that Hitler finally acquiesced. The result was that the Nazi assault upon Soviet territory was launched on the 22d of June 1941, instead of on the 8th of May. Because the Germans were aware of what the Greeks had done to upset their timetable, they wreaked every barbaric form of vengeance that they could possibly conceive upon the Greek people. I know, therefore, how dire is their distress and how great is their need.

Relief for Greece could have been continued through UNRRA, which was set up by the United Nations Organization, and to which we generously contributed. But the Government of the United States is responsible for the termination of UNRRA, giving some justification for asserting that, in the dispensation of relief, we were not thinking solely about human need and the suffering of men, women, and children, but those who obtained relief had to be politically acceptable to our dispensation. Relief could have been provided through an international relief fund set up in the United Nations, as other nations wished to do, upon the recommendation last year of former Mayor Fiorello LaGuardia, the head of UNRRA, pursuant to the directive of UNRRA itself in the United Nations.

But, Mr. President, United States representatives prevented that resolution setting up an international relief fund from being adopted, though Mayor LaGuardia asserts that he had visited Stalin beforehand and that the head of the Soviet Government had given his commitment that the Soviet Union would participate in setting up such an international relief fund.

I hold in my hand the resolutions and official documents showing who proposed to set up an international relief fund and who killed it. This material comes to me, upon my request, from the United Nations Organization itself.

We are already undertaking to provide $50,000,000 outside this bill for immediate relief to Greece, and that is all that is asked to relieve distress in Greece. It will be recognized that I refer to the general relief bill providing $350,000,000 for relief of other distressed nations and peoples of the world. But again, Mr. President, while that bill allows $50,000,000 for Greece, there is some justification for the assertion that we recognize human misery and need only when it happens to occur in a country whose political policy is agreeable to the State Department of the United States.

When the Good Samaritan was on the way to Jericho and heard a cry to his conscience, he did not ask whether the recipient of his charity was on his political side. It is a good lesson for America to recall today like other Biblical illustrations, in the dispensation of Christian charity.

The $150,000,000 which this measure requests for economic rehabilitation in Greece should be and can be provided through the World Bank in the form of a loan, a part of which, at least, could be paid back, and would not in the first instance be an outright gift, provided at the expense of the American taxpayers.

It is well known that the International Food and Agricultural Organization set up under the United Nations organization sent a mission to Greece to make a study of short-term and long-term needs in that war-torn country. That mission submitted a report, which was recently published. In its report, it asked for two kinds of relief—perhaps I should say three kinds: First, they appealed to the Economic and Social Council of the United Nations and to the United States and Britain, to provide Greece with short-term relief in the matter of food and other imports which they were not otherwise able to get to cover the period following UNRRA's withdrawal until international assistance and an expanding economy would no longer require such special aid. I understood that type of aid referred to the kind of relief contemplated in the $50,000,000 appropriation which is being made available by Congress for assistance to the distressed Greek people, outside the proposal which is now before us. But, the burden of the recommendation of that mission of the Food and Agricultural Organization was that the World Bank make a loan of $100,000,000 to Greece for long-term rehabilitation of her economy.

It is said that the World Bank cannot give this assistance, that it cannot extend this loan. No one denies that it has many billions of dollars in its treasury. One reason it is not able immediately to give this assistance is because there has been some delay on the part of our Government in recommending some of the officials of the institution. It is said it is a lending organization. Several weeks ago the bank announced that the Greek Government had notified it that it intended to apply for a loan and would do so as soon as it completed a study of its needs and its reconstruction program. Surely the Greeks could pay something back. The United States is the major stockholder in the World Bank. If the bank should lose the fund, we would lose the major part. But is not that preferable to giving it all without any hope of reimbursement to the American taxpayers?

So I say, Mr. President, that the relief needs of Greece, short term and long term, could have been taken care of through UNRRA had we continued it. They could have been provided for in an international relief fund had we not killed it. They could be aided now in connection with the $50,000,000 which Congress is in the course of providing. The long-term relief can and should be provided through the World Bank set up for the express purpose of giving such assistance to those who require it.

Even if the President had asked the Congress to make a direct grant of money to Greece for both relief and rehabilitation, he could have got the money by a simple request. Congress is not going to deny a request of the President that we do our duty in an economic way to the other peoples of the world. But—

What has deeply moved and disturbed the American people and people all over the world is the unprecedented proposal, first, that we send a military mission to Turkey, second, that we give Turkey $100,000,000 for the equipment and support of her army for the next 15 months, third, that we send a military mission to Greece, fourth, that we give Greece $150,000,000 to equip, train, and support a Greek Army of 125,000 for the next 15 months.

I know we are moving in a fast world. I knew especially that the international scene is kaleidoscopic in its changes; but I will say candidly, Mr. President, that, if 6 weeks ago anyone had suggested to me that the President would propose or that the American Congress would countenance our sending a military mission to Turkey, paying the major part of the support for the equipment and maintenance of a Turkish Army, I would have thought that the suggestion was unthinkable. It is so linked with the animosity that is directed against some nations and some peoples, it is so delicately interwoven with a nation like Greece for which we have such supreme respect and affection, that we seem to take it as a matter of course that today there are no geographic limits to where America may go in giving aid and armed support for things which we approve of in various parts of the world.

There is an axiom in the law that what we do by another we do ourselves. If we finance another nation's army by providing money for its support, by giving them the equipment, by providing training in the use of the equipment, through the medium of an American military mission, can it be denied that to a very practical degree the foreign army becomes our army because we are financing it, we are equipping it, we are training it, and we are providing supervision in certain ways through an American mission? Above all, we are helping to continue its existence.

What deeply frightens the American people is that, if Congress adopts this measure, it will make the United States, the principal founder of the United Nations, repudiate its solemn covenant to act through the United Nations for the prevention and removal of threats to the peace and for the suppression of acts of aggression or other breaches of the peace, and to bring about by peaceful means and in conformity with the principles of justice and international law, adjustment or settlement of international disputes or situations which might lead to a breach of the peace.

I have before me the Charter of the United Nations Organization. I merely want to read article I of that Charter:

The purposes of the United Nations are:

1. To maintain international peace and security, and to that end to take effective collective measures for the prevention and removal of threats to the peace and for the suppression of acts of aggression or other breaches of the peace, and to bring about by peaceful means, and in conformity with the principles of justice and international law, adjustment or settlement of international disputes or situations which might lead to a breach of the peace.

Mr. President, the effect of this proposal, if enacted, is officially to brand the United Nations as a failure, and of no force or power to achieve the sacred functions for which it was founded—the protection of the security of peoples and the preservation of the peace of the world. This proposal has disappointed the hopes of the American people for peace more than any other single event since the establishment of the United Nations.

Mr. President, let me summarize the results from the last Gallup poll on that subject. The poll indicated that 56 per cent of the people queried favored the bill asking for $250,000,-000 to give aid to Greece, but the poll report also indicated that a majority of the people regretted that we had not gone, in the first instance, through the United Nations Organization, and the poll further disclosed that an overwhelming majority opposed our sending military missions to Turkey and to Greece.

Mr. President, the question of sending military missions might be adverted to at this point. At the present time there is no statute which authorizes the President of the United States to send a military mission to any country outside the Western Hemisphere. There was a statute, enacted several years ago, which permitted us to send military missions within the Western Hemisphere, but not outside it. On the contrary, the fact that the Executive recognizes that he has no authority to send military missions outside the Western Hemisphere is best attested by the fact that there is now pending in the present Congress a bill to authorize the President to do that very thing—to send military missions outside the Western Hemisphere.

I recall that in 1945 I was visiting in Syria and was talking to the highest officials of the Syrian Government. To the American minister whom I accompanied in the conference and to me —with the idea that in some way I might be able to help in the accomplishment of their recommendations—they pleaded that two American officers in American uniforms be permitted to go there, to help them achieve their emancipation—from the Russians, Mr. President? No; from the British troops. But our officials had to report to them that our Government had no authority to send military missions outside the Western Hemisphere, even though they sympathized with their aspirations. Help later was given. The Senator from Michigan [Mr. Vandenberg] and the Senator from Texas [Mr. Connally] had a very great and excellent influence in the United Nations in bringing about a decision by which British and French troops did leave Syria and Lebanon.

But I am saying that this bill proposes a new principle; namely, to allow military missions to be sent outside the Western Hemisphere. Where will that course lead us?

We are told that not more than 30 or 40 American officers will be sent. Mayor LaGuardia has said that that will mean the sending of 300 or 400 personnel, because every officer will have at least 10 aides. But, Mr. President, if an American officer in the uniform of the United States Army or Navy is placed there America will be there, with all that that means and with all that it should mean. In many instances it will mean that the American uniform will be the leverage by which reactionary and perhaps corrupt governments may at least psychologically intimidate the opposition to their own domestic policies.

Mr. President, it is not true that the United Nations is incapable of meeting the present problems of the eastern Mediterranean unless the United States makes it so.

If we rob the United Nations of the stalwart support of the strongest nation in the world and then condemn it as being incapable of acting, the fault is upon us, not the United Nations. We shall have to bear upon our hearts and consciences the immeasurable consequences, not only of this new doctrine which now is proposed, but the mortal blow that we strike at the United Nations, which is our one great gain from all the blood and treasure the war has just cost us.

The leaders who have proposed this measure to us, however earnest and sincere and patriotic, I fear are not aware of what they have done. In an honest but misguided zeal to strike out against what they call communism, as one does against horrible shapes and forms which accost one in a nightmare, they would sabotage the United Nations, destroy any hope of reconciliation with Russia, launch the United States upon an unprecedented policy of intervention in remote nations and areas of the world unilaterally, ally us with the reactionary and corrupt regimes of the world, subject this Nation to the serious accusation of aspiring to become the new Rome or the old Britain, and risk for the American people a war which may destroy civilization.

Against such a policy, small wonder that the protests of those groups who believe in peace and the United Nations, those who want America to hold firm to its old democratic traditions, are rising to a higher and higher pitch.

Surely the Senate will not adopt in haste this policy, the end of which no Senator can forsee.

Mr. President, let me digress here to observe that, as I said to the Foreign Relations Committee the other day, a committee characteristically courteous in their reception, I supported lend-lease. I saw Senators on this floor search their souls for the right decision on that policy. They saw its implications and where it might lead. So did I. But I supported it. I thought that at that time, under those circumstances, there was nothing else to do. But, Mr. President, to those who too rashly condemn some of us who were so hardy in our support of lend-lease and are so reluctant in any support of this measure, let me remind them of the action I took about the 20th of May 1940, when I stood on this floor and announced to the Senate that the Germans had reached Abbeville, nearly on the Atlantic coast of France; and that they were about to pinch off the whole British Army and that Dunkerque was in prospect. I did not announce that, but that was what was inevitable. Then I announced the purport of a resolution I contemplated submitting, not upon the direction of President Roosevelt, but at least having communicated it to him and having advised him that I would submit it on my own responsibility at noon that day unless he requested me not to. I read it over the telephone to Miss Margaret Le Hand, his personal secretary. After I had finished she probably disclosed what may have been the thinking of the President, when she said, "It would be great if we could get that, wouldn't it?"

We authorized the President to let any allies who were the victims of Hitler's aggression have any airplanes in our own possession that could be replaced by manufacture in the United States. A little later the authority was extended until it embodied the spirit and the purpose, if not the letter, of the eventual lend-lease law.

What I wanted to emphasize, Mr. President, was that on that day Denmark was under the cruel heel of the Hitler hordes, as was Norway, likewise Holland, likewise Belgium, likewise all eastern France, and it was inevitable that the German Army should sweep over probably all of France. It was thought by a great many at that time that it was only a question of time until Britain herself would fall.

I will say, therefore, that, whenever Russia undertakes, even in a small way, to do the same thing, I shall try to be as diligent in rejection of such action on her part as I was at that time in resisting the actual military aggression of Hitler's hordes upon the people of western Europe.

Let me remind the Senate that there was no United Nations in 1940. Today military assault has been undertaken, and to my knowledge, no ultimatum prophesies of such an assault in the immediate future. Today we have taken a solemn covenant that we will collectively keep the peace of the world through the United Nations Organization.

I say, Mr. President, against a policy such as that now proposed, small wonder that the protests of the groups who believe in peace and in the United Nations, those who want America to hold firm to its old democratic tradition, are rising to a higher and higher pitch. Surely the Senate will not adopt in haste this policy, the end of which no Senator can forsee.

Let Senators who give their unreserved approval to the pending measure be prepared for the full implications of it, as those of us who supported lend-lease were prepared to accept the utmost implications of that measure.

The American people believe in the United Nations for they know it is the only rock upon which they can base their hopes of any peace. A majority of the people have recently attested their grievous disappointment that the United Nations was bypassed, and their overwhelming opposition to our sending military missions, without precedent, to Turkey and Greece. Now the Foreign Relations Committee, in an attempt to assuage the grief and to satisfy the protest of the American people, ingenuously, and with the best motives—and undoubtedly the committee wishes the matter had been handled differently from the beginning—proposes that the United States go ahead sending military missions to Turkey and Greece, supporting Turkish and Greek armies, and for all practical purposes administering the Government of Greece, but that it be subject to the veto of the United Nations by a majority vote.

Mr. President, this may soothe our consciences, but it does not correct our conduct. There is no substitute for the United

Nations; there is nothing just as good. It is like going through the courts of law—you either do or you do not. You either act according to law or you act outside the law. This proposal, despite the Committee amendment, is still outside the charter of the fundamental law of the United Nations.

It does not discharge our solemn obligation to act through the UN "for the prevention and removal of threats to the peace and for the suppression of acts of aggression" and for the "adjustment or settlement of international disputes or situations which might lead to a breach of the peace" by acting unilaterally and then telling the UN we will stop if a majority of the UN ask us to discontinue what we are doing. . . .

What is the occasion of our alarm respecting the security of Greece? It is that Albania and Yugoslavia and Bulgaria are alleged to have given training, encouragement, and some equipment to certain Greeks alleged to be led by Communists in the northern part of Greece, said to number 13,000. So far as I am aware, nobody has charged that these "armed bands" so-called consist of anything but Greeks in Greece. But Greece appealed to the United Nations against this aggression. The United Nations took jurisdiction, quite properly, and appointed a Commission of Inquiry. The Commission has been on the spot, made its findings, and is now preparing to report. Can anyone with justice say that the United Nations has failed in this matter? Shall we, before the report of the Commission has been filed, before the United Nations has had a chance officially to know the facts and to take any action, presume that it will not act at all? Can anyone justify the United States in unilaterally sending a military mission to Greece, equipping and training a Greek army of 125,000 as an answer to an alleged intervention now being investigated by the United Nations? On the allegation of small-scale intervention in Greece, I am afraid, Mr. President, we in Congress are being asked to authorize the unprecedentedly large-scale intervention by the United States.

And what is the aggression, or what is the situation threatening the independence and the security of Turkey? There have been no excursions into Turkish territory by the forces of Russia or any nation. There is no Communist threat in Turkey. The totalitarian government there has seen to that. The assumed threat in Turkey is that certain requests have been made by the Soviet Union to Turkey that the four Black Sea powers—Turkey, the Soviet Union, Rumania, and Bulgaria—without the western powers having anything to do with it, shall determine the control of the Dardanelles. For over 200 years Russia, feeling that the Dardanelles is essential to its security as well as to its welfare in affording access to the Mediterranean, has either been trying to acquire or to obtain a dominating influence in the control of the Dardanelles. That may be bad policy, but it is not Communist policy—it has been Russian policy for over two centuries. It will be recalled that Russia won the Dardanelles in 1854 in a war with Turkey, and the British and the French then sent their fleets into the Black Sea, sank the Russian Fleet, and forced the Russians to agree to a new treaty taking away from them the Dardanelles, which they had secured by their victory over Turkey and through their treaty of peace with Turkey.

In World War I the Allies solemnly agreed to give Russia the Dardanelles in compensation for Russia entering the war on the Allied side against Germany, while Turkey fought with Germany. And I need not add that Turkey did not fight with us in this war at all, so far as I know, although she did declare war technically toward the end of the conflict. Russia got out of World War I before it was over through her revolution, although, said Sir Bernard Pares, the brilliant British historian, she gave two and one-half million killed and two and one-half million wounded to the Allied victory before she got out, and the British historian Pares says she saved Paris twice by what she did in World War I. But Russia did not get the Dardanelles, and it is my information that the revolutionary government did not ask for it.

Since World War I, the Dardanelles have not been controlled exclusively by Turkey; they have been controlled by a convention of powers called the Montreux Convention, and the dominating powers in that convention have been Britain and France. In short, western European powers have used Turkey as a bastion against Russia. The United States was not a party to the Montreux Convention, but it was agreed at Potsdam that Great Britain and the United States support liberalization of the Montreux Convention and that concessions be made to Russia. This is one of the pending issues yet unsettled among the big powers. But there has never been any ultimatum. There has been no new demand to my knowledge. What precipitated the present proposal was not a new threat by Russia, but notice to Turkey by Great Britain that she was no longer able or willing to pay the major part of the expense of maintaining the Turkish Army. That expense we now propose to assume.

Mr. President, I do not presume to pass judgment on what Great Britain does, but I think the British imperial record discloses to fair critics of history that the British have played the game of power politics, having been in power for centuries. In international affairs they do not have the same tradition we have. If they support a revolution to aid British prestige or further British interests, that is not a strange doctrine to them. If they finance a foreign army to serve their ends, their people and apparently their parliaments do not object to that. If they even influence internal affairs of other peoples, they have precedents, Mr. President, for such policy, which America, thank God, does not have. And it is a peculiar thing that Britain, which has been in Greece for years, has been there, I dare say, more to serve British policies than to save Greece; and if Britain has been in Turkey helping to support the Turkish Army as well as backing up the Turkish position with the British Fleet and with British bases in the eastern Mediterranean, I presume, Mr. President, that Britain has been doing it to serve Britain's national interest. Call it "imperial," they have not objected to that.

The strange thing is that, though we may be activated by different motives—and I know we are—when we do substantially the same thing, yet is there not some justification for suspicion being attached to our own motives of serving similar purposes on the part of the United States?

I say, Mr. President, let the British do what they choose to do; that is their business. But I have the greatest reluctance to have the charge made against my country that, to a phenomenal degree, we are stepping into empty British footprints in the imperial quicksands of the world.

Mr. President, before I get away from the Dardenelles, though I do not have the clipping before me, let me say that I remember reading last year, about September or late August, in the *Richmond Times-Dispatch,* the integrity of which no Senator would question, an editorial which said that Americans in considering the Dardanelles' problem might well think of it as if a foreign power possessed the mouth of the Chesapeake Bay. How would we feel about that? And how would we feel if we asserted the right of this government and that government to determine the defense and the control of the mouth of the Chesapeake Bay, and Britain, France, or Russia said, "No, you are not going to arrive at that settlement unless we have a voice in it."

Mr. President, I live down in that golden part of this country, that blessed part of this earth called Florida. Instead of thinking about the mouth of the Chesapeake Bay, as does the *Richmond Times-Dispatch,* I think of the Gulf of Mexico. I look at it on the map. I see that Mexico and the United States of America are the powers which border on that great body of water. I see the mighty Mississippi, which opens up the heart of America, emptying its colossal waters into that great gulf. I see, Mr. President, the Straits of Yucatan and the Straits of Florida, which form the mouth of the Gulf of Mexico. Suppose —God forbid—that in an earlier day we had not wisely acquired Florida and made it a part of the United States of America, but having been Spanish in its early settlement it had remained Spanish in association and come to belong to the Republic of Mexico. Suppose, therefore, the mouth of the Gulf of Mexico was controlled by Mexico, except insofar as it was regulated by a convention which was entered into, we will say, in the old days when the great European powers were the mighty forces of the earth.

Then suppose that, looking backward historically we saw a great giant—Mexico—arising upon this continent, growing stronger and stronger, and suppose, becoming more and more sensitive to our own security, we had said to Mexico, "The mighty Mississippi opens its arteries to the heart of America. We demand, Montreux convention or no Montreux convention,

Congress of Vienna or no Congress of Vienna, compact of the nations of Europe or no compact of the nations of Europe—we demand that America, as the mightiest nation on this waterway, the mouth of which is in your control, shall share it with you, if not dominate it with you, to the exclusion of all the powers of the Old World altogether." Would men who proposed that in the American Congress, would those of our military and naval staffs who advocated it, would those of our State Department who urged it, be called warmongers, subject to denunciation around the world as aggressors against Mexico? I can hear Senators making these steel rafters ring with the defense of American policy calculated to secure the heartland and the homeland of America.

Mr. President, I am not saying that in any case the Soviet Union is justified in coming down and attacking the Dardanelles. I think if she were to do so it would raise the supreme test of what the United Nations would do. For my part I would vote to furnish America's share of the forces necessary to resist that kind of an aggression. But so far it is still in the stage of negotiation. It is a request—call it a demand, if you like—made by Russia upon Turkey. We ourselves admitted that the Montreux convention should be changed. The Russians truly feel—and there is much ground for such feeling—that the Turks, who in the last war gave raw materials to the Germans and aided them, permitted German ships to slip through this waterway which they presume to protect.

Stop to think about Russia's situation. Take a map and study it. It will be seen that a merchant ship today cannot leave any Russian port and go across any sea of this earth without the permission of the British or the American or the British and the American Fleets.

If I may quote it without impropriety, I will say that I was rather amused at a point of view expressed to me by a lady in Great Britain one evening in 1945 at a dinner. She had heard I had been to Russia as well as to some other countries. She said, "Senator, what do you think of these Russians wanting a navy and everything?" That lady was honestly shocked at the suggestion that Russia should even have a navy.

The other day our own Secretary of the Navy was testifying before the Foreign Relations Committee. I was by the great kindness of that committee permitted to ask a few questions. I said, "Mr. Secretary, I have read in the papers from time to time about American naval craft going into the eastern Mediterranean. Have we a squadron or task force of any sort in the Mediterranean? I was just wondering if we are correctly informed by the press from time to time, which tells us about certain demonstrations made by American naval forces."

The Secretary, with the ability which is characteristic of him, immediately replied by making a very patriotic statement: "I said last autumn that it was my feeling that we should accustom ourselves and the world to the sight of the American flag anywhere in the world that it would not be conspicuous where it went—wherever there is a sea."

I said, "So you deem that that is the role of this country to have the naval craft wherever there is a sea?"

He answered, "I think so; yes, sir."

I said, "Do you deny to other powers the same right?"

He indicated that the seas were free and accessible to all nations.

I wondered what those naval forces would do if the Russians decided to put a navy in every ocean and sea of the world—I wondered if that would be considered an act of aggression on their part. Suppose a Russian ship wanted to leave Murmansk, which is icebound for many months of the year, to go through the Atlantic Ocean, the North Sea, either through the English Channel or to the north of Britain. Does anyone think it could do so without the approval of the British Navy?

Suppose a Russian ship desired to leave a Balkan port, for which Peter fought a war, to go out through the Baltic, through the Kattegat and the Skagerrak, the entrance to the North Sea from the Baltic, does anyone think it would be able to do so without the permission of other powers?

Suppose a Russian ship started from the Black Sea, which leaves Russia's homeland to go into the Mediterranean, could it get through the Dardanelles without Turkey's permission?

If a Russian vessel got through the Dardanelles, could it pass the eastern Mediterranean without the permission of the British Fleet established at Cyprus and with access to Greek bases?

I think if Senators will look at a map they will not have serious cause to wonder why it is that the British have always been so interested in Greece. For, if they will examine closely, they will see that it is not so much the adjacent shores but the Greek islands in the eastern Mediterranean that really dominate the Dardanelles and keep ships from coming through from the other side. Suppose, Mr. President, Russian ships came out of the Black Sea and got through the Dardanelles; suppose they got past Cyprus and it was intended that they should go to the Indian Ocean; could they get through the Suez Canal without British permission?

If the ships got through the Suez Canal and down into the Red Sea, could they negotiate the Indian Ocean without British permission?

Suppose the ships decided to go straight west in the Mediterranean, could they get by the British Navy based at Alexandria? Could they pass Malta, a British base? Could they, without British approval, get through Gibraltar, which, so far as I can read the map, is a part of the Spanish mainland, but has been a British bastion for centuries? If they got into the Atlantic Ocean, how far could they go without the approval of the British or the American Navy? If they started from the other side, at Vladivostok, and came across the Pacific, we know, of course, that it is our country which dominates that ocean.

If the Russians do what Hitler did, I shall try to do against them what I tried to do against Hitler. The Sudetenland had never been a part of Germany in history. Neither had Denmark. Neither had Norway. Neither had Holland. Neither had Belgium. Neither had eastern France, which Hitler had overrun with force of arms and with Nazi barbarity, when I introduced the genesis of lend-lease and later fought for the bill which was introduced by someone in a position of leadership. However, while I will oppose the exertion of Russian armed force in the acquisition of the Dardanelles, what I think my country should do toward recognizing some elemental justice in her claim is another proposition.

I am not unaware of all the epithets I have had to bear, all the contumely I have had to bear, all the bitter denunciations that I have had to experience from certain sources, to the delight of some publications which call themselves fair, but wish to apply one appellation or another.

All I have ever said is what I think is good policy for the United States of America. As a citizen and as a United States Senator I have the right, if not the duty, to express my opinion. I am saying that it is an act of fairness and justice for the United States of America, in determining what a sound policy shall be, to take into consideration the aspirations, aims, and situations of other peoples of the world, their background, their history, their peculiarities, and their interests and fears. . . .

Let America remember, as we make this solemn decision, that we cannot, with arms, cram democracy down people's throats. They must want it and be willing to fight for it, either to be able to gain it or to deserve it.

Today our great country stands at the Rubicon. Flushed with our victories with our loyal legions clamoring to follow us, we can, like Caesar, not only take Rome, but begin what some historians have called, the glorious journey down the glamorous path of empire. No nation started out to be a great empire, but those who came to the purple and the ermine took decision after decision, never going at once the whole way, until eventually there was no turning back, short of their tragic dissolution. Is there anything about any empire of the past that America desires to emulate? Could anybody seriously suggest that we should follow that fool's gold or that our quest would end differently from that of all others who have pursued it? Yet this proposal so hastily urged upon us would clearly set us on the path of empire.

Can the world's greatest empire, now our contemporary, teach us nothing? Have we not the good sense and the good spirit to curb our own power and to make it humble, to make America come as humbly to world leadership, in the Council of Nations, as Thomas Jefferson came riding on his horse to his inaugural?

The implications of this measure reach beyond the prediction of any man. Senators declaring their support of it with honest candor have said it might mean war. Is this issue one upon which we can hazard that event?

Does the pending issue in the Dardanelles demand that we challenge in mortal combat a nation occuping one-sixth of the earth and containing one-tenth of the world's people? Is Russian access to the eastern Mediterranean such a violent invasion of our rights and interest that it demands we risk war? Are we prepared to thicken the sands of the Middle East with American blood as the price of our exclusive enjoyment of the oil resources of that area?

America's role is to lead the world to peace, not war; to help mankind up, not to push it down; to build, and not to destroy. If there be those who will not hearken to the appeal of right or respect the sentiments of justice, if there be those who would trample upon their fellow men as aggressors, we shall not be slow to defend the cause of the oppressed. But we have not been singled out alone to stand in the Thermopylae of right against the invading hosts of wrong. We have solemnly pledged that we will work—and, if needs be, fight—with the other members of the United Nations against war makers if all possible methods of peaceful adjustment have failed. That is the kind of team ball to which we have already committed ourselves. That is truly befitting the American character. That is in the American tradition. There, in the United Nations, is America's rendezvous with destiny.

It has been said that our refusal to adopt this measure would repudiate our President. The world knows that we do not differ here in this debate about objectives; it is essentially about methods that we argue. We have in the Congress the sacred duty to determine the best way to preserve the Nation's peace and security, the peace and security of all peoples. We do not have the fearful alternative of rejecting the President or repudiating the United Nations, for the President, too, is wedded to the United Nations. Congress has the power—yes, the challenging opportunity—to make the United Nations able to function as it was intended to function. We can give it the strength it is alleged to lack. We can supply the very force which it is alleged not to have. With the unstinted support of this Congress, the United Nations can realize its full vigor and promise. It can become, as it was intended to be, the last best hope of peace on earth. The question is, Shall Congress destroy the United Nations, or shall it build it?

I proclaim that there is nothing that this Congress could do in its whole life which would so hearten mankind as to rededicate this country to the United Nations and to its high purpose to maintain international peace and security. The world would know that when required to take effective collective measures for the prevention and removal of threats to the peace and for the suppression of acts of aggression in the name of this noble charter, we have again pledged our lives, our fortunes and our sacred honor; that America is, and before God and man will continue to be, a democracy dedicated to the people, the servant of their hopes and their dreams, the friend of all the peoples who live in the houses, big and little, beside the roads of the world; that no overweening ambition, no lure of profit or power, no fool's gold of empire shall tempt us to betray our dead or our destiny; that America is not soft, that it is not afraid to fight either for the poor, the oppressed, or the victims of aggression, that we realize that we can neither lift up mankind nor protect their security, strong as we are, alone; and that therefore we shall keep our pledge to achieve international cooperation in solving international problems of economic, social, cultural, or humanitarian character and in promoting and encouraging respect for human rights and for fundamental freedoms for all without distinction as to race, sex, language, or religion; that we turn our faces toward the future with confidence; that we are on God's side because we are on man's side, and as our cause is just we are strong in His strength. If, God forbid, we shall ever have to fight, let us fight to save the Union, as did Lincoln, because the Union is all that can save men. As Washington said, "Let us raise a standard to which the wise and the just may repair." And now, as it was when Washington rose to defend the new Charter of the United States, "The event is in the hands of God."

MOSCOW PEACE CONFERENCE [15]

George C. Marshall [16]

Secretary of State George C. Marshall gave this radio report to the American people on Monday night, April 28, 1947. Less than forty-eight hours before, he had arrived by plane from Russia and had given President Truman and other Washington leaders a preview of his public statement.

The address was a simple, uncomplicated summary of the conference of Russia, Great Britain, France, and the United States that began in Moscow on March 10. General Marshall analyzed clearly and acutely the problems facing the four conferees. He gave a discerning, if slightly veiled, condemnation of Russia for her obvious failure to cooperate in any settlement of the major issues. Marshall also hinted at what he proposed to do.

Any interpreter needs to read between the lines of this State Department utterance. Marshall himself wrote the speech by hand, on the plane returning from Europe—"the first time anyone has done such a thing in a long time," commented James Reston (*New York Times,* April 29, 1947). His reference to "disintegrating forces" was more ominous than might seem apparent. The activities of the Communists in the British-American-French sectors of Germany were doubtless part of those sinister forces of disintegration. Russia, at Moscow, he suggested, had substituted passion and propaganda for reason. Stalin, he observed, had held out hope for eventual compromise and agreement. Marshall, however, bluntly drove home the major idea that the European crisis could not wait on indefinite deadlock and mutual exhaustion. The speaker thus warned Americans that the united policy in those zones would henceforth be directed to the building up of a separate British-American Germany to combat the Soviet *fait accompli.*

On Tuesday, April 29, John Foster Dulles, special Republican adviser at Moscow, gave his own report of the Conference. The two statements are similar. Dulles, however, should be read as further interpretation of the Marshall position. The former, speaking as a private citizen, was far more outspoken. He frankly declared, for example, that Russia was out to absorb all of Germany. His proposals were, in effect, that Congress should implement a policy of immediate democratizing of Germany and should strengthen that unit as part of a Western European bloc against Russia.

[15] Text furnished by the Department of State. Corrected from the radio version as recorded by this editor.

[16] For biographical note see Appendix.

Marshall has slow Virginia speech and clipped military inflection and articulation, but he projects vocally and convinces by his lively and sincere expression. He gives the impression of extempore speaking—even when he reads his prepared text.

Tonight I hope to make clearly understandable the fundamental nature of the issues discussed at the Moscow conference of Foreign Ministers.

This conference dealt with the very heart of the peace for which we are struggling. It dealt with the vital center of Europe—Germany and Austria—an area of large and skilled population, of great resources and industrial plants, an area which has twice in recent times brought the world to the brink of disaster.

In the Moscow negotiations, all the disagreements which were so evident during the conferences regarding the Italian and Balkan treaties came into sharp focus and remained, in effect, unsolved.

Problems which bear directly on the future of our civilization cannot be disposed of by general talk or vague formulae—by what Lincoln called "pernicious abstractions."

They require concrete solutions for definite and extremely complicated questions—questions which have to do with boundaries, with power to prevent military aggression, with people who have bitter memories, with the production and control of things which are essential to the lives of millions of people.

You have been kept well informed by the press and radio of the daily activities of the Council, and much of what I have to say may seem repetitious. But the extremely complicated nature of the three major issues we considered makes it appear desirable for me to report in some detail the problems as I saw them in my meetings at the conference table.

There was a reasonable possibility, we had hoped a probability, of completing in Moscow a peace treaty for Austria and a four-power pact to bind together our four governments to guarantee the demilitarization of Germany. As for the German peace treaty and related but more current German problems, we had hoped to reach agreement on a directive for the guidance of our deputies in their work preparatory to the next conference.

In a statement such as this, it is not practicable to discuss the numerous issues which continued in disagreement at the conference. It will suffice, I think, to call attention to the fundamental problems whose solution would probably lead to the quick adjustment of many other differences.

It is important to the understanding of the conference that the complex character of the problems should be understood, together with their immediate effect on the people of Europe in the coming months.

To cite a single example, more coal is most urgently needed throughout Europe for factories, for utilities, for railroads and for the people in their homes. More coal for Allied countries cannot be mined and delivered until the damaged mines, mine machinery, railroad communications and like facilities are rehabilitated.

This rehabilitation, however, depends on more steel, and more steel depends in turn on more coal for steel making. Therefore, and this is the point to be kept in mind, while the necessary rehabilitation is in progress, less coal would be available in the immediate future for the neighboring Allied states.

But less coal means less employment for labor, and a consequent delay in the production of goods for export to bring money for the purchase of food and necessities. Therefore, the delay necessary to permit rehabilitation of the mines so vitally affects France that the settlement of this matter has become for her a critical issue.

All neighboring states and Great Britain and the Soviet Union are directly affected in various ways, since coal is required for German production of goods for export sufficient to enable her to buy the necessary imports of foods, et cetera, for much of which the United States is now providing the funds.

Moreover, in the background of this coal issue, which is directly related to steel production, is the important consideration of the build-up of heavy industry in Germany, which could later again become a threat to the peace of the world. I cite this single example to illustrate the complications which are involved in these negotiations.

The Allied Control Council in Berlin presented a detailed report of the many problems concerned with the political, military, economic and financial situation under the present Military Government of Germany. In connection with these matters, the Ministers considered the form and scope of the provisional political organization for Germany, and the procedure to be followed in the preparation of the German peace treaty.

The German negotiations involved not only the security of Europe and the world, but the prosperity of all of Europe. While our mission was to consider the terms of a treaty to operate over a long term of years, we were faced with immediate issues which vitally concerned the impoverished and suffering people of Europe who are crying for help, for coal, for food and for most of the necessities of life, and the majority of whom are bitterly disposed toward the Germany that brought about this disastrous situation.

The issues also vitally concern the people of Britain and the United States who cannot continue to pour out hundreds of millions of dollars for Germany because current measures were not being taken to terminate expeditiously the necessity for such appropriations.

The critical and fundamental German problems to which I shall confine myself are: the limits to the powers of the central government; the character of the economic system and its relation to all of Europe; the character and extent of reparations; the boundaries for the German state; and the manner in which all Allied states at war with Germany are represented in the drafting and confirmation of the treaty.

All the members of the Council of Foreign Ministers are in apparent agreement as to the establishment of a German state on a self-supporting, democratic basis, with limitations imposed to prevent the re-establishing of military power.

This issue of the degree of centralization of the future German state is of greatest importance. Excessive concentration of power is peculiarly dangerous in a country like Germany which has no strong traditions regarding the rights of the individual and the rights of the community to control the exercise of governmental power.

The Soviet Union appears to favor a strong central government. The United States and United Kingdom are opposed to such a government, because they think it could be too readily converted to the domination of a regime similar to the Nazis. They favor a central government of carefully limited powers, all other powers being reserved to the states, or Laender as they are called in Germany. The French are willing to agree only to very limited responsibilities for the central government. They fear a repetition of the seizure of power over the whole of Germany carried out by the Hitler regime in 1933.

Under ordinary circumstances, there are always strong and differing points of view regarding the character of a governmental reorganization. In this case there are great and justified fears regarding the resurrection of German military power, and concern over expressed or concealed desires for quite other reasons.

Regarding the character of the German economic system and its relation to all of Europe, the disagreements are even more serious and difficult of adjustment. German economy at the present time is crippled by the fact that there is no unity of action, and the rehabilitation of Germany to the point where she is self-supporting demands immediate decision.

There is a declared agreement in the desire for economic unity in Germany, but when it comes to the actual terms to regulate such unity there are wide and critical differences.

One of the most serious difficulties encountered in the effort to secure economic unity has been the fact that the Soviet-occupied zone has operated practically without regard to the other zones and has made few if any reports of what has been occurring in that zone. There has been little or no disposition to proceed on a basis of reciprocity and there has been a refusal to disclose the availability of foodstuffs, and the degree or character of reparations taken out of this zone.

This unwillingness of the Soviet authorities to cooperate in establishing a balanced economy for Germany as agreed upon at Potsdam has been the most serious check on the development of a self-supporting Germany, and a Germany capable of providing coal and other necessities for the neighboring states who have always been dependent on Germany for these items.

After long and futile efforts to secure a working accord in this matter, the British and American zones were combined for the improvement of the economic situation, meaning the free movement of excess supplies or produce available in one zone to another where there is a shortage. Our continuing invitation to the French and Soviets to join in the arrangement still exists.

This merger is bitterly attacked by the Soviet authorities as a breach of the Potsdam Agreement and as a first step toward the dismemberment of Germany, ignoring the plain fact that their refusal to carry out that agreement was the sole cause of the merger. It is difficult to regard their attacks as anything but propaganda designed to divert attention from the Soviet failure to implement the economic unity agreed at Potsdam. Certainly some progress toward economic unity in Germany is better than none.

The character of the control over the Ruhr industrial center, the greatest concentration of coal and of heavy industries in Europe, continues a matter of debate. It cannot be decided merely for the purpose of reaching an agreement. Vitally important considerations and future consequences are involved.

The question of reparations is of critical importance as it affects almost every other question under discussion. This issue naturally makes a tremendous appeal to the people of the Allied states who suffered the terrors of German military occupation and the destruction of their cities and villages.

The results of the Versailles Treaty of 1919 regarding payment of reparations on a basis of dollars, and the difficulties encountered by the reparations commission appointed after Yalta in agreeing upon the dollar evaluation of reparations in kind, convinced President Truman and his advisers considering the question at Potsdam that some other basis for determining reparations should be adopted if endless friction and bitterness were to be avoided in future years. They succeeded in getting agreement to the principle of reparations to be rendered out of capital assets—that is, the transfer of German plants, machinery, et cetera, to the Allied powers concerned.

It developed at the Moscow conference that the Soviet officials flatly disagreed with President Truman's and Mr. Byrnes' understanding of the written terms of this agreement. The British have much the same view of this matter as the United States.

We believe that no reparations from current production were contemplated by the Potsdam Agreement. The Soviets strongly oppose this view. They hold that the previous discussions and agreements at Yalta authorize the taking of billions of dollars in reparations out of current production.

This would mean that a substantial portion of the daily production of German factories would be levied on for reparation payments, which in turn would mean that the recovery of Germany sufficiently to be self-supporting would be long delayed. It would also mean that the plan and the hope of our Government, that Germany's economic recovery by the end of three years would permit the termination of American appropriations for the support of the German inhabitants of our zone, could not be realized.

The issue is one of great complications, for which agreement must be found in order to administer Germany as an economic whole as the four powers claim that they wish to do.

There is, however, general agreement among the Allies that the matter of the factories and equipment to be removed from Germany as reparations should be re-examined. They recognize the fact that a too drastic reduction in Germany's industrial set-up will not only make it difficult for Germany to become self-supporting but will retard the economic recovery of Europe.

The United States has indicated that it would be willing to study the possibility of a limited amount of reparations from current production to compensate for plants, previously scheduled to be removed as reparations to various Allied countries, which it now appears should be left in Germany; it being understood that deliveries from current production are not to increase the financial burden of the occupying powers or to retard the repayment to them of the advances they have made to keep the

German economy from collapsing. The Soviet Government has made no response to this suggestion.

The issue regarding boundaries to be established for Germany presents a serious disagreement and another example of complete disagreement as to the meaning of the pronouncement on this subject by the heads of the three powers.

In the rapid advance of the Soviet Armies in the final phase of the war millions of Germans in eastern Germany fled to the west of the Oder River. The Soviet Armies, prior to Potsdam, had placed Poles in charge of this area largely evacuated by the German population. That was the situation that confronted President Truman at Potsdam.

Under the existing circumstances the President accepted the situation for the time being with the agreed three-power statement, "the heads of government reaffirm their opinion that the final delimitation of the western frontier of Poland should await the peace settlement."

The Soviet Foreign Minister now states that a final agreement on the frontier between Germany and Poland was reached at Potsdam and the expression I have just quoted merely referred to the formal confirmation of the already agreed upon frontier at the peace settlement, thus leaving only technical delimitation to be considered.

The United States Government recognized the commitment made at Yalta to give fair compensation to Poland in the west for the territory east of the Curzon Line incorporated into the Soviet Union. But the perpetuation of the present temporary line between Germany and Poland would deprive Germany of territory which before the war provided more than a fifth of the foodstuffs on which the German population depended.

It is clear that in any event Germany will be obliged to support, within much restricted boundaries, not only her pre-war population but a considerable number of Germans from Eastern Europe. To a certain extent this situation is unavoidable, but we must not agree to its aggravation. We do not want Poland to be left with less resources than she had before the war. She is entitled to more. But it will not help Poland to give her frontiers which will probably create difficulties for her in the future.

Wherever the frontiers are drawn, they should not constitute barriers to trade and commerce upon which the well-being of Europe is dependent. We must look toward a future where a democratic Poland and a democratic Germany will be good neighbors.

There is disagreement regarding the manner in which the Allied powers at war with Germany are to participate in the drafting and confirmation of the German peace treaty. There are fifty-one states involved. Of these, in addition to the four principal Allied powers, eighteen were directly engaged in the fighting, some of course to a much greater extent than others.

It is the position of the United States that all Allied states at war with Germany should be given an opportunity to participate to some degree in the drafting and in the making of the peace treaty, but we recognize that there would be very practical difficulties, if not impossibilities, in attempting to draft a treaty with fifty-one nations participating equally at all stages.

Therefore, the United States Government has endeavored to secure agreement on a method which involves two different procedures, depending on whether or not the state concerned actually participated in the fighting. But all would have an opportunity to present their views, and rebut other views, and all would sit in the peace conference to adopt a treaty.

It is difficult to get the agreement of the countries that have suffered the horrors of German occupation and were involved in heavy losses in hard fighting to accept participation in the determination of the treaty terms by countries who suffered no losses in men or material and were remote from the fighting. The United States, however, regards it as imperative that all the States who were at war with Germany should have some voice in the settlement imposed on Germany.

The proposal for the four-power pact was advanced by the United States Government a year ago. It was our hope that the prompt acceptance of this simple pact insuring in advance of the detailed German peace settlement that the United States would actively cooperate to prevent the rearmament of Germany would eliminate fears as to the future and would facilitate the making of a peace suitable to Europe's present and future needs.

It was our hope that such a commitment by the United States would relieve the fear of the other European powers that the United States would repeat its actions following the first World War, insisting on various terms for the peace settlement and then withdrawing from a position of any responsibility for their enforcement. It was thought that the compact of the four powers to guarantee the continued demilitarization of Germany would reassure the world that we were in complete accord in our intention to secure the peace of Europe.

However, the Soviet Government met our proposition with a series of amendments which would have completely changed the character of the pact, making it in effect a complicated peace treaty, and including in the amendments most of the points regarding the German problem concerning which there was, as I have pointed out, serious disagreement.

I was forced to the conclusion by this procedure that the Soviet Government either did not desire such a pact or was following a course calculated to delay any immediate prospect of its adoption.

Whether or not an agreement can finally be reached remains to be seen, but the United States, I think, should adhere to its present position and insist that the pact be kept simple and confined to its one basic purpose—to keep Germany incapable of waging war.

The negotiations regarding the Austrian treaty resulted in agreement on all but a few points, but these were basic and of fundamental importance. The Soviet Union favors and the other Governments oppose the payment of reparations and the cession of Carinthia to Yugoslavia.

But the Soviet Government attached much more importance to its demand that the German assets in Austria, which are to be hers by the terms of the Potsdam Agreement, should include those assets which the other three Powers consider to have been taken from Austria and the citizens of the United Nations by force or duress by Hitler and his Nazi Government following the taking over of Austria by military force in March 1938.

The Soviet Government refused to consider the word duress, which in the opinion of the other three Powers would be the critical basis for determining what property, that is, business, factories, land, forests, et cetera, was truly German property and not the result of seizures by terroristic procedure, intimidation, fake business acquisition, and so forth.

The Soviet Union also refused to consider any process of mediation to settle the disputes that are bound to arise in such circumstances, nor would they clearly agree to have such property as they receive as German assets subject to Austrian law in the same manner as other foreign investments are subject to Austrian law.

The acceptance of the Soviet position would mean that such a large portion of Austrian economy would be removed from her legal control that Austrian chances of surviving as an independent self-supporting state would be dubious. She would in effect be but a puppet state.

All efforts to find a compromise solution were unavailing. The United States, in my opinion, could not commit itself to a treaty which involved such manifest injustices and, what is equally important, would create an Austria so weak and helpless as to be the source of great danger in the future.

In the final session of the conference, it was agreed to appoint a commission to meet in Vienna May 12 to reconsider our disagreements, and to have a committee of experts examine into the question of the German assets in Ausaria. Certainly prompt action on the Austrian treaty is necessary to fulfill our commitment to recognize Austria as a free and independent state and to relieve her from the burdens of occupation.

Complicated as these issues are, there runs through them a pattern as to the character and control of Central Europe to be established. The Foreign Ministers agreed that their task was to lay the foundations of a central government for Germany, to bring about the economic unity of Germany essential for its own existence as well as for European recovery, to establish workable boundaries, and to set up a guaranteed control through a four-power treaty. Austria was to be promptly relieved of occupation burdens and treated as a liberated and independent country.

Agreement was made impossible at Moscow, because, in our view the Soviet Union insisted upon proposals which would have established in Germany a centralized government, adapted to the seizure of absolute control of a country which would be doomed economically through inadequate area and excessive population, and would be mortgaged to turn over a large part of its production as reparations, principally to the Soviet Union. In another form the same mortgage upon Austria was claimed by the Soviet delegation.

Such a plan, in the opinion of the United States delegation, not only involved indefinite American subsidy, but could result only in a deteriorating economic life in Germany and Europe and the inevitable emergence of dictatorship and strife.

Freedom of information, for which our Government stands, inevitably involves appeals to public opinion. But at Moscow, propaganda appeals to passion and prejudice appeared to take the place of appeals to reason and understanding. Charges were made by the Soviet delegation and interpretation given the Potsdam and other agreements which varied completely from the facts as understood or as factually known by the American delegation.

However, despite the disagreements referred to and the difficulties encountered, possibly greater progress toward final settlement was made than is realized.

The critical differences were for the first time brought into the light and now stand clearly defined so that future negotiations can start with a knowledge of exactly what the issues are that must be settled. The deputies now understand the precise views of each Government on the various issues discussed. With that they can possibly resolve some differences and surely can further clarify the problems by a studied presentation of the state of agreement and disagreement.

That is the best that can be hoped for in the next few months. It marks some progress, however painfully slow. These issues are matters of vast importance to the lives of the people of Europe and to the future course of world history. We must not compromise on great principles in order to achieve agreement for agreement's sake. Also, we must sincerely try to understand the point of view of those with whom we differ.

In this connection, I think it proper to refer to a portion of a statement made to me by Generalissimo Stalin. He said, with reference to the conference, that these were only the first skirmishes and brushes of reconnaisance forces on this question. Differences had occurred in the past on other questions, and as a rule, after people had exhausted themselves in dispute they then recognized the necessity of compromise. It was possible that no great success would be achieved at this session, but he thought that compromises were possible on all the main questions, including demilitarization, political structure of Germany, reparations and economic unity. It was necessary to have patience and not become pessimistic.

I sincerely hope that the Generalissimo is correct in the view he expressed and that it implies a greater spirit of cooperation by the Soviet delegation in future conferences. But we cannot ignore the factor of time involved here.

The recovery of Europe has been far slower than had been expected. Disintegrating forces are becoming evident. The patient is sinking while the doctors deliberate. So I believe that action cannot await compromise through exhaustion. New issues arise daily. Whatever action is possible to meet these pressing problems must be taken without delay.

Finally, I should comment on one aspect of the matter which is of transcendent importance to all our people. While I did not have the benefit, as did Mr. Byrnes, of the presence of the two leading members of the Senate Foreign Relations Committee, I did have the invaluable assistance of Mr. [John Foster] Dulles, a distinguished representative of the Republican party as well as a recognized specialist in foreign relations and in the processes of international negotiations and treaty-making.

As a matter of fact, the bipartisan character of the American attitude in the present conduct of foreign affairs was clearly indicated by the strong and successful leadership displayed in the Senate during the period of this conference by Senators [Arthur H.] Vandenberg and [Tom] Connally in the debate over a development of our foreign policy of momentous importance to the American people. The fact that there was such evident unity of purpose in Washington was of incalculable assistance to me in Moscow.

The state of the world today and the position of the United States make mandatory, in my opinion, a unity of action on the part of the American people. It is for that reason that I have gone into such lengthy detail in reporting my views on the conference.

PEACE SETTLEMENT WITH RUSSIA [17]

WALTER LIPPMANN [18]

Walter Lippmann delivered this address at the first general session of the thirty-fifth annual meeting of the Chamber of Commerce of the United States, at Washington, D. C., on the evening of April 29, 1947. At the opening session James Forrestal, Secretary of the Navy, and C. Gordon Sockshutt, president of the Canadian Chamber of Commerce, talked on foreign affairs. President Truman sent a message, read by John R. Steelman, his assistant, urging price cutting. The "keynote" speech to the convention was given by Early O. Shreve at the closing session.

Lippmann is chiefly prominent as a columnist, with his "Today and Tomorrow" published in some 182 newspapers. He was educated in Europe and at Harvard. Since the publication of his first volume, *A Preface to Morals,* in 1912, he has produced many volumes on morals, economics, contemporary history, and social problems. He was an editor of the *New Republic,* worked with the War Department in World War I, and later was on the American Commission to Negotiate Peace. He is currently with the *New York Herald Tribune.* Much more than a journalist, he is a philosopher.

As a speaker, Lippmann is intellectual rather than emotional. He avoids oratorical display, gestures, or other marks of conscious training. He states that he does not think of himself as a public speaker, but he is nevertheless in constant demand. His quiet, well-modulated tones, originality of phrasing, analytical insight, and mature interpretation of contemporary problems combine to give him unusual effectiveness before audiences. [19]

Gentlemen: I am sure you would have me come directly to the crux of the matter—that is to say to our relations with the Soviet Union.

We can best see where we are today by recalling how the situation has developed since the Allies were able to plan for a complete victory over Germany, Japan, and the satellites. That was in the autumn of 1943, when the Big Three met at

---

[17] Reprinted through the courtesy of Mr. Lippmann. Text furnished by the author.

[18] For biographical note see Appendix.

[19] For further comment on Lippmann as a public speaker see *Representative American Speeches: 1940-1941.* p. 292-3; *1943-1944.* p. 248.

Teheran. Then for the first time they were able to think not about how to hold on in the British Isles, at Stalingrad, at Alamein, and in New Guinea and to avoid being defeated, but how the war was to be won, and what the postwar world was to be.

Before that the differences which were to divide the Allies were submerged by their common danger and the sheer struggle to survive. But from then on, with ultimate victory in sight, it was clear that there could be no peace until and unless there was a settlement among the victorious Allies. The Allies had to make peace with each other before they could make peace with their enemies.

In the work of attempting to make a settlement among the Big Three, we may say that there have been two periods, and that we are now at the beginning of a third. For the sake of clarity and brevity I shall call them the Roosevelt-Churchill-Stalin period, the Byrnes-Bevin-Molotov period, and the Marshall period.

Reduced to its permanent elements, stripped of all secondary matters, the net result of the Roosevelt-Churchill-Stalin period was an agreement on the military boundary line where the British-American and the Russian forces were to meet as the fighting ended, and were then to stand still and to advance no farther. That military boundary ran through Europe from Stettin on the Baltic Sea to the suburbs of Trieste on the Adriatic, then along the northern frontier of Greece, north of Turkey and the Black Sea, along the northern boundary of Iran for the Russians and along the southern boundary of Iran for the British. In the Far East it ran through Korea at the 80th parallel. In China the line was not clear because, though theoretically under the agreement the National Government of Chiang Kai-Shek was supposed to recover the whole of China, including Manchuria, in fact Chiang Kai-Shek was unable to do that. For China was divided by a civil war, one side deriving support from the Russians and the other from the United States. Nevertheless, though there was no agreed boundary line within China, as there was in Europe, between the Soviets and ourselves, there was, and is a de facto boundary along the line which separates Red China from Nationalist China. For neither side in China has been strong enough to win the civil war.

The military frontier established during the Roosevelt-Churchill-Stalin period has endured. It still stands virtually unchanged since it was agreed to with Stalin during the war. It has endured not because it satisfies any of the Big Three but because it registers the actual line where their armed forces met at the end of the war. None of them could cross that line without opening up a battle. None of them has crossed it with military forces. This line, which registered the military situation, became also the political frontier between the Soviet orbit or sphere of influence, and that of the western nations.

The Byrnes-Bevin-Molotov period, which began with the London Conference of September 1945, lasted until the beginning of this winter. During this period each side worked to consolidate its own sphere of influence, and at the same time to push forward into the other sphere of influence.

The Russians tried to cross the line by fomenting a revolution in the Iranian province of Azerbaijan, by pressure on Turkey, by infiltration into Greece, by supporting Tito's effort to obtain Trieste, by laying claim to an Italian colony in Africa, by supplying the Chinese communists with the Japanese weapons captured in Manchuria. Yet all these attempts to advance beyond the old Roosevelt-Churchill-Stalin line were repulsed.

We, too, have tried to cross the line, and to advance our influence into the Russian orbit. With the British we waged a diplomatic campaign for free elections in Poland, Rumania, Hungary and other satellites, and gave our moral support to non-Communist and anti-Communist parties which, if they came into power, would no longer take their orders from Moscow. This campaign was unsuccessful, and in the long tedious negotiations by Messrs. Byrnes, Bevin and Molotov over the satellite countries ended in treaties which register the stalemate at the old military line.

One side or the other, or both tried to change the boundaries of the spheres of influence by infiltration, by propaganda, by economic pressure, by political intervention and by diplomatic negotiation.   But the striking thing about the Byrnes-Bevin-Molotov period has been that all our attempts, and all the Russian attempts to change the boundaries of the two spheres of influence have failed.

In China the result has been the same.   The dividing line between Red China and Nationalist China stands approximately where it was at the end of the war.   It has not been possible to unify China by a Nationalist victory with our support, or by a Red victory with Russian support, or by the agreement which General Marshall tried to bring about.   The status quo is essentially unchanged, and the upshot of General Marshall's mission to China was a decision to accept this fact, and to limit our intervention in China for the present to supporting Chiang Kai-Shek enough to maintain the status quo, but not enough to enable him to win the civil war.   Thus far the Soviet Union has limited its intervention to supporting Red China enough to hold what it has, but not enough to overrun the rest of China.

This decision, which marks what I have called the beginning of the Marshall period, was to limit our intervention to the status quo.   It was taken just before General Marshall became Secretary of State.

The China decision was followed by an event which had been foreseen for some time, and could not be postponed much longer.   This was the decision of the British government that they no longer had the military and economic resources to hold all their sectors on the old Roosevelt-Churchill-Stalin boundary line.

The reasons which have compelled the British to retire from the front line of the Middle East are, of course, well known to you, and I shall not discuss them at length.   They are in brief that the Empire, of which India was the great central asset, is liquidating itself, and that the United Kingdom is so gravely weakened by the two wars of this century that it no longer has the manpower, the military strength, the productive capacity and the financial resources to hold and to use all the strategic positions of the old empire.

Among these strategic positions none was more important than the eastern Mediterranean and the Middle East.   Greece, and above all Turkey, are like a door which can swing open both ways. Through that door Russia can come down to the great oil regions of the Middle East and also into the Mediterranean, and can act against the soft under-belly of Europe. But through this same Turkish door, if it is swung open the other way, it is possible for a great sea and air power to pass up into the Black Sea, and to act against the soft under-belly of Russia.

For these reasons the decision of the British government that they could no longer hold the Turkish door was an event of transcendent importance. It was the greatest event of the postwar era. For it meant that unless the United States intervened to replace the British, the old Roosevelt-Churchill-Stalin boundary line, which at least fixed the limits of Soviet expansion, would no longer hold. That, of course, is why President Truman went to Congress last March to ask not only for money, but in fact for authorization to have the United States replace Britain and confront directly the Soviet Union in the Middle East.

Though the situation compelled the President to act, though American intervention in the Middle East became unavoidable once the British were compelled to retire, there is no disguising the difficulties, the costs, and the risks of our position today.

In the first place, though we are not without friends and moral supporters, we now stand virtually alone as respects military power and money confronting the Soviet Union in Asia and in Europe. The weakness which has compelled Britain to withdraw in the Middle East will almost certainly compel her to turn over to us her main responsibilities and commitments in Germany as well. Thus our burdens are immensely extended while the risks of conflict have been sharpened because everywhere the issue is a direct one between Russia and ourselves.

In the second place, as the issue is sharpened there is of course no peace in the world and no recovery and reconstruction, but only a steady economic deterioration which, if it continues, if it is not arrested, and reversed, must inexorably lead, and at no distant date, to the economic collapse of Western Europe, including Britain, France, Italy and Western Germany. Moreover, within all the countries of Europe and elsewhere the great struggle between Russia and America,—combined with economic misery and hopelessness—has become an internal domestic struggle. The result will be, can only be, that the more we drift towards the supreme crisis of our relations with the Soviet Union and to the possibility of war, the greater becomes the probability that the countries which we should have to count upon as allies would be incapable because they were divided, and unwilling because they cannot face another war, to help us.

In the third place, as things are developing now, both Moscow and Washington are in the gravest danger of losing control over the choice between war and peace, of losing their power to decide whether they will settle by negotiation or will fight to the bitter end. We are both playing the most dangerous game in the world, which is to deal with one another through satellites and puppets and weak clients. We are dealing through agents, and it is never certain that an agent will follow instructions, that he will not through stupidity or some sinister reason act on his own, and force your hand, and then leave you in a position where you have to back him up.

There, I believe, lies the greatest danger of war. There are desperadoes, gangsters, conspirators in both camps; there are hotheads who are trigger-happy, there are fanatics, and there are speculators who have lost power and position and hope to recoup in a war.

The balance of power which was fairly stable in the Roosevelt-Churchill-Stalin period, has now become extremely and dangerously unstable.

The United States stands virtually alone, holding in check the military power of the Soviet Union without effective allies and obligated also to maintain the economic life of Western Europe and of a considerable part of the world. There is still a balance. But we can no longer count on it. For we cannot hold defensively such an immense part of the world against the slow pressure and infiltration of the Soviet Union. If the present position continues much longer, we shall be at the mercy of incidents which could lead to war. The fact that the attempt to hold the line is so exhausting, so expensive, and so dangerous, will increase to a dangerous degree the tension in this country and in the world.   This will bring with it the idea of a crusade and of preventive war to end the anxiety and uneasiness.

The position may be compared to the situation during a war when neither side is willing to state the terms on which it is ready to settle, and when, therefore, the prevailing view is that the war must be fought to the bitter end and must terminate in unconditional surrender.   We must not let things drift that far.   In my view the world cannot stand another war now, and if war comes, it will be a kind of war which will spread everywhere and be not an international war that could end in a peace treaty, but a general civil war which would end in universal anarchy.

Our national interest requires that in resisting the expansion of Russia and even in attempting to reduce the expansion that has already occurred, we should not drift into the position where we and the Russians believe that the conflict can end only with the unconditional surrender of one or the other.   In our dealings with Russia we must take our stand firmly.   But we must take it clearly for a negotiated settlement and for a modus vivendi. We must refuse to appease the Russians and to surrender Europe and Asia to them.   But we must refuse also to enlarge and embitter the conflict by asking of them unconditional surrender. We must, in other words, proceed at once to state the terms on which we believe a settlement should be made, the terms for which we are maintaining and deploying our military forces, the terms on which we are prepared to make our economic contribution to the reconstruction of the world.

These terms, I believe, should be the following:

1.   We should say to the Soviet Union that in the Far East we propose that the status quo be maintained in China; that neither Red China nor Nationalist China shall be supported by either of us to the point where it can conquer the other.

2.   In the Middle East we should state that our special guarantees of assistance and support to Turkey and Greece are for the object of achieving a treaty which concludes the disputes over the Dardanelles, the boundaries of Turkey and the boundaries of Greece.   We should say that in the terms of that treaty we are prepared to acknowledge the special interest of the Soviet

Union in the security of the Dardanelles, and in the freedom of passage in time of peace, and of military operations sanctioned by the United Nations. In denying her right to physical possession of the straits, we should be prepared to consider any proposal which involves international civilian control and guarantees.

3. In Europe we should demand—without compromise— agreement on the political decentralization of Germany and we should be prepared if necessary to federate the three western zones of Germany even if the Soviet Union refuses to permit the Germans of its zone to enter such a German federation. But the constitution of the new Germany which we set up in the western zones should be clearly designed to admit the German states in the Russian zone on equal terms whenever the Russians are ready to permit it.

4. We should also say to the Russians that as far as continental Europe up to their frontiers is concerned, we propose that they, the British and ourselves evacuate all of Europe—leaving only token forces in Germany. We should then ask them to join us in sponsoring the formation of a European economic union. We should ask them to permit the countries of their orbit to enter this economic union, and to instruct the Communist parties in the rest of Europe not to oppose the formation of such a union.

5. We should say, then, that when such a union is formed, we shall be prepared on terms equivalent to lend-lease to provide it with the working capital required to start the economic life of Europe on a productive basis. We should then say that on the basis of such a general world agreement, we are prepared to consider assistance to Russia in her reconstruction—in the form both of current reparations from Germany, which would then be able to work productively, and also of credits from the United States.

My thesis, in short, is that we must resist the expansion of the Soviet empire, that we must press for the withdrawal of the Red Army within its own borders, but that we must accompany this pressure—which is dangerous, expensive and difficult—with clear and realizable terms of peace.

The statement of these terms of peace will not please the Russians. Nevertheless, the knowledge of what concretely we want, and that we want no more than that, will make their own resistance weaker. They will know the price on which they can have a peaceable settlement.

The statement of these terms of peace, which are reasonable and constructive, will assure the support to our side of the great masses of the people of continental Europe and of the British Isles. This is vitally important. For these masses will not support us in an unlimited crusade against the Soviet Union. They will, on the contrary, turn increasingly towards neutrality and towards distrust of our motives, and to resistance to our intervention in Europe and the world.

The statement of our terms, moreover, will unify the American people in support of our foreign policy. This support exists, but it is on the surface. It is not so deep and so well founded as it needs to be, if our people are to remain united and strong in the difficult and dangerous days to come.

ATOMIC ENERGY

AGAINST THE APPOINTMENT OF LILIENTHAL [1]

ROBERT A. TAFT [2]

In March 1946, the State Department Committee on Atomic Energy, headed by Under Secretary of State Dean Acheson and including David Lilienthal, issued the Acheson-Lilienthal report for the control of atomic energy.

The report proposed to set up an International Atomic Development Authority with exclusive jurisdiction over atomic materials, plants, and research, with power to inspect facilities throughout the world, with "moderate controls" over national atomic agencies, and with "step by step" abandonment by the United States of its atomic monopoly. This document became in effect the Baruch proposal which Russia rejected.[3]

On October 28, 1946 President Truman appointed Mr. Lilienthal and four others to the United States Commission and in January sent their names to the Senate for confirmation. The Joint Congressional Committee on Atomic Energy, with Senator Hickenlooper as chairman, conducted six weeks of lively hearings on these appointments.

On March 24, 1947 the Senate debates on the nominations began and reached a climax during the first days of April. The issue was not simply the consideration of Lilienthal's personal fitness as chairman of the Commission. The overshadowing question involved policies of public versus private control of public utilities, civilian versus military control of atomic energy, militant versus moderate attitude toward Russia, and Democratic versus Republican leadership in shaping postwar military and other policies.

On April 1, Mr. Taft arose in an extended condemnation of the appointment. He continued his argument on April 2, with many sharp give-and-take interruptions as the debate developed.

The section here included was delivered on April 2 and raised this issue: Did Lilienthal have a major responsibility for the Acheson-Lilienthal Report? After an analysis of the authorship, Taft concluded that he had. The complementary issues developed: If this report were adopted, would it threaten the security of the United States? If so, should it be rewritten? Although Taft handled his argument with skill and convic-

---

[1] *Congressional Record.* 80th Congress, 1st session. 93:3127-33. April 2, 1947 (daily edition).

[2] For biographical note see Appendix.

[3] See *Representative American Speeches: 1945-1946.* p. 120.

tion, he was constantly harried by Senator Brien McMahon. The latter asked whether Taft had a better solution than the Baruch plan. Taft contented himself with a "negative" attack.

As usual, the Ohio Senator spoke somewhat rapidly, at times excitedly, tightened his voice, and elevated the pitch unnecessarily. He was a debater rather than an orator. His material was fairly well grounded on facts, but his critics concluded that he had strayed from the immediate argument of Lilienthal's nomination when he ventured into extended criticism of foreign policy.[4]

Mr. President, I have only one other point to make. I do not purport to pass on or claim even that Mr. Lilienthal is a Communist or a fellow traveler. I do think that the group of which he was a part took an unduly friendly attitude toward communism. Like Mr. Henry Wallace, they felt that communism was merely another form of democracy, and, as Mr. Wallace often said, "a little better form of democracy than our democracy." I think most of them have seen that that is not the fact, but that was the condition, that was the attitude of many of this group throughout the government, and it was for that reason that they were soft toward the admission of Communists into government departments. The fact that many Communists are here is not evidence of Communist ability, Communist aggressiveness; the fact is that we had plenty of people in the government who thought that communism was just as good as American democracy. Therefore when a Communist came along they did not exclude him, and just as in the TVA, there was a Communist cell for a while, Mr. Lilienthal not doing much about it, so the same attitude existed in the government until the President of the United States himself recently was forced to issue an order in which he said that now the time has come when we must get rid of Communists. He admitted that many of the departments of government have proceeded to admit Communists. Why? Not because perhaps the heads of those departments were Communists but because they were soft on the subject of Communists, because they did not regard Communists as being threats to the American security. That was exactly Mr. Lilienthal's attitude. I think that is the only way to explain the report known as the

⁴ For further comment on Taft as a speaker see *Representative American Speeches: 1945-1946.* p.154.

Acheson-Lilienthal report on the subject of international control of atomic energy. It is a very interesting report. Senators will find copies of it on their desks, placed there today by the Senator from Connecticut [Mr. McMahon]. I think it is said that many others joined Mr. Lilienthal in this report. That is true. But if Senators will read it, I do not think they can have any doubt that Mr. Lilienthal wrote the report. The others went along with him in the report. The others, for the most part scientists without great experience in the subject of power, without great experience in governmental questions, were inclined at the time to believe that the only solution of the whole problem of atomic energy was in effect to give it away to Russia or any other country that wanted it.

The report in essence proposed that we set up an international atomic development authority, which is described as something as like TVA as two peas in a pod, except it is on an international scale. This atomic development authority is to take over all mines of uranium and thorium; it is to take over all plants; to operate the plants; to conduct all atomic research of every kind, and all atomic manufacture of every kind except some vaguely denatured products at the end of the process which might be left to the individual nations to develop. That atomic development authority was to be substantially independent.

On page 45 of the report—and I am not sure whether my copy is the same edition as the one on the desk of Senators— Mr. Lilienthal does recognize the desirability of having it responsible to somebody; he does not know exactly who. He says:

> There are many ways of assuring this necessary degree of accountability on the part of the Authority to the nations and peoples whose instrument it will be. Some integral organ of the United Nations, perhaps the Security Council itself, will need to serve as the overseeing body for the Authority. But it could do so in ways generally comparable to those employed by congressional appropriations and investigating committees and the Bureau of the Budget in relation to governmental institutions in the United States.

In other words, he envisages the same independent authority that he had as chairman of the TVA.

Detailed measures would have to be worked out to assure the proper connection between such overseeing or "accountability" body and the Atomic Development Authority itself.

Of course an international Atomic Authority would be even more independent, I think, than the TVA, because the rather vague Security Council control would be something exceedingly indefinite. Certainly this authority would be completely independent of the United States. It would be so far away from the United States that there would be nothing we could do about it. We would not control the personnel. We would have only one voice among many in deciding what its powers should be, or how they should be changed. We would have only one voice among many in selecting the personnel. As Mr. Lilienthal says in his report:

One of the important problems will be the question of personnel. It will be of the essence to recruit that personnel on a truly international basis, giving weight to geographical and national distribution.

That means that the great bulk of the personnel would be foreigners so far as we are concerned, and would not be Americans. The head of the organization might be a Russian; he might be a Yugoslav; he might be a Frenchman, a French Communist; or anyone else that the United Nations might conceivably agree upon. We have seen recently that an attack was made on Mr. Trygve Lie. The charge was made that the members of the secretariat or commission which Mr. Lie sent to Greece to look into the Greek problem is dominated largely by Soviet members.

When Mr. Lilienthal has set up this organization, it is to move in and take over all our plants. It is to take over Oak Ridge, Tenn., with 59,000 acres and 49,000 Americans. Apparently it is to take over the Hanford Engineering Works, with 400,000 acres in Pasco, Wash., and take over 45,000 acres at Los Alamos, N. Mex., and a number of smaller plants throughout the United States. I suppose in making the deal we might cut down the acreage somewhat, although if the organization is to conduct the necessary experiments which it is prepared to conduct, I do not see how we can help turning over all this land to an international authority conducted by an international force to operate the plants existing in the United States, or how we can prevent foreigners from other nations having full access to all those plants.

Furthermore, this body would have complete regulation of a growing industry in the United States as well as in the other countries throughout the world. The organization would, in effect, have to say what possible activities with some denatured products, if there is such a thing, could be conducted by American business, and under what conditions, and that international check would exist, of course, throughout the United States. That may be necessary. I have some doubt as to whether there is really any field for denaturing.

The other side of the picture is that the Atomic Development Authority would build in Russia, and in other countries throughout the world, plants exactly like our plants. On page 47 the report says:

In strengthening security, one of the primary considerations will relate to the geographical location of the operations of the Authority and its property. For it can never be forgotten that it is a primary purpose of the Atomic Development Authority to guard against the danger that our hopes for peace may fail, and that adventures of aggression may again be attempted. It will probably be necessary to write into the charter itself a systematic plan governing the location of the operations and property of the Authority so that a strategic balance may be maintained among nations. In this way, protection will be afforded against such eventualities as the complete or partial collapse of the United Nations or the Atomic Development Authority, protection will be afforded against the eventuality of sudden seizure by any one nation of the stock piles, reduction, refining, and separation plants, and reactors of all types belonging to the Authority.

This will have to be quite a different situation from the one that now prevails. At present with Hanford, Oak Ridge, and Los Alamos situated in the United States, other nations can find no security against atomic warfare except the security that resides in our own peaceful purposes or the attempt at security that is seen in developing secret atomic enterprises of their own. Other nations which, according to their own outlook, may fear us, can develop a greater sense of security only as the Atomic Development Authority locates similar dangerous operations within their borders. Once such operations and facilities have been established by the Atomic Development Authority and are being operated by that agency within other nations as well as within our own, a balance will have been established. It is not thought that the Atomic Development Authority could protect its plants by military force from the overwhelming power of the nation in which they are situated. Some United Nations military guard may be desirable. But at most, it could be little more than a token. The real protection will lie in the fact that if any nation seizes the plants or the stock piles that are situated in its territory, other nations will have similar facilities and materials situated within their own borders so that the act of seizure need not place them at a disadvantage.

Except that the other fellow will have all the bombs he does not now possess.

MR. CAPEHART. Will the Senator admit that there is today no organization in the world to which it can be turned over, and will the Senator not admit that until such an organization is established the smartest thing to do is to return it to where it was originally, that is, the Army and the Navy?

MR. TAFT. Mr. President, I refuse to yield further. I would favor returning it to a military commission. The Panama Canal was to be built by civilian engineers, but before we got through with it, we said to the Army, "You build the Panama Canal"; and the Army built it. I think the Army is competent to handle a job that civilians are competent to handle. But at the moment I am not discussing that particular question.

The Senator from Connecticut has raised the question as to whether I am opposing the whole plan submitted to the United Nations. I think at the present moment I would withdraw that plan, at least until the world is in a more peaceful state. I want to show, however, that when Mr. Baruch presented this plan on June 14, 1946, to the United Nations, he described in about seven lines what the Lilienthal report was. He said:

I offer this as a basis for beginning our discussion—

He was not accepting it with any tremendous enthusiasm—but I think the peoples we serve would not believe—and without faith nothing counts—that a treaty merely outlawing possession or use of the atomic bomb constitutes effective fulfillment of the instructions to this commission. It would be a deception to which I am unwilling to lend myself were I not to say to you and to our people that the matter of punishment lies at the very heart of our present security system. It might as well be admitted here and now that the subject goes straight to the veto power contained in the charter of the United Nations so far as it relates to the field of atomic energy.

The very heart of the problem was ignored by the Lilienthal report. Is assumed, apparently, that all we were going to do was to set up an international authority and everything would be wonderful. No man could have had such a belief except a man who naively believes in the good faith of the U.S.S.R. and their willingness to enter a peaceful world. I say that it is Mr. Lilienthal's softness toward communism which led him to make this report, which got us into the position in which we now find ourselves.

This report discusses the question of other nations seizing plants. It discusses the question of security, but it does not say a word about any nation giving up the veto. It does not discuss in any way the manner in which we are successfully to enforce this control, except for one thing. It says that if we build a plant and it is seized, that is a danger signal. Then we will know that the enemy are going to war. Of course we will know it. We will know that they are going to war with the bombs which we let them build and for which we built the plants. The report discusses the question of security, but it wholly fails to realize the seriousness of the problem, the difficulty of an international agency, the fact that an international agency is shot through with every kind of nationality. If Communists can infiltrate into TVA they can certainly infiltrate into any international agency. They will know every detail of the atomic bomb. Those who come into the United States and operate the plants can arrange to blow them up at any time the Russian Government tells them to do so.

MR. McMAHON. Mr. President, will the Senator yield?

MR. TAFT. No; I shall not yield to the Senator from Connecticut.

If this international authority happens to be more Russian than American there is no way by which we can restrain them from developing in Russia bigger and better bombs than in the United States. It seems to me that this is the most naive report that could be made by any man who has ever dealt with an international problem, and it can only arise from the fact that Mr. Lilienthal considered communism just another form of democracy. He considered Russia a nation like ours, desiring to reach every possible agreement and eliminating every possibility of war. In that Mr. Lilienthal was completely mistaken.

Let me read what President Truman said this year:

This is no more than a frank recognition that totalitarian regimes imposed on free peoples by direct or indirect aggression undermine the foundations of international peace, and hence the security of the United States. The peoples of a number of countries of the world have recently had totalitarian regimes forced upon them against their will.

By the U.S.S.R., of course—

The Government of the United States has made frequent protests against coercion and intimidation in violation of the Yalta agreement, in Poland, Rumania, and Bulgaria. I must also state that in a number of other countries there have been similar developments.

How foolish a report looks which was made a few years ago, when we were proposing not only to turn over all bombs to Russia but to build plants in Russia so that they could construct them to carry out the plans described by the President.

Mr. President, I say that until the situation changes, and certainly until the position of Russia, as described by the President, is changed, we cannot undertake to give them the atomic bomb. That is all I have said, and that is the fact. It is perfectly obvious today. I have talked to scientists, and even they are beginning to say, "We had better withdraw this whole report until we can work out with the Russian Government something better than we have today."

Mr. President, in conclusion, I wish to say that I think the only explanation for this report is a submission on the part of its authors to the theory which spread so rapidly through the United States. I cannot help thinking that it had some foreign support or initiative, but it reached many Americans well beyond the influence of Communist propaganda—the theory that there is no defense against the atomic bomb, there is no way to prevent other people from getting it, therefore we might as well give it away at once. The conclusion was so desirable to the Communist group that I cannot help thinking that to some extent the arguments for it were at least propagandized by them, and the conclusion from that was, "therefore, if that is so, keep the military out of it."

We had this tremendous propaganda last year against any military touch apparently of the whole subject of the atomic bomb, and we have it again today. We have the same propaganda today for the confirmation of Mr. Lilienthal, on the theory apparently that in some way, if we go ahead with this policy, there will be a wider distribution of the atomic bomb throughout the world. Mr. President, all I say is this: We in this body have the responsibility practically of appointing the Atomic Energy Commission. We ought not to confirm anybody we would not be willing to appoint. There are plenty of people in the United States, in the first place, who are believers in the system of free enterprise, who are believers in the American division of constitutional powers between the legislative and the executive; there are plenty of people in the United States who believe that our form of government can handle the atomic energy question as well as any other question that may confront us.

In the second place, there are plenty of people today who are realists about Russia, who realize that Russia has a form of government which is a threat to the welfare of the world and of the United States, who are not going to be soft toward Russia, and who are primarily concerned with seeing to it that we have absolute and complete protection against any threat from any foreign nation.

Finally, Mr. President, there are plenty of people in the United States who are open, frank, and truthful. I think we can choose one of those people rather than Mr. David Lilienthal.

FOR THE APPOINTMENT OF LILIENTHAL [5]

Arthur H. Vandenberg [6]

In "perhaps the most dramatic session of the Eightieth Congress," the Senate on April 3, 1947 refused to table President Truman's six appointments to the United States Atomic Energy Commission.

Senator John W. Bricker of Ohio was the author of the defeated motion to recommit the nominations to a committee. In effect, the vote, 52 to 38, was an endorsement of the nominations and foreshadowed the final vote of the following week.

Senator Vandenberg, yielding his chair as president pro tem to Senator Irving M. Ives, of New York, took the floor on that day for what was generally judged to be one of the most forceful and effective speeches of his career. The Michigan Senator "flung out sizzling challenges" to Senators Taft and Bricker and ably defended the personal and political character of Lilienthal. The debater refuted with general effectiveness the major arguments against the appointment. When he called for confirmation "in the interest of the national welfare and for the sake of a square deal," the crowded galleries, contrary to the rules, applauded vigorously. Plainly the spectators were with Vandenberg, rather than with the Ohio senators.

Vandenberg had again demonstrated his ability to express ideas in colorful language, to appeal both emotionally and logically, to refute with skill, to rely on the mastery of his subject both in general and in detail, and to dominate with animated delivery.[7]

On Wednesday, April 9, by a vote of 50 to 31, the Senate confirmed the nomination of Lilienthal to be Chairman of the Commission. The nominations of Robert F. Bracher, Sumner Pike, Lewis L. Straus, and William W. Waymack to be members of the Commission, and of Carroll L. Wilson to be General Manager were confirmed by voice vote. Thus these five civilians were entrusted with one of the most important programs ever given to such a group. They were placed in charge of operations of atomic plants at Oak Ridge, Tennessee, and Hanford, Washington; they were given control over the secret stock bombs, raw materials, atomic experiments, 180,000 scientists, engineers and other workers, and a budget for the year 1947-1948 of $450,000,000.

[5] *Congressional Record*. 80th Congress, 1st session. 93:3204-6. April 3, 1947 (daily edition).

[6] For biographical note see Appendix.

[7] For further comment on Vandenberg as speaker see *Representative American Speeches: 1937-1938*. p. 39; *1944-1945*. p. 43; *1945-1946*. p. 45.

Mr. President, I wish briefly to make a matter of record my reasons for believing that under all existing circumstances Mr. David E. Lilienthal should be confirmed as Chairman of the Atomic Energy Commission without further delay. I do so with no illusions that any Senator, at this late hour, after weeks and months of bitter controversy, is still open to persuasion. I do so with complete respect for the good conscience with which every Senator will take his position. I quarrel with none. I do so chiefly because it is my only way of advising my own constituents of my views in response to thousands of letters on both sides of the issue, which it has been a physical impossibility for me to answer.

Mr. President, I have been a member of the Senate Atomic Energy Committee which sat as a jury in the Lilienthal case from January 27 to March 4. I have heard or read every word of the testimony. As a result, I have been driven away from the adverse prejudice with which I started. I have been driven to the belief that logic, equity, fair play, and a just regard to urgent public welfare combine to recommend Mr. Lilienthal's confirmation in the light of today's realities.

I say this with full appreciation of the earnest zeal with which others hold a contrary view, including many of my warmest friends. I say it with a candid expression of regret that other possible nominees whom the President first unsuccessfully sought declined to serve. I agree it would have been a happy thing if this Commission could have been long since launched with the benediction of universal approval. On the other hand, I must summarily reject the frequently quoted doctrine that no nominee is eligible if he is attacked. It seems to me that any such doctrine would surrender to "hue and cry," regardless of truth and justice.

Since it is impossible for all Senators intimately to know the record developed in seven weeks of utterly exhaustive hearings, I respectfully suggest that fair-minded men cannot wholly ignore the impact of the cold, hard fact that eight out of nine of the Senate's own jury, commissioned by the Senate to pass upon the facts, report, regardless of party lines, in favor of confirmation. I remind the Senate that these jurors consisted of the Senator from Iowa [Mr. Hickenlooper], the Senator from Colorado [Mr. Millikin], the Senator from California [Mr. Knowland], the Senator from Connecticut [Mr. McMahon], the Senator from Texas [Mr. Connally], the Senator from Georgia [Mr. Russell], the Senator from Colorado [Mr. Johnson], and the senior Senator from Michigan.   At least in respect to the others, Mr. President, I am surely entitled to say that a more representative or competent Senate jury could not have been impaneled.   It seems to me that it would be highly improbable that such a jury would almost unanimously go wrong.   At any rate, I plead a reasonable presumption—and I say this with deepest respect for the good conscience of our lone dissenter, the distinguished Senator from Ohio [Mr. Bricker].

In the climax of this long investigation, almost without parallel in Senate history, the "jury" agrees—8 to 1—that it is in the public interest for the Senate to confirm Chairman Lilienthal and order him officially to the intensive atomic labors which, for the sake of the public welfare and the national security, have too long lagged.

I repeat that I recall no such thoroughness of inquiry by a Senate committee in all my nineteen years of service here.   I am unable to believe the process has not been adequate or that we would be warranted in prolonging it.

I can summarize my own feeling, Mr. President, by reading one of the countless telegrams which I have received from unimpeachable Americans.   This has been read before.   It is worth repeating because of its source, and I repeat it because it happens to be addressed to me.   It comes from a great free enterpriser— a great industrialist, who long headed General Electric.   It comes from a great citizen whose broad devotions to the public weal cannot be gainsaid.   It is from Owen D. Young:

> Because of my interest in public utilities I became associated with David E. Lilienthal nearly twenty years ago.   I regarded him as an adversary and so naturally watched him with a critical eye.   Because of my interest in the international problems of this Nation, I have also watched Lilienthal's work in the atomic field.   As a result, I wish to say that he is a man of clear vision, of executive ability, of firmness and unquestioned loyalty, and in a unique position to serve effectively in the position for which he is nominated.

But, Mr. President, with varying shades of emphasis, he is charged with either sympathy for communism or too easy toleration of it. After weeks of testimony, I find no basis for this charge. I hope my own record, plus the fact that I am in the top bracket of all Communist blacklists all round the world, demonstrates that I am not calculated to be "soft" on such a subject. But I do not want to emulate the intolerance of communism itself by condemning to some sort of Siberia all persons who do not happen totally to subscribe to my own view as to how America ought to be run; nor would any of us, I hope, use communism as an excuse for verdicts otherwise unjustified.

It is the opinion of our committee that Mr. Lilienthal is no part of a Communist by any stretch of the imagination. There were a few youthful intriguers in one minor department of the Tennessee Valley Authority who were juvenile Communists. I have no doubt they were there, an infinitesimal percentage of the total TVA personnel. I am sorry the Chairman of TVA did not find this tiny group and root them out. But let us be fair about it, Mr. President. If I were to hold every top executive in American industry personally responsible for the underground communism which exists in every large employment, I would denude most American industry of its leadership. I even read recently that no less reliable a witness than former Senator Robert M. LaFollette charged that we had some highly questionable characters in the staffs of some of our committees right here in the Senate of the United States. I take it, however, that this does not warrant the impeachment of Senators.

I do not minimize these things. They put us on notice as to our necessities for eternal vigilance. It has been useful to rip all these matters to their bare bones. I can guarantee that the Joint Congressional Atomic Energy Committee will make this matter its special business. But I am unable to find anything in the record in respect to this phase of the case which indicts Mr. Lilienthal. Thank heaven this is so because if he were unreliable, he has already had at least three months in which to subvert our atomic secrets and sell us down the river; and if we were to reject his nomination he would be under none of the special restraints of the Atomic Energy Act to still hold his tongue. We would, indeed, be in a bad way if we could not honestly, conscientiously, and conclusively give him a clean bill of health in respect to communism.

I add, Mr. President, that there is another far graver alien danger that our own development of atomic energy shall slow down to a point where we shall not everlastingly keep ahead of the rest of the world in nuclear physics. Already we have been relatively stagnating far too many months while the famous Manhattan Project has been in the twilight zone of uncertain transition from military to civilian control. It will remain in this uncertainty until the Commission is firmly in the saddle. This is a hazard to which every American scientist testifies. This has been told to our committee in plain, blunt language by those who know, and by those to whom the American people must look for responsibility in respect to national security as related to this awful contemplation. We have been put on notice. This would not justify us in confirming a bad commission. But it may well temper our pursuit of perfectionism, if such there be. Certainly it calls for action now without further delay.

I may say at this point, Mr. President, that when I hear suggestions now made that we should repeal our present atomic energy law, which provides super-control of atomic energy in this country by civilian auspices, and when I now begin to hear again that it must all be subordinated to military control, my mind goes back to the many months during which the Atomic Energy Committee of the Senate struggled with that problem.

Mr. President, if we found out one thing truer than another, it is that in peacetime we cannot drive science into its laboratories with bayonets.

Now let me come to a second charge against Mr. Lilienthal. It is said he is such a devotee of public ownership that he will endanger free enterprise. Mr. President, I confess that that gave me pause. I am one of those who do not want the Government to complete with private enterprise unless it is an indispensable public necessity. But what are the realities in the instant case?

We, the Congress, have declared by law that the control of atomic energy must be the tightest Government monopoly ever set up in the United States—pending the day when the destructive use of atomic energy shall be outlawed for keeps. You all voted for it. It passed the Senate unanimously. We solemnly and unavoidably decreed that Government ownership and management, no matter how much we dislike it in other aspects of our national economy and life, is an indispensable public necessity for the sake of national security in respect to the control of atomic energy.

To leave this world-wrenching mystery, involving life and death, in private hands or under private enterprise at the present time would be a shocking outrage upon human values. It would violate every element of public trust. So we, the Congress, declared for a primary Government monopoly. Therefore one of the most available men to run it is the successful manager of the greatest existing comparable example of public ownership and management. Whether we like it or him or TVA, this sequence leads logically to David Lilienthal's door. His liability under other circumstances thus becomes an asset for the time being.

It seems to be a fact, despite incidental arguments, that TVA is one of the most successful public institutions of its sort on earth. It is the nearest thing, if not the only thing, comparable in general character to the far-flung empire of the Manhattan project with its vast public investment and its vaster personnel. It is not Mr. Lilienthal's chairmanship which makes the job a public project. We, the Senate, did that unanimously months ago. Rather, it is because we made the job a public project that Mr. Lilienthal becomes peculiarly eligible.

But we did something else when we passed the original atomic energy bill. We set it down that, when the world is freed of the hazard in the destructive use of fissionable material, we propose to turn this new power back into the relatively free control of competitive American initiative. Indeed, the law requires the Commission to report back to Congress for new instructions whenever the nonmilitary use of fissionable material becomes feasible. Mr. Lilienthal could not escape the many mandates of the bill in this direction even if he would, and he will never get a chance because his appointment runs only for seventeen months; and unfortunatley there is no possibility of international agreements dependably to outlaw atomic bombs, under adequate disciplines against bad faith, within this time. In 1948 this appointment, if renewed by the President, will again pass under free and untrammeled Senate review. Meanwhile, the more expertly the phase of "public monopoly" is run, the nearer we shall be to creating maximum atomic opportunities for transfer to the domain of free enterprise, when that happy time comes.

I pause at this point to add that I expect the Joint Congressional Committee on Atomic Energy to be something more than a collection of dummies in the evolution of all these plans. It is clothed with every authority to know what goes on. It will walk sentry post at all times. It is our constant congressional liaison. I confess that I am not heavily impressed with the idea that, once confirmed, Mr. Lilienthal is going to become such a superautocrat that even Congressmen and Senators will suddenly disintegrate into impotent pygmies. That is several miles from true, if I know my Congressmen and Senators. Yet, it is some kind of a compliment to Mr. Lilienthal, from his critics, when, however fatuously, he is assigned such giant stature.

Now I come to the third charge. The charge is made that this nominee's connection with the Acheson-Lilienthal report, covering the problem of physical atomic controls, discloses a flaw in his reliability as a guardian of our atomic secrets because this report did not go to a finality in prescribing the ultimate security system demanded by the later Baruch report. It seems to me this criticism is irrelevant, incompetent, and immaterial. The Acheson-Lilienthal report was offered, according to its own language, merely as a place to begin. Clearly, its authors were charged with the exploration of physical mechanisms for atomic control; not with the exploration of political mechanisms which became the subsequent responsibility of the Baruch group. But they made an invaluable and indispensable report, without which the Baruch report and the ultimate finished American plan would have been impossible, and—this ought to end this part of the argument—Lilienthal wholeheartedly endorses the Baruch report and the American plan, and Baruch wholeheartedly endorses Lilienthal.

The Acheson-Lilienthal report was a vital milestone on the journey to this final goal.

It was approved precisely for what it was by a very distinguished board of consultants. Prominently among those consultants who put their stamp of integrity upon this report which is now subjected to critical attack was the very man who is the idol of all the speeches I have heard here against the Lilienthal confirmation. It is signed by Maj. Gen. Leslie R. Groves, who says:

> In our opinion this report furnishes the most constructive analysis on the question of international control we have seen and a definitely hopeful approach to a solution of the entire problem.

It is signed by three other great Americans, any one of whom, if he was nominated for the post of Chairman of the Atomic Energy Commission, I am sure would be confirmed unanimously and in the twinkling of an eye.

Such being the case, I am unable to find Mr. Lilienthal any less acceptable on account of a report for which these and four other distinguished men are equally responsible. On the contrary, I think his intimate association with these men and with this report actually underscore his unique eligibility for the equally unique responsibilities which this task entails. In equity and logic, I must dismiss this charge.

In doing so, Mr. President, an additional observation seems pertinent. I have mentioned a few names, now associated with Mr. Lilienthal, without which Hiroshima might have been too late. I think it is important to mention a few others who have richly earned the right to be special consultants in this matter. Dr. Bush, the Government's chief atomic consultant, flatly testifies that in his opinion Mr. Lilienthal is the best available American for this pending assignment; and he bluntly asserts that his rejection by the Senate, under all existing circumstances, would be serious disservice to the public welfare at a critical moment in atomic history. Mr. Bernard M. Baruch, whom I suspect the Senate would instantly have confirmed for this appointment, endorses Mr. Lilienthal. Mr. John M. Hancock, Mr. Baruch's trusted assistant in many an enterprise dedicated to the public welfare, endorses Mr. Lilienthal. Dr. Karl Compton, president of Massachusetts Institute of Technology and one of the great figures in our atomic history, vigorously urges Mr. Lilienthal's confirmation. Dr. Thomas, the great scientific engineer representing the Monsanto Chemical Co., which played a key role in this gigantic enterprise, endorses Mr. Lilienthal. So does Mr. Chester Barnard, chairman of the New Jersey Bell Telephone Co., and another keyman in our atomic history.

I do not know of one single scientific, engineering, or industrial authority who has had anything to do with our wartime triumph in atomic energy and who has testified in this celebrated cause who has not joined in this unbroken record of approval. Where are the comparable witnesses against him, Senators? I ask that again. Where are the comparable witnesses against him? I confess that these are things that count with me, Mr. President. I am unable to forget what we owe these men. They know whereof they speak. They are not speculating in episodes of ancient history or relative inconsequentiality. They bring to us from the rich experience of their devoted loyalty to their country the advice that this is the thing we should do. They know at first hand. They are not likely to jeopardize their own transcendental achievements. They are not likely to desert their country's welfare.

I cannot count them as less reliable or less patriotic than we found them to be in war. If Mr. Lilienthal is good enough for them, he must be good enough for the Senate to confirm, even though he may not be one whom we might have preferred. I realize that it is a great responsibility to confirm him—or anyone else. Under the circumstances, however, it may be an even greater responsibility to turn him down and thus further prolong our dangerous era of atomic drift.

There were other complaints against the Lilienthal record, such as the charge, way back in the early 1930's, that when he was Public Utility Commissioner of Wisconsin he held another job in Chicago in violation of the Wisconsin statutes. What he did, however, was to make a contract with his erstwhile private employers to compensate him subsequently, not for current services, but for adjustments due him on account of services previously rendered.

Mr. President, when I confront matters of ancient history, as to which it is very difficult, because of the lapse of time, to know all the facts intimately, it occurs to me that if I can find a key witness of impeccable morality to testify, I am entitled to take his word. Who is it who testifies in this particular situation? It is the then Governor of Wisconsin, Philip La Follette. He testified that he knew all about the contract, that it did not violate the law, that it was entirely appropriate and satisfactory, and that it was approved by him before Mr. Lilienthal took office. On a moral and legal question of this nature, I know of no better reliance than Governor La Follette himself.

Mr. President, there are many other incidental controversies involved in this situation. My time is running out, so I can refer to only one more. The other day in the debate it was suggested that the military liaison which will be available for the protection of the national security, under the operation of Mr. Lilienthal, administering this responsibility, will be inadequate. It was pointed out that in his examination in respect to the military liaison committee he was somewhat confused at points in respect to the direct answers—the confusion being, I submit, Mr. President, that he was perfectly honestly confused as to how he could fit his administrative responsibilities into the very unusual requirements of military liaison which the law requires of him. But when it came to the key questions upon which the correct answer depends, Mr. President, I submit that there is no doubt about the answer. Those who were on the committee when this law was written know that the whole argument turned on the question as to who was to decide what the military liaison committee could contact itself with in respect to the operations of the Commission.

Here are the questions to which the telltale answer was given:

MR. LILIENTHAL. The answer to that is definitely that it is up to the military liaison committee to decide what it regards as an appropriate military field.

SENATOR MILLIKIN. And there are no impediments which will be put in its way?

MR. LILIENTHAL. No impediments will be put in its way.

How can that be called equivocation?

The PRESIDING OFFICER (Mr. Dworshak in the chair). The time of the Senator has expired.

MR. VANDENBERG. Mr. President, I ask the Senator from Iowa whether I may have five minutes more.

MR. HICKENLOOPER. I yield five more minutes to the Senator from Michigan.

MR. VANDENBERG. Mr. President, further in his examination Mr. Lilienthal said: "There will be nothing withheld from the military liaison committee."

That is all the Military Liaison Committee requires, Mr. President; and even if that guaranty were not written into the text and the body of this law, I respectfully submit to the Senators who are fearful that the Military Liaison Committee will not have adequate approach to information, that they scan the membership of the Military Liaison Committee. There, once more, they will find their great friend and their idol—I do not speak of him with any disrespect; on the contrary, I think he rendered his country one of the greatest services ever rendered by any American in time of war—Maj. Gen. Leslie R. Groves. He is part of the Military Liaison Committee. If anyone wishes to try to make me think that General Groves will stand impotent or silent in front of closed doors when the welfare of his country is at stake, such a person has a far less valid opinion of General Groves than I have. Mr. President, there is no possibility of any menace or threat in respect to the Military Liaison Committee under the Lilienthal appointment.

Mr. President, I thank the Senator from Iowa for giving me additional time. I wish to return as much of it to him as I can.

I simply say, in conclusion, that I have substantially reviewed the record which many weeks of testimony unfolded. In dismissing the complaints I have in almost every instance found an affirmative reason, a positive reason, for supporting Mr. Lilienthal's confirmation. It seems to me that the preponderance was in his favor overwhelmingly.

I have no quarrel with those who disagree. I know there is a deep-seated prejudice against Mr. Lilienthal in many earnest,

sincere minds. I have no quarrel whatever with those feelings.
But for myself, in the presence of the evidence I have no alternative except to say to my colleagues that I have no doubt that in
the interest of the national welfare and for the sake of a square
deal, Mr. Lilienthal is entitled to be confirmed.

ATOMIC ENERGY [8]

David E. Lilienthal [9]

Mr. Lilienthal, confirmed on April 9, 1947 by the Senate as Chairman of the Atomic Energy Commission, gave this address on April 19 at the closing banquet of the three-day session of the American Society of Newspaper Editors, held at the Hotel Statler, Washington, D. C.

The speaker impressed the editors profoundly when he held aloft a cylinder of pure uranium and warned them that the United States "actually has gone downhill" in the race for the development of atomic energy. Dr. Vannevar Bush, president of the Carnegie Institution, also on the program, concurred in the Lilienthal proposition that the United States was lagging in its atomic program.

The editors applauded the new chairman of the Commission as he declared, "We can best serve mankind not by unreal dreaming, not by assailing the motives of our President, but by strengthening this nation as the only remaining bulwark of democracy."

General Dwight Eisenhower, also a speaker at the three-day conference, explained the function of the Army High Command in adapting its methods to the prospective era of the "super blitz."

Mr. Lilienthal is a dominating and persuasive speaker, thoroughly extempore, pleasing in voice quality, inflection, and other vocal qualities. His skill in speech composition is an additional factor in his speaking effectiveness. He was a debater at Depauw University, and a member of Delta Sigma Rho, honorary forensic society. His speech instructor was Professor B. Gough, at one time President of the National Association of Teachers of Speech. With his oration on "The Mission of the Jew" Lilienthal won the Depauw, the Indiana State and the midwest contests and placed "second or third" in the final interstate contest at Topeka, Kansas (1918). [10] As lawyer, publicist, public administrator, he has engaged with success in many a debate and occasional address.

It is a great honor and one I highly prize to have this opportunity to speak to this gathering of newspaper editors from all parts of this broad land. I am especially appreciative of your invitation because of certain recent events of a rather

[8] *Congressional Record*. 80th Congress, 1st session. 93:A1922-4. April 22, 1947 (daily edition). The text here reprinted was furnished by the Atomic Energy Commission.

[9] For biographical note see Appendix.

[10] Letter to the editor of this volume. May 7, 1947.

tumultuous character in which I played a not too happy part. I am told by more experienced criminal defendants than I am, that it is not considered the best form to thank the jury after they have brought in a verdict of "not guilty," the idea being, apparently, that they only did their duty and therefore thanks are not good form. Nevertheless I cannot refrain from commenting that had it not been that the press of the United States is overwhelmingly fair, decent, independent, and above narrow partisanship, your present speaker would almost certainly not be talking to you tonight as Chairman of the Atomic Energy Commission. Now this result may or may not be a good thing, but as a statement of fact about the press of this country it is something I felt I should like to say to you directly.

This black object that I hold in my hand is a cylinder of pure uranium. The amount I hold here is small as you can see. It is harmless. Five years ago no man had even seen even this much pure uranium. Not that it was rare, but it was simply of little importance. Tonight this black metal, this inanimate substance is the central figure in the councils of the peoples of the world.

Why this should be so is not difficult to understand. Look at this small cylinder for a moment. It weighs about 2½ pounds. That much coal or oil, burned under the boilers of industry, would provide a trifling amount of useful energy. Compare the technical opportunities of the controlled release of nuclear forces. The energy resulting from the fission of the 3 million billion billion atoms in this small cylinder, converted into electricity would equal about the total daily use of electricity in the city of Washington, which now requires about 2500 tons of coal.

This amount of TNT would produce only a small explosion. But the destructive power of the energy in the nuclei of this handful of material is very great, is catastrophic, the equivalent of many many tons of TNT. As you know, one bomb derived from this stuff destroyed an entire city in a single blast. This material is so dense, so heavy that 60 tons—about the capacity of a railroad coal gondola—could be piled up here in a block about 8 feet long by 3 feet high by 4 feet thick. Yet the energy in that material, if only 25 per cent of its heat were converted to electricity, would provide an amount of electricity as great as the entire country uses in a year.

Now these are opportunities that lie in the future and I cite them only to show how great are the economic stakes of further development to bring these opportunities into living reality.

But there are even more important reasons why the recently acquired knowledge about this black cylinder is so vital. Uranium and certain other substances can be put into a kind of furnace called a reactor, or pile, in a particular way so that a terrific radiation is created, a fantastically intense and powerful bombardment by infinitesmal particles that makes the beam from X-ray machine or piece of radium seem faint. This violent barrage of particles and the resulting radio-activity can perform scientific miracles. Materials, familiar materials like iron or carbon or gold, are thrust into that furnace. They go into that bombardment one substance, they frequently come out another. Transmutation of the very elements, the dream of the ancient alchemists, is realized at last, in the day when you and I are living. The characteristics of familiar substances can be changed—made more or less brittle, more or less electrically conductive, and so on. Even more important in terms of human benefit, this intense radiation is a means whereby we can expand our knowledge of nature, push back the frontiers of darkness in a hundred fields—in medicine and the knowledge of how to conquer disease, in industry, in nutrition, in agriculture. It uncovers new concepts of the nature of the universe, brings new skills, new professions, new ideas into being, as basic knowledge always does.

Now, the present discoveries of the controlled release of nuclear energy are the barest beginning. Almost nothing yet is known of the nucleus of the atom; almost everything lies ahead. In our own day the knowledge thus far acquired can be used to unfold vast new understanding of the world, bringing human benefits in its wake.

Our knowledge of the nucleus, of the development of nuclear heat and energy, of neutron bombardment, of the secrets of all physical matter—these are in their earliest stages. The atomic bombs thus far used are also only a beginning, perhaps but a crude beginning, when compared with what further research and development may produce. This may seem rather grim. But what I am talking to you about are the facts and possibilities in the world, regardless of whether they appear grim or pleasant. And the fact is that only a beginning has been made in the destructive potentialities of nuclear weapons. As to the military uses of nuclear energy this must always be remembered: atomic energy research and development—whether for the uses of war and destruction or for beneficent and creative purposes—is virtually an identical process; two sides of the same coin. It is only in the very final stages that a difference arises between destructive and peaceful uses, a difference between what you need to know to make the forces within the nucleus serve the interest of human kind and what you need to know to make them destroy it. Up to that final point the road is the same.

The United States has a head start on the rest of the world. Are we to maintain that preeminence, maintain and increase it, or are we to fall behind? Will we fool along or politic along, or are we to press forward in the vigorous tradition of a pioneer nation?

The answers to such questions depend largely upon you. This is the theme of what I have to say to you of the American press. What our course shall be in the development of this portentous discovery will depend upon how important forward strides in atomic development appear to the American people, depend upon how well the whole American people understand the essential facts, understand the human implications of this discovery.

How well the people understand depends largely upon our institutions of education and communication, the schools and universities, the churches and religious organizations, the radio, and most of all the press.

This great venture into new fields of knowledge can progress no more rapidly than the public's understanding. The American people must know in broad terms what is at stake for themselves and their children.

Our problem is first to *understand*. This is not easy. It is not easy for any of us—it is not easy to sense that a profound change has taken place in the world. And it is not enough that a few people understand, a few grasp the facts. This comprehension must become widespread. And in the process we must come to grips with reality but without hysteria.

This is not only a large order for the press and for educational forces. This, my friends, is a large order for humankind.

What are the essential facts that must be known? Let me illustrate with a few. And may I say that none of these facts are highly technical. None of them are secret scientific data. At the threshhold of progress in public understanding we must overcome the prevalent feeling that—all this atomic energy business is over my head! That is simply not true.

First, take the present condition of our atomic energy development as of this 19th of April 1947. This is a vital fact for the American public to know and to understand in broad outline.

We all know that when the first atomic bomb was dropped on Hiroshima August 6, 1945, the United States had a very considerable head start on the rest of the world. It was estimated that we had a start of between five to fifteen years. What's the situation today? It is this painful fact, that since Hiroshima, the United States has lost momentum in atomic energy development. For from the level of V-J Day we have actually gone downhill, measured in such vital factors as scientific personnel, depreciation of plants, intensity of effort, and in other important ways.

This is wholly understandable, for a relaxation in a transition period was inevitable. But it certainly presents a state of affairs that is not compatable with our conception of the responsibilities that the country has now laid upon this new Commission. Accordingly the Atomic Energy Commission has appraised the situation and initiated steps to change these conditions. Nothing less than a major effort is called for, a program under full head of steam, carried forward jointly by American science, industry, the armed forces and government.

We have lost time and momentum. It is clear that much

of this lost time was quite unavoidable. But to face the facts of lost drive, the dribbling away of time, this is the beginning point of any understanding by realistic men of what America's course should be from here on out.

What other facts must become widely understood? I would say high on the list is an understanding of this country's official proposal to the world for international atomic control, the Baruch Plan, now being carried forward by Senator Warren Austin and Mr. Frederick Osborne. This must become known to all of us. The physical facts that make the safeguards in that proposal, if agreed to and put into effect, a protection to the American people, must be understood. These are scientific and technical facts that make anything less than those controls and safeguards no protection to us at all. These too must also be widely known.

The alternatives to no international atomic agreement are grim. You know what they are as well as I do. You know too that statements are made, and they will continue to be made, abroad and at home, that tend to confuse the American people on these issues. Therefore we must all know the facts that make our proposal a fair, a decent basis for other peoples— as well as a protection to us. For in view of these alternatives to no agreement, it is essential that the American people should be in no doubt as to the solid moral ground on which the American proposals rest.

Then there is a somewhat different kind of knowledge that must become widespread.

Bear in mind that the decision to develop atomic energy as a weapon was made in utmost secrecy. The American people knew nothing of it and measures were taken to see that they did not know. Over two billion dollars were spent without public participation or a chance to criticize the manner of spending. This was a war necessity. But it is no precedent nor example of the working of peacetime democracy. The fact is— and we might as well face it—that it has yet to be demonstrated that in peacetime the necessarily cumbersome and time-consuming processes of our Federal Government can make a success of such a scientific and technical undertaking as this. It has yet to be demonstrated that in peacetime the United States Government can retain in its service and attract to its service the top creative brains of science and of industry and of management that we simply must have if we are to maintain our preeminence. It has yet to be demonstrated how much secrecy the American people and its representatives will accept in peacetime, since it is their money that is being expended and their destiny that is at stake. And yet it is perfectly clear—no one has suggested an alternative—that atomic energy is an undertaking that under present world conditions must remain in government hands. It is clear too that under present conditions a large area must be kept secret at all costs.

We of the Atomic Energy Commission—which happily includes your fellow editor Bill Waymack—firmly believe all these things can be demonstrated. We realize fully that it will be an accomplishment without precedent, but it can be done if the American people are constantly aware of how vital it is to our country that it shall not fail. Here is your great function.

There are other situations that the public should understand. Thus, it must be recognized, for it is true, that this is an ever-changing field, that what we have today in the way of plants, of research and development, may be obsolete tomorrow—indeed it should be a measure of our success that we strive to acquire new and better ways that will make today's plants and processes obsolete. There should also be the fullest understanding of the identity, or virtual identity, of research and production for peaceful uses and for military uses, an identity that reaches a parting of the ways only at the very end of the course. There should be a clear understanding of the possible ways in which, in the future, nuclear science can contribute to the everyday life, health and prosperity of our people—a fascinating story. These things lie ahead. The country should know that they can be brought to fruition, by good, solid imaginative work.

A final illustration of the kind of knowledge that must become general is this: that the scientific basis of nuclear energy release is not an American monopoly; that this scientific knowledge about atomic energy is part of a basic store of knowledge that is world-wide, and that other nations, including Russia, will inevitably in time have learned on their own what we know today. The truth of this comment is not new to you, but anyone who reads public statements these days will agree with me that it needs to be better understood. There are still those who think that what we have is the kind of scientific secret that can be put in an envelope and locked in a vault, and thereby kept as our sole possession for all time. It is not that kind of secret.

These then are some of the facts that the American people must know. For the vitality of our democracy rests upon the widest public participation in those majestic decisions of policy which determine the course of the republic.

Probably among the most important decisions in our history as a nation will be those made concerning the course and direction of atomic energy development, and the uses to which this new force is put. These decisions will affect our most cherished institutions. They will have a deep and all-important effect upon our relations with other nations and peoples of the world and upon the very preservation of civilized life. These are not scientific nor industrial decisions. They are human decisions, decisions about human organization, about our way of life, about the relations of science to well being, about the issues of peace, or of war, war of a destructiveness beyond our imagination.

Those decisions will be made with wide understanding by the people of the facts, of the consequences of the decisions, that is to say, in accordance with the democratic process, or these decisions will be made without understanding, made in the dark, made under the compulsions of hysteria, and fear, not of reason and judgment.

The first decision to be made may be the most important of all. It is an answer to this question: "How important is it to the security and well-being of this country that atomic energy development be pressed forward urgently and vigorously?" For the country to answer this question will require knowledge on the part of the people of *what is at stake*. If they do not know what is at stake, then the chances are great that this development will slow down, even more, that it will be exposed to all kinds of petty frustrations. Top scientists will adjure it;

good administrators will have nothing to do with it. It will become a fine nesting place for industrious mediocrity.

It is true that the American people on their own, without the agreement of other nations cannot develop international action which will remove the threat of atomic warfare. But, if we as a people thoroughly understand the implications, both destructive and creative, of this new force—if we keep way in the forefront in its development—it is not fantastic to hope that the time will come when in spite of all political obstacles to the free flow of news, the peoples of the whole world will also come to realize that there is no security for anyone unless international agreement safeguards the whole world against the misuse of atomic energy. And this decision will come about among our people and among the peoples of the world through the educational forces of which a free press is the most vital.

It is because of the American people's faith in public knowledge that alone of all our private business institutions the freedom of the press has been enshrined in the very Bill of Rights itself. We as a people have a faith in knowledge, have a belief in the beneficent consequences of an expanding area of reason based upon knowledge. Never in our long history has it been more important that we live that faith, that faith in the principles of self-education.

What I am proposing is a great and sustained program of education, at the grass roots of every community in the land. And this leads at once to the question: Who shall be responsible for the dissemination of the facts concerning atomic energy? Clearly it should not be the Atomic Energy Commission. The Commission does not plan and we are opposed to the idea of a large information staff. Clearly it should not be any branch, executive or legislative, of the Government of the United States. This is a high function of the people's institutions of education and communication. It is a heavy and I may say a sacred responsibility of a free press. It will be your job, in my opinion, not only to disseminate the facts, within the limits of security, but to interpret and give meaning to those facts. It will be your job to see that your public servants, legislative and executive, are held to the highest standards of performance, to see to it that atomic energy shall never become the victim of petty politics or narrow partizanship. It will be your job not simply to increase public knowledge but to make it effective. It is for such a historic and fateful function as this that through 150 years this nation has never wavered in its determination that the schools, the churches and the press shall remain vigorous, independent, and free.

NATIONAL ATTITUDES

PUBLIC OPINION AND DEMOCRATIC GOVERNMENT [1]

FELIX FRANKFURTER [2]

Associate Justice Felix Frankfurter gave this address on February 28, 1947, at the second Willkie Awards for Journalism dinner, in the auditorium of the National Press Club in Washington, D. C.

Two hundred writers, editors, and publishers of the white and Negro press and representatives of the three branches of government were present. President Truman presented the awards for public service in the community, for objective reporting, and for individual writing other than news reporting. The President also praised the Negro newspapers for the "courageous and constructive way in which they had dealt with race relations." In addition to Justice Frankfurter and President Truman, Frank L. Stanley, president of the Negro Newspaper Publishers Association, spoke.

The Frankfurter address is a condensed and unhackneyed interpretation of the political philosophy underlying the American form of government. Students of public address and of American principles will find here an example worthy of oral interpretative reading.

Justice Frankfurter, with a reputation of political liberalism, is a dynamic conversationalist. He is described as "brilliant, talkative, . . . warmhearted, preoccupied, effervescent, learned, . . . wise, and exasperating." [3] These qualities of personality are obvious in his public address.

The unfolding of America's destiny may be said to fall thus far into five stages. There was the founding of our Nation. Washington's character was indispensable to keep the Thirteen Colonies together for achieving independence. After the military victory, his character was equally indispensable to fuse the thirteen independent states into a nation.

---

[1] *Congressional Record.* 80th Congress, 1st session. 93:A843. March 3, 1947 (daily edition).

[2] For biographical note see Appendix.

[3] *Current Biography.* 1941:307-8.

Jefferson gave the nation its democratic mission. His claims on posterity summarize the three indispensable aims in the unceasing effort to realize democracy: the Declaration of Independence symbolizes political freedom; the Virginia Statute for Religious Freedom sought to put an end to tyranny over the inner life of man; the founding of the University of Virginia expressed the realization that neither political nor religious freedom can long be enjoyed without the continuous systematic pursuit of truth through free inquiry.

Lincoln saw that freedom within a nation must be indivisible and his compassionate nature did not flinch even from the awfulness of war in order to establish that the republic cannot survive half free and half slave.

Fifty years later it became clear that the country's inner strength is not sufficient safeguard for our great democratic experiment—that we are part of the world and that the world must be safe for our democracy.

But even that turned out not to have been enough. And so, within less than another quarter century, war came again for millions of Americans scattered all over the globe, on land, in the air and on sea, because the nation had come to realize that totalitarian regimes imperiled our democracy. This does not mean, of course, that other nations must copy our form of government, or that there is no such thing as a long and painful historic process, or that overnight we can turn democratic formulas into a working civilization. It does mean that democratic aims must be pursued with passion and pertinacity.

Democracy is neither a mystical abstraction nor a mechanical gadget. It is the teaching of experience, and is vindicated by nature herself. Nature plants gifts and graces in ways that defy all the little artifices of man, and in the long course of human history democracy has proven itself beyond any other form of social arrangement that which evokes these gifts in the largest measure. All the devices of political machinery—votes and parties and platforms—are merely instruments to enable men to live with one another under conditions which bring forth the maximum gifts of each for the fullest enjoyment of all. The kind of civilization we cherish is the society which was launched by the Declaration of Independence, which was to move within the spacious framework of the Constitution, which was rededicated by Lincoln at Gettysburg and in his second inaugural. It is a society in which the dignity of every individual is central, regardless of the accidents of antecedents; a society in which there is no unimportant people; a society in which institutions are progressively to be shaped so as to bring to maximum fruition the potentialities of men. One does not have to think too well of what our civilization has thus far achieved to refuse to destroy its good together with its evil in arrogant and humorless hope of writing in the future nothing but good on a clean slate. The answer to the defects of our society is not denial of the democratic faith. The answer is more loyal practice of that faith. If one faith can be said to unite a great people, surely the ideal which holds us together beyond any other is our belief in the moral worth of the individual, whatever his race, color or religion. And the glare of war revealed fissures in our spiritual structure, deeper ones than we had heretofore realized.

Until recently men did not talk much about these great simple themes. The pace of material development preoccupied the energies of men; it too often overawed their thoughts. The deficiencies of democracy became a favorite jibe of the worldly wise, and the promise of democracy was too romantically conceived. We are desperately in need not of new truths but of passionate devotion to old truths. Not so long ago we used to hear a great deal about a new plateau of commercial values, and almost imperceptibly it was assumed that we were also being elevated to a new plateau of moral values. The law of political and economic institutions is the law of change. But there are eternal verities—those conditions without which freedom is outraged and faith replaced by cynicism. Ultimately, there can be no freedom for self unless it is vouchsafed for others; there can be no security where there is fear; and a democratic society presupposes confidence and candor in the relations of men with one another and active collaboration for the common ends of life.

For we are enlisted in a common enterprise—the bold experiment of freedom. It involves the most exacting collaborative effort. It demands the exercise of reason on the largest scale and self-discipline of the highest order. For its utlimate reliance in achieving the common good is the responsibility of the individual. No office in our land is more important than that of being a citizen.

We are, in short, engaged in the most difficult of all arts—the art of living together in a gracious society. For this it is not enough to be literate; it is not even enough to be literary. While mankind is literate as never before, environment for reason is least congenial. Thus, while the conditions for a good life have not changed, they now operate in a much more complicated setting. We talk glibly about the annihilation of distance. Speed of communication has, of course, brought many gains, but these triumphs of science have brought in their train farreaching and subtle problems which we have not solved because we have hardly begun to face them. The mobility of words too often brings in its train immobility of reflection.

In our jealous regard for freedom of the press we pay little heed to the vast change of circumstances in which that freedom operates. It touches uncritical sensibilities even to recognize the potential opportunities for arousing prejudices, confusing judgment, and regimenting opinion represented by chain newspapers, syndicated articles, headline exploitation, the movies, the radio and private polls. Moreover, we now know better than did the Eighteenth Century, in which the modern democratic faith was born, how slender a reed is reason—how recent its emergence in men, how deep the counterveiling instincts and passions, indeed how treacherous the whole rational process. Moreover the whole temper of our society is hurried; its atmosphere and appurtenances are hostile to reflection. Thus, while mankind is literate as never before, reason is asked to flourish when the conditions for it are least favorable. And yet democracy beyond any other form of society is dependent on reason.

Without respect for freedom of inquiry and freedom of opinion there is no democracy. But no less indispensable is the assurance of the means by which opinion really remains free.

Modern instruments of dissemination may unwittingly make the public the victims either of gullibility or of cynicism or of both. But only critically disciplined readers and listeners can generate that healthy public opinion which a democratic government expresses. Informed opinion and free activity cannot issue without an atmosphere in which free and informed thoughts are dominant.

CREDO [4]

David E. Lilienthal [5]

David Lilienthal gave this statement before the Joint Congressional Committee on Atomic Energy on February 4, 1947.

This nominee had been facing the committee for the second week on the question of whether he should be confirmed as chairman of the Commission on Atomic Energy. For more than an hour he had been goaded by sharp questions from Senator Kenneth McKellar, of Tennessee, ancient foe of Lilienthal and an opponent of the Tennessee Valley Authority project. McKellar's bitter opposition was allegedly due to the fact that Lilienthal tolerated no political patronage in the operation of the Authority.

Senator McKellar accused Lilienthal of communistic leanings and of operating the Authority as a socialistic-communistic enterprise. One point in the cross examination apparently cut Lilienthal deeply—the reference to the European origins of his parents. They were born near Pressburg, now Bratislava, Czechoslovakia, the witness explained in reply to a McKellar question. McKellar insinuated that Lilienthal was communistic because his parents came from a neighborhood now under communistic domination.

"As a matter of fact, Czechoslovakia is now under the domination of Russia, is it not?" asked McKellar.

"That is a complicated question," the witness replied. "I might say my parents were born in this area quite a long time ago. My father is seventy-eight, and my mother, seventy-two. And I am sure you are giving them very great pain by the maltreatment you are giving me in these hearings, Senator."

"You said here the other day that you thought they lived in Austria-Hungary."

"The record shows that I said they were born in Austria-Hungary and that is true," replied Lilienthal. He did not bother to expound the territorial changes that affected the Lilienthal ancestral home.

In reply to the Senator's question, "The truth is that your sympathies are very leftist, are they not?" the witness gave the extemporaneous, unrehearsed expression of his beliefs printed below. The brief defense was one of the "most moving and eloquent definitions of democracy heard on Capital Hill in many a year." This Lilienthal political

4 Hearings before the Senate Section of the Joint Committee on Atomic Energy on confirmation of the Atomic Energy Commission and the General Manager. 80th Congress, 1st session. p. 131-2. February 4, 1947. Government Printing Office. Washington, D. C.

5 For biographical note see Appendix.

creed was widely reprinted, lauded in many an editorial and radio commentary, recommended for study by every school pupil, and regarded as one of the major reasons for the consolidation of American public opinion behind the confirmation of Lilienthal.[6]

I will do my best to make it clear. My convictions are not so much concerned with what I am against as what I am for; and that excludes a lot of things automatically.

Traditionally, democracy has been an affirmative doctrine rather than merely a negative one.

I believe and I so conceive the Constitution of the United States to rest, as does religion, upon the fundamental proposition of the integrity of the individual; and that all government and all private institutions must be designed to promote and to protect and to defend the integrity and the dignity of the individual; that that is the essential meaning of the Constitution and the Bill of Rights, as it is essentially the meaning of religion.

Any forms of government, therefore, and any other institutions which make men means rather than ends in themselves, which exalt the state or any other institutions above the importance of men, which place arbitrary power over men as a fundamental tenet of government, are contrary to this conception; and therefore, I am deeply opposed to them.

The communistic philosophy, as well as the communistic form of government, falls within this category, for its fundamental tenet is quite to the contrary. The fundamental tenet of communism is that the state is an end in itself, and that therefore the powers which the state exercises over the individual are without any ethical standards to limit them.

That I deeply disbelieve.

It is very easy simply to say that one is not a Communist. And, of course, if despite my record it is necessary for me to state this very affirmatively, then this is a great disappointment to me.

It is very easy to talk about being against communism. It is equally important to believe those things which provide a satisfying and effective alternative. Democracy is that satisfying, affirmative alternative.

[6] For further comment on the Lilienthal nomination see above, p. 113-33.

And its hope in the world is that it is an affirmative belief, rather than being simply a belief against something else and nothing more.

One of the tenets of democracy that grows out of this central core of a belief that the individual comes first, that all men are the children of God and that their personalities are therefore sacred, is a deep belief in civil liberties and their protection; and a repugnance to anyone who would steal from a human being that which is most precious to him—his good name —either by impugning things to him by innuendo or by insinuation. And it is especially an unhappy circumstance that occasionally that is done in the name of democracy. This, I think, is something that can tear our country apart and destroy it if we carry it further.

I deeply believe in the capacity of democracy to surmount any trials that may lie ahead, provided only that we practice it in our daily lives.

And among the things we must practice is this: that while we seek fervently to ferret out the subversive and antidemocratic forces in the country, we do not at the same time, by hysteria, by resort to innunendo, and smears, and other unfortunate tactics, besmirch the very cause that we believe in, and cause a separation among our people—cause one group and one individual to hate another, based on mere attacks, mere unsubstantiated attacks upon their loyalty.

I want also to add that part of my conviction is based on my training as an Anglo-American common law lawyer. It is the very basis and the great heritage of the English people to this country, which we have maintained, that we insist on the strictest rules of credibility of witnesses and on the avoidance of hearsay, and that gossip shall be excluded in the courts of justice. And that, too, is an essential of our democracy.

Whether by administrative agencies acting arbitrarily against business organizations, or whether by investigating activities of legislative branches, whenever these principles—of the protection of an individual and his good name against besmirchment by gossip, hearsay and the statements of witnesses who are not subject to cross-examination—are violated, then, too, we have failed in carrying forward our ideals in respect to democracy.

THE INDEPENDENT IN POLITICS [7]

WAYNE L. MORSE [8]

While ratification of the conference report on the Taft-Hartley labor bill was under consideration in the United States Senate on June 5, 1947, Senators Taft, Murray, Ball, Pepper and others referred to the activities of strong pressure groups, including both labor and management. In extended debate, Senator Morse delivered an eloquent analysis of his own position in opposition to the bill and gave his concept of the senatorial voting principles in view of his relations to his constituency.

Something of the political philosophy of Edmund Burke, in his statement to the electors of Bristol, England, September 6, 1780, in his declaration of his right to exercise independent judgment unswayed by "instructions," underlies the Morse argument.

Senator Morse was one of the three or four outstanding senatorial speakers of this session of Congress. His speech training under Professor Andrew Weaver at the University of Wisconsin, his intercollegiate debating, his experiences as debate director at Minnesota, his study of law, his speaking career as Dean of the Law School at Oregon State University, and especially his turbulent and successful activities as a member of the War Labor Board, well fitted him for immediate leadership in the United States Senate. He is a powerful extempore debater, an unusually effective speaker, mature and well informed in his handling of facts and issues.[9]

The Senator [Ball, of Minnesota] is right when he says some of the union ads have not presented all of the facts. I am trying to balance the scales in this criticism of mine. Of course the millions of dollars spent by employers to spread falsehood and propaganda is what has poisoned public opinion.

The advertisements which have been published by employer representatives involve the Communist and Fascist technique—statements of half truths. It is the technique of omitting relevant facts which ought to be placed in the advertisements in order to give a true picture of the problem which is being discussed.

---

[7] *Congressional Record.* 80th Congress, 1st session. 93:6607-08. June 5, 1947 (daily edition).

[8] For biographical note see Appendix.

[9] For comment on the outcome of this bill see introduction to President Truman's radio address denouncing the proposed legislation, p. 191.

As the Senator from Minnesota has so correctly pointed out, when we pick up the advertisements of the labor organizations and read their propaganda, we frequently find more propaganda which falls into the same errors which characterize the type of propaganda and the techniques used by the United States Chamber of Commerce and the National Association of Manufacturers.

As I see it, these two great economic forces, management and labor, have girded themselves for battle. We have an economic war ahead of us. We are to have a test of economic strength.

One of the reasons why I oppose this bill is that, in my judgment, an attempt is being made so to change the law that it will not carry out the principles of equality in collective bargaining for which I have pleaded in this session of Congress. One of the objections I shall make is that I believe that the bill will not result in a fair equalizing of the rights of labor and management. Management under this bill will be given such an advantage over labor that it can prevent effective collective bargaining by unions. I want to see those rights equalized. I am such a firm believer in government by law rather than by men that I do not want to see legislation enacted which in many cases will force a test of defiance of law because enforcement of it would result in great injustices. When a large body of people believe that a law is unjust, they are going to exert the basic, fundamental right which exists in a free society to oppose the administration of such a law.

That will not produce labor harmony. I do not condone such noncompliance with law but I cannot ignore the fact that human beings will resist the enforcement of unjust laws.

Mr. President, I believe that all of us, on both sides of this issue, must rise above political pressure and propaganda, and make it very clear to management and labor that our duty in the Congress of the United States is to vote on the merits of these questions as we see them, and that we have no intention of yielding to political pressure. I am sure that such is the attitude of my opponents on this question, and I know that it is my attitude and that of my associates on the side opposed to the conference report.

Let me cite a typical telegram urging me to yield to the majority on this issue. I have received many from businessmen in Oregon. This one is more kind than most of the others. Nevertheless it shows the effect of the type of propaganda which I have been discussing. It is a telegram from a very dear friend, one of the outstanding industrialists in my State. He is very much disturbed because I am going to vote against the conference report, and because I am going to vote to sustain a veto if a veto is handed down. Senators can see what is bothering him when he writes as follows:

I hope, Wayne, that you will be able to vote favorably upon the conference-reported labor bill. I recognize with you the weak spots in this legislation, and I too am sorry that your arguments before the Senate were not fully supported. However, I am convinced after checking with many people in various fields, including farmers, laboring men, and employers in Oregon, that the people of your State want this legislation passed, rather than lose corrective legislation at this immediate session. I hope you will recognize what I am sure is the desire of your constituents in this matter. Regards.

There is not a more sincere or finer employer in the State of Oregon than is the sender of that telegram. I think I know what has happened. It has happened to hundreds of my friends within the employing class in my State. They have the notion that unless we pass this legislation we shall not have any legislation at all in this session of Congress. But I say, Mr. President, that such need not be true. We can vote down this conference report, or, if it is agreed to, we can vote to sustain a veto if a veto is handed down; and there is still ample time by August 1 to pass fair and constructive legislation. So I do not accept the premise that it is this bill or not any. There is another premise which I do not accept, and that is that it is my obligation or my responsibility to sit here and vote in accordance with what I think a majority of my constituents want at this time. I just do not accept that principle of representation in the Senate of the United States.

Therefore I replied to the sender of that telegram as follows:

Thank you for your wire. Deeply regret that I cannot vote for conference report bill. I am satisfied that it is unsound legislation in its present form. However, if I knew that every person in the State of Oregon wanted the bill passed, I would still vote against it because my obligation in this job is to vote for what I consider to be sound legislation in the public interest and not for legislation which a temporary majority may think it wants when you and I know that a majority of the people of Oregon have not analyzed the weaknesses and limitations of this legislation. I can assure you that it is not an easy decision for me to make because I agree with you that undoubtedly a majority of my constituents think they want this legislation. However, what they really want is legislation which will check the major labor abuses and bring about a maximum degree of industrial peace. Unfortunately this legislation will not accomplish those objectives and hence I cannot and will not vote for it. Regards.

Mr. President, it is not at all pleasant, it is not at all politically comfortable, to find oneself in a position in which he is satisfied that the majority of the people of his State have been so propagandized with regard to a piece of bad legislation that they really believe it is the piece of legislation that should be passed.

On the other hand, as I read the constitutional debates on the basis of which this government came into being it was not contemplated that under a representative form of government a man in the Senate of the United States should vote in accordance with the dictates of a majority as determined by a Gallup poll or some other method of determining a temporary majority opinion. Rather, the basic theory of representative government requires a Senator to assume the solemn obligation, intended by the founding fathers, and vote for legislation which he believes to be in the public interest, even though he knows that as of that moment a majority of his constituents would vote contrary to his judgment. Then it is his obligation of political leadership to stand up and tell his constituents why he took the action which he did. If his reasons are not satisfactory to them then it is their opportunity and privilege to remove him from his seat at the next election. I think the people of my State want me to represent them by exercising an honest independence of judgment on the merits of issues as I find them back here. They want me to weigh the views of those constituents who write and wire to me, but cast my votes free of political pressures and unmoved by threats of loss of political support if I do not do the bidding of some pressure groups.

It is only on the basis of that principle of representative government, Mr. President, may I say from this platform today to the people of my State, that I desire to remain in the Senate of the United States. It was on the basis of that principle that I ran for this office and the people of Oregon elected me on the basis of that abstract principle. I believe they will keep me here to apply it. If we cannot exercise that type of independence of judgment in representing the people of our states, then I want to say that I do not desire to serve in the Senate of the United States if I have to serve subject to yielding to the type of pressures that management and labor groups are seeking to bring to bear upon the members of the Senate for votes on this labor bill. I have a hunch, Mr. President, that after the present wave of emotion passes and after the people of my State come to see in actual operation the effects of such legislation as is now being proposed, if it is placed on the statute books, a large majority of them will come to thank me for exercising the independence of judgment which I intend to exercise in casting my vote against this bill.

I shall vote against the bill that has been reported by the conference committee because, after careful study, I am completely convinced that the amendments added in conference make it an impracticable and unadministrable law. Virtually every amendment which has been made threatens the legitimate rights of the American workingman; the net effect is to discourage and stifle collective bargaining and to impede, if not make impossible, effective enforcement of the National Labor Relations Act.

I supported the Senate committee bill, which was a fair, reasonable, constructive, and enforcible bill, and I opposed the amendments that were made on the floor of the Senate because they seemed to me to strike serious blows at the rights of labor and to impair the efficient administration of the law. The amendments which have been made in conference not only infinitely aggravate and multiply every serious vice of the Senate amendments but they add such restrictive and administratively unfeasible provisions of their own that even if I believed the bill we passed was sound and helpful, I would be compelled to vote against the conference bill, because of the inevitably disastrous effects I am sure it will have on industrial peace in this country. I say with every emphasis at my command that this bill will be causative, not preventive, of labor difficulties.

IS THE AMERICAN PRESS REALLY FREE? [10]

GEORGE V. DENNY, JR., ERWIN CANHAM, MORRIS ERNST,
MICHAEL STRAIGHT, AND REAGAN MCCRARY [11]

This debate was presented on Thursday evening, October 17, 1946, as one of the regular Town Hall programs, and originated in the Akron Armory, Akron, Ohio, from 8:30 to 9:30 P.M., Eastern Standard Time, over the American Broadcasting Company network.

These programs have been given without interruption since May 30, 1935. Some five million usually listen. The series has provided an impressive demonstration of American democracy. Crucial issues of national and international importance have been debated and discussed; the speakers have presented unequivocally their respective cases. The only limitation apparently has been that both (or all) sides be adequately presented. An important feature has been the introduction of the "Interrogators" and the question-and-answer period with audience participation.

Mr. Denny has shown rare skill in handling all sorts of audience hecklers and contributors. His programs have been so directed that complicated issues are stated simply; all speeches are comparatively short; only top-notch and seasoned speakers lead the debates; and audiences, both invisible and face-to-face, are stimulated to further study. Mr. Denny, defending radio "showmanship" in these programs, suggests that it is more desirable to have several million listeners attending a somewhat popular discussion than it is to have a comparatively small audience tuning in on a more academic and technical debate.[12]

Erwin Canham at Bates College was a brilliant intercollegiate debater, member of Delta Sigma Rho, and a member of a Bates team that visited seven British universities in 1925. Later he was a Rhodes Scholar and a participant in the debates in the Oxford Union. In addition to his journalistic activities as editor of the *Christian Science Monitor*, Canham continues to speak on the platform and conducts a weekly radio news commentary. As this Town Hall report shows, he is effective in rebuttal. His delivery is conversational, but alert and impressive. He has a wide command both of ideas and of language.

[10] Reprinted from *Bulletin of America's Town Meeting of the Air.* Vol. 12, no. 25. October 17, 1946. By permission of the speakers, by special arrangement with the Town Hall, Inc., and through the courtesy of the American Broadcasting Company.

[11] For biographical notes see Appendix.

[12] For further comment on these programs see *Representative American Speeches: 1937-1938.* p. 52; *1938-1939.* p. 138; *1939-1940.* p. 233; *1940-1941.* p. 209; *1945-1946.* p. 165-7.

Morris Leopold Ernst was also an intercollegiate debater, at Williams College. He received a law degree from the New York Law School. He is well known as a lecturer before clubs and colleges and over the radio. He is highly intelligent in his treatment of major problems. He organizes his material clearly and injects elements of informality and audience interest.

Michael Straight is an editor on the staff of the *New Republic*, author of *Make This the Last War*, and a frequent participant in informal discussions and more formal lectures. A graduate of Oxford, he has the characteristic wit, repartee, and originality of phrasing, combined with penetrating logic.

John Reagan McCrary, now a radio commentator, was formerly executive editor of the *American Mercury* and at one time chief editorial writer for the *New York Daily Mirror*. He was Public Relations Officer for the Eighth Army Air Force.[13]

MODERATOR DENNY: Good evening, neighbors, and our thanks to Mr. and Mrs. Berk of Station WAKR and our Town Meeting host committee for turning out such a fine audience on a rainy night. They are packed and jammed on the stage and along the walls of this Armory and it's raining cats and dogs outside.

We're about to discuss a very vital question that concerns one of our basic freedoms, friends. Most of us today get our news from the pages of the daily press or over the radio.

Now are these two great media giving it to us straight? Are they free from government censorship or any other restraint that might color or distort the news? You'd be surprised how this audience here answered that question tonight when I asked them in the preliminary meeting.

In a few weeks, we'll discuss this question in relation to radio. Tonight, we're concentrating principally on the press.

Of course, I know that many of us pick up the news of the day as we hurriedly turn to the sports pages and our favorite comic strips, and I must confess that I, too, would like to know how Lena, the Hyena, is going to look.

Fortunately, here in America, we're not limited to reading a state-issued *Pravda* or *Isvestia*. There are more than 1,700

[13] The limits of this volume prevent the reprinting of the "Questions, Please" from the audience, following the debate.

dailies and approximately 10,000 weeklies which are read by an estimated audience of 50 million people.

No one seriously charges our government with controlling or censoring what is printed in these papers. But questions have been raised by men like Mr. Morris Ernst and Mr. Michael Straight as to the possible dangers of too little competition and too great concentration of power in the hands of a few owners of big newspapers and great newspaper chains.

Mr. Ernst, who has represented the Newspaper Guild of America, and is author of a recently published very provocative book, *The First Freedom*, believes that the present situation does constitute a threat to a really free American press.

Mr. Erwin Canham, editor of the *Christian Science Monitor*, whom many of you have just heard on the preceding program over most of these ABC stations, takes strong exception to Mr. Ernst's position, and takes the affirmative of tonight's question.

Facts will play an important part in tonight's discussion, so I suggest that each one of you, our listeners, view the statements of our speakers in the light of your own experience.

I'm going to ask our special interrogators, Mr. Michael Straight, who's one of the editors of *The New Republic*, and author of a book called *Make This the Last War*, and "Tex" McCrary, radio commentator, and former editor of a New York daily having one of the largest circulations in the country, to point out the significance of these facts as they understand them.

As Mr. Ernst leads in the attack on the present situation and has some definite remedies to suggest, we'll ask him to speak first. Mr. Morris Ernst, prominent New York attorney, author of *The First Freedom*. Mr. Ernst.

MR. ERNST: Two different theories of freedom of the press exist in the modern world. One is the bible of the Communists. They do not trust the common man. They fear competition of ideas in the market place of thought. Our theory of a free press is a national religion. We adopt that gospel as an act of faith—faith that by matching of wits, truth will win out. In other words, the only corrective of life is criticism.

We can be proud, for you and I, Americans, are substantially free of governmental restraints. All of us tonight agree on this position.

Moreover, we in the United States have done a magnificent job quantity-wise. Fifty million circulation of daily papers is a great compliment to the ingenuity of the publishers of America.

But in another sense, a deeper sense, our press is less than free. A free press means that the market place of the printed word is as wide as the economics permit. We have staked our all on the philosophy that only out of conflict of thought can truth arise.

Let us see what is happening to our press in such terms.

How much competition is left?

In how many areas has difference of opinion disappeared?

Have you or I a chance to start a small newspaper in our home town?

Where are the odds for a small-town newspaper survival?

I make no point tonight of what is good or bad. I do not talk of whether a paper is reactionary or conservative, Republican or Democratic.

Here is the indictment I make in behalf of the readers of the nation: We have lost 1,000 daily newspapers in 20 years. We are down to only 1,700. More than 2,500 weeklies have disappeared. There are only 117 cities left in this vast country where there is any competition left in daily newspapers.

I ask what price freedom and what price free enterprise? One boiler plate company supplies the inside pages for 3,000 weeklies, and even these pages are sold packaged with advertising.

One man owns about one half of all the independent papers of his state. What if he owns all the papers in the state? Do we sit by idly until that happens?

Twenty-five per cent of the total circulation of all our daily papers is owned by a handful of chains. In 10 states, there is not a single city with daily newspaper competition today, and in 22 states there is not a single city with any Sunday competition.

Now I submit that it is no answer for you to say, but we have done well in total circulation.

Take Springfield, Massachusetts, for example. It has four papers, but all owned by the same interests. What good does total national circulation do to the people of that area? It is no answer to say that the papers that are left are better than those of 20 years ago. Let's admit it. The question and the answer duck the issue. Even if better, what would keep the few remaining papers on their toes without competition if monopoly continues?

Nor is it an answer to say that only the inadequate newspapers have folded up. It just ain't true. Papers are bought up usually because they are prosperous and the buyer wants to get rid of his competitors.

But if all these facts don't worry the people of America, how about those hundred areas where the only newspaper left owns the only radio station? I ask what about freedom of the press, freedom of democracy in that area?

How do the people in such districts develop critical capacities to decide issues such as a new park, school, a mayor? Bear in mind that the wealth of the nation depends solely, solely on the growth of critical capacity of the common man.

The leaders of the press make no sense when they tell me to listen to the radio or to read the magazines. I think far more of the press than they do. And let me make one point perfectly clear. I am peculiarly concerned with the smaller communities, west of the Hudson, for in a real sense Manhattan is a hick island, scarcely aware of the problems of the villages and the farms of this nation.

It is no answer to say that the little country newspapers are worthless, for if the small communities are devitalized by the monopoly of the press, it is inevitable that the National Government will have to expand in power. Maybe that is the way we'll go totalitarian.

I'm tired of liberals who talk in terms of doom and shout about "modern man is obsolete." Rather do I suggest that we are on the eve of a mass renaissance. We can sweep back this tide of antifreedom. We can restore free enterprise for the press.

Here are just a few samples, only seven, but they would surely help.

1. We can reexamine our postage subsidies so as to give the little papers a fair break. Did you know that we, the taxpayers, give 100 million dollars a year to the publishers of newspapers, magazines, and books? We, as taxpayers, give that money.

It's the difference between what the publishers pay for postage and what the delivery costs the Post Office Department.

I would gladly increase this subsidy, but here is where your town papers and you readers come in for a chance at survival. Why not have a sliding scale subsidy like our income surtaxes? No postage on the first 20,000 circulation; a quarter of a cent a pound of the next 20,000; half a cent on the next 50,000, etc.

I ask why should the giant, with vast circulation and great economies get a present from the budget of the nation of tens of thousands of dollars each year.

Why should one magazine owner, for example, get a check of over two million dollars a year from the Federal Treasury? Why shouldn't the little town weekly be allowed to compete on a surtax theory of life?

2. We can revise our tax laws. It costs one million dollars to buy one press for one daily in one big city. Under our tax laws, again bearing down on small free enterprise and favoring those giants with large capital, a simple shift would make it possible for the first time, for a growing vital publisher, to gather enough capital together to get into the area of competition.

If we don't revise our tax laws, only the inheritors of vast wealth can ever enter into the newspaper field in big cities.

3. We can really prevent newsprint being dominated by a few giants. Much of the forest of Canada is owned by the large newspapers of the United States.

We divorced railroads and coal mines many years ago. Surely we must look into the stranglehold of a few over the pulp of the nation. Ask your local editor about the squeeze on him for newsprint.

4. Long ago we declared that a bank may not own a security affiliated company. A bank might do the job cheaper, might do

it better, but we ordered economic divorces to prevent excess power in the market places. Should we not declare that no newspapers shall own the only radio station of its area?

5. Congress forbade absentee control of local light and power plants in the utilities act. Is it unreasonable for Congress to apply the same principle to absentee ownership of newspapers? Why should we let an Akron publisher, no matter how nice or decent, own a paper in Florida? Would you like your Akron papers to be edited from Florida?

6. We have only three press associations and they should be compelled to give their services to all papers at a fair price and a decent profit.

7. Let's look into the featherbedding rules of the trade unions which are an insurmountable burden for many employees.

In conclusion, let me say if we don't restore economic freedom for small publishers and for the readers, we may well go totalitarian by the mere process of concentration of the power of the press into a handful of giants, a handful too small for 140 million people.

MODERATOR DENNY: Now for the other side of the case we'll hear from Mr. Edwin Canham, editor of the *Christian Science Monitor* and ABC news analyst. Mr. Canham.

MR. CANHAM: We have been talking for eight or ten minutes and we have not yet had a definition of freedom of press. Don't you think it is time we knew what we are talking about?

Freedom of the press is not a right bestowed upon the newspapers. It is a duty they owe to the people. It is a duty to provide the people with the facts of the modern world, as nearly as any imperfect human institution can dig out those facts and explain their meaning.

Mr. Ernst believes the press is not free. I believe it is free, relatively speaking and with due regard for all its imperfections.

Mr. Ernst bases his argument, in the main, on the shrinkage in numbers of American newspapers since their high point in 1909. Many of our listeners tonight, perhaps, will remember something of the newspapers in 1909. Do you think that they more adequately discharged their duty to the people then?

Do you think they conveyed the facts of the world to the people in 1909 more adequately than they do today with their larger numbers and greater diversity?

It is not a question here of good newspapers and bad newspapers. It is a question of performing a service to the American people. I assure you with all the emphasis I have that American newspapers are today discharging their obligation to the people, are paying their debt of freedom of the press far more adequately than they have ever done before.

To return to Mr. Ernst's "golden age" of 1909 would not enable American newspapers to perform that obligation any more ably than they are doing today. It is seldom a good thing to try and set back the hands of the clock and it is usually impossible.

Indeed, to try and produce again the fringe newspapers of 1909—and they account for most of Mr. Ernst's figures, although there were some strong and vital newspapers included, too— would not enable the American press to discharge its duty of freedom today.

Mr. Ernst was himself active in the effort to save the *New York World*, one of the major newspaper casualties of our time. I ask him would any of his proposals tonight have been able to save the *New York World*?

I think he will agree that they would not, but he has told us that he is not interested in those provincial, limited newspapers of Manhattan Island, that his heart warms to the great west country and he's interested in little towns west of the Hudson. But I assure you that the situation there is in many respects comparable to that concerning the *New York World*.

You cannot breathe the breath of life into a straw man. You cannot prop up a newspaper which has incompetent management, nepotism, lack of genuine vitality, lack of real ideas. Mr. Ernst, there isn't enough money in the RFC to perpetuate inadequacy.

I agree with Mr. Ernst, entirely, that the government should not stack the cards in favor of consolidation. With him, I would like to see the government a fair and impartial umpire, but for the most part, his proposals simply ask that the cards be stacked in favor of incompetence and against the irresistable force of sound, technological change.

Let us ask Mr. Ernst to try and prove his point. He tells us that diversity, numbers, and freedom are the same thing. I don't think he proves it. He assumes it. But I suggest to you that freedom is much more fundamental than numbers and diversity, and that the hard facts of American newspaper life are against Mr. Ernst.

I can take him to large metropolitan areas in the United States where a maximum of diversity in newspapers exists and where the press is less free by far than it is in comparable areas where newspaper concentration exists.

Some of the freest newspapers in the United States are published in so-called monopoly cities and towns. I mean by that newspapers that most adequately discharge their duty of providing their public with the significant facts of the modern world, and some of the least free newspapers in the United States are published in highly competitive towns.

Sometimes the excesses of competition produce the very opposite of freedom. Sometimes highly competitive newspapers will make concessions much more damaging to newspaper freedom than anything that happens in a one-paper town. That is the plain fact of the matter and can be attested by millions of you listeners who live in these cities and towns.

I am not decrying competition. We must always have it on a broad scale, but the excesses of competition, the fringe areas which account for most of Mr. Ernst's figures did not and cannot produce press freedom.

We are speaking tonight in Akron, a one-newspaper city. My good friend, John S. Knight, publisher of the *Akron Beacon Journal*, has often publicly declared that he would welcome competition. He did not embark upon a sinister plot to kill off all other newspapers in Akron. His position in some respects would be much more comfortable if he had competition, and he has said so. He would not be so much at the mercy of pressure groups as he is now, publishing the only newspaper,

But Mr. Ernst, in effect, asks that the government tie one of Mr. Knight's hands behind him so that he will not have published so effective, so hard-hitting, yes, so free a newspaper, so that some competitor can come in and survive.

That doesn't make sense to me. It is not a fair umpiring. When daily newspaper competition returns to Akron—and I hope it will—it will be because somebody has an idea so vital and a know-how so practical that it cannot possibly be stopped, and it may return by means of new technological developments not precisely in the form of a daily newspaper. But competition will not return by means of a government subsidy crammed into the pockets of a straw man.

But I agree wholly with Mr. Ernst that government subsidy to existing publishers, if it exists and if it is unfair, should be removed.

As a matter of fact, there is much more competition among American newspapers than these figures we have heard would indicate. Naturally, and inevitably, that competition has shifted from the crossroads town to the whole county, or to the state, or to the region.

Journalism has grown up out of the horse-and-buggy days. For competition to be strong and healthy in modern newspapers, you do not need a whole flock of weak, unstable, separate publications. The competition can be concentrated effectively in somewhat fewer, somewhat larger units.

Obviously there are some areas where there is certainly too little competition, but Mr. Ernst's figures, I think, fatally overstate his case.

On the basis of the technological changes to which Mr. Ernst objects, the American press has built up domestic and foreign news coverage which is unparalleled.

Of course, it isn't perfect, but it is better than any other people have ever had in the history of the world. It is better than we had in 1909, or at any time in our history. American newspapers are reporting the news of their communities better than they have ever done before, better than in 1909.

They are interpreting this news with more background and acumen. I invite Mr. Ernst, I invite anyone who thinks the

American press is not going forward to take a little trip with me to the back files.

We will find that the good old days never did exist. We will find more standardization today, but standardization in the sense of higher quality standards and of broader outlook. The diversity of the old days often meant narrowness and provincialism, instead of genuine local color and interest.

We will find newspapers crusading today, serving their communities today, and striving earnestly to tell the complex story of the modern world. We will find also, as you well know, many shortcomings for we are dealing with a human institution in a democracy.

The press is increasingly and constructively self-critical. It had better be, for newspapers need all the strength they have to help their readers through the problems of the atomic age. To break newspapers down technologically, into what I'd like to call the "Balkanization" of 1909 would solve no problems. It would be disastrous.

We must retain the essential values of competition. We must accept the duty which free press owes to a free people. We must go forward. We are going forward, and we will continue to go forward.

MODERATOR DENNY: Thank you, Mr. Canham, and I must congratulate you and Mr. Ernst both for actually joining issues on this question, a feat that is not always characteristic of Town Meetings and other forums.

Now we're ready for the analysis by our special interrogators. Mr. Straight, I'm sure you are going to take exception to some of Mr. Canham's claims, but will you tell us just how they stack up beside Mr. Ernst's arguments in your opinion? Mr. Michael Straight, editor of the *New Republic*. Mr. Straight.

MR. STRAIGHT: That was a flattering speech of Mr. Canham's. In just seven minutes he had Morris and myself stacking cards, setting the clocks back, propping up dead men, breathing life into straw men, cramming subsidies into people's pockets, taking America back to 1909, resisting irresistible forces, and best of all, tying up John Knight's hands behind his back. That's not bad for two men. I wish Mr. Denny had let him go on. Another five minutes, and he might have had us dressed up in coon skins, trading with the Ohio Indians.

We agree, of course, that there has been progress in the American press since 1909. We agree that competition has declined in that time. But is Mr. Canham suggesting that competition is not the main reason for that progress? Mr. Canham maintains that our press is really free because it is adequately providing our people with the significant facts about the world.

Let's take one significant fact—the meat shortage. Let's look at the stories this morning in the *Chicago Tribune*, the Hearst press with its 30 million readers, and even the *Akron Beacon Journal*.

We read these stories, and we learn that there isn't any meat today because of price control. Every time there is a strike in America, these same papers have a front-page headline, "No Production—the Strikers Are to Blame."

One interpretation of the meat shortage might be that the meat packers and the ranchers have been on strike against the OPA.

But no reader of these newspapers ever heard of a strike except by a union. Is that adequately reporting the facts about the world today?

Eighty per cent of our readers are big city readers. Some part of the duty of the press that serves them is to express their point of view. It is not expressing it.

Mr. Canham says, "All right, if you don't like these papers, start a new paper."

He looks at Akron and he says, "When someone gets a great idea and some know-how, Akron will get a second paper." I wonder.

Suppose after this meeting a group of citizens here in the front row come up to Mr. Canham. They say, "Mr. Canham, we are going to take your advice. We've got a great idea, we've got the know-how, what do we do?"

"Well," Mr. Canham says, "First of all, you lay down five million dollars in the bank, and then you get a reserve of another ten million."

"Well," they say, "what do we do then?"

Mr. Canham says, "Then you wait for two years until you get some newsprint."

You say, "Then what?"

Mr. Canham says, "Well, you try to get the news services, and the wires, and the features, and that's pretty tough."

And you say, "Well, what do we do then?"

Mr. Canham says, "Well, just a minute, before you go on. What is this great idea of yours?"

You say, down here, "Our idea is to really express the desires of the rubber workers of Akron."

Mr. Canham says, "And you expect with that great idea to be like other papers and make 70 per cent of your income out of advertising?" And they nod.

Mr. Canham says, "Then that's not a great idea."

Well, I'm the interrogator and I'll put my question to Mr. Canham—of course, it's a loaded question as it ought to be. Mr. Canham, would you be worried if Mr. Knight owned all the papers in Ohio, and if you would be, what would you do?

MR. DENNY: Thank you, Mr. Straight. Mr. Canham?

MR. CANHAM: Yes, Mr. Straight, I would be very much worried if Mr. Knight owned all the newspapers in Ohio, but I would not be half as much worried as Mr. Knight would be.

As to what I would do about it, I certainly would not advocate governmental regulation. I certainly would not advocate interference by government in the production of newspapers in Ohio to prevent control.

I would, on the other hand, do everything possible to stimulate the production of newspapers or competitive media from the ground up. That brings me to all the interesting spots which Mr. Straight has just put between quotation marks and attributed to me.

I don't say very many of those things—very few of them.

But I do say that a medium expressing the point of view in Akron that he wants expressed, I firmly believe could be established if it had the dynamism of a proper concept and idea behind it. I don't say, in the slightest degree, that it would have to be based upon department store advertising, and so on, to be a success. I don't say that at all.

I say there are ways by which public expression can come and in our own time. In the last two or three decades, we have seen several important new innovations in the field of expression, in the field of publication, come along on a shoestring or less, and have become great successes. Therefore, the door is not as closed as it would seem to be. I am not as defeatist as my two able friends.

Mr. DENNY: Thank you, Mr. Canham. Well, now, it's come time when we're going to hear from Mr. "Tex" McCrary, but because we've gone a little over our time in the first part of this program, we're going to pause briefly for station identification.

Mr. DENNY: Now, Mr. "Tex" McCrary was to have been with us here tonight but due to the bad weather Mr. McCrary is still in New York, but through the magic of radio are going to hear from him and he is going to heckle Mr. Ernst from New York. So, now, will you cut in, "Tex" McCrary in New York.

Mr. McCRARY: Well, George, I'm very sorry that I couldn't be out there because of the weather, because it sounds like it's a good fight—inside as well as out. Mr. Morris Ernst is concerned about the declining amount of competition and diversity in the business of informing the American people.

Now, please forgive me for injecting jokes into a serious debate, but I think this story has a bearing on the discussion. A benevolent old gentleman, seeing a little boy carrying a big stack of newspapers down the street, stopped and patted him on the head and said, "Goodness, my boy, don't all those papers make you tired?"

The little boy grinned and replied, "No, I don't read 'em."

That's the constant threat that hangs a perpetual nightmare over the newspaper business—the threat that people will stop reading newspapers—stop reading papers and start getting their news and entertainment and general information from radio, movies, magazines, and ultimately, perhaps, television.

That's why editors and publishers keep pumping new features into their papers to earn higher circulation prices—not to compete against each other, but to compete against the increasing attractiveness of other media, new and aggressive media—radio, movies, magazines—all of them competing for readers and listeners, and lookers, and equally important, competing for the advertising dollar.

Competition, diversity, has never been keener than it is today.

There are lessons to be learned from a post mortem of a newspaper and other publications that have died in the last 25 years. Mr. Ernst has learned the wrong lessons.

In New York City since I can remember, two newspapers have died. One was the old *World*, owned by the Pulitzers out in St. Louis; the other was the *New York American*—pet paper of the Hearst chain. Now both of those papers were absentee-owned, but they died. One was liberal, one was conservative, but both died.

My point is this: Newspapers die, not as the result of some sinister, monopolistic trend. That is not the common cause of death, you'll find, in post mortems on newspapers. They die for the same reason that men and businesses and political parties, and even nations, die—loss of vitality, laziness. Those that are still alive were never more alive than they are today.

To me what seems a far more serious problem, Mr. Ernst, is this one: The fact that the great liberal papers in America today are subsidized by inherited wealth. How do you feel about that, Mr. Ernst?

MR. DENNY: All right, Morris Ernst, here in Akron.

MR. ERNST: I think the inherited-wealth newspapers are the last defensive line of Americans. I don't like it, but it's the last defense other than the cooperative movement or the labor movement going into the field.

I'm interested in Tex's shift of position from his associate's position. He says, in effect, there is no more competition between newspapers, but the newspapers pick up the competition from the radios and the movies.

I think they are different media. They can learn from each other. But is Tex happy when one man owns half the newspapers of a state, and there are only 117 cities left with any competition *locally* in those cities? I want to know from both my opponents, how do they feel about the 100 cities where the only newspaper owns the only radio station. Won't they go that far and ask for diversity to that extent?

MR. DENNY: All right, Tex McCrary.

MR. MCCRARY: I'll go along with you on that last question, Morris. I think there should be diversity to that extent. But again I'd like to say that the freedom of quotation here—this is a little bit licensed—for I didn't really say that there's no more competition among newspapers. There's terrific competition among newspapers right here in New York City as you know. The paper that I used to work with—

MR. ERNST: Tex, I don't know whether you heard me—

MR. MCCRARY: What?

MR. ERNST: There are only 117 cities left with competition of newspaper ownership—out of all this vast country only 117. Do you think that's too few or too many?

MR. MCCRARY: The competition among newspapers will be the competition in the smaller cities against the newspapers in larger cities. The competition is still between newspapers.

MR. ERNST: Now, Tex, you don't mean for a moment that in a small town where they're discussing a new sewer system they can pick up the merits of that debate in the Chicago or New York or Detroit papers?

MR. MCCRARY: I don't mean that at all, Morris, but we'll get on to cases. In the state where I was born and raised, in a town that was a whistle-stop between Dallas and Houston, that little town of about 500 people had a fine weekly newspaper which dealt adequately with the problems of that community and still does. But, that town was covered for its information on national and international affairs by papers in Dallas and Houston, and the papers in Dallas and Houston competed for circulation in that town.

MR. ERNST: I agree with you entirely. But I ask you this one. We have lost 2,500 such little weeklies in towns that have none left. Are you happy about that on the level of your little town?

MR. McCRARY: I'm not happy about that, Morris.

MR. ERNST: Why not move forward to see what we can do to give the little guy a break?

MR. DENNY: It looks like, Tex, he's turned interrogator on you.

MR. McCRARY: It ain't fair! I can't see him!

MR. DENNY: Well, come ahead, have you got another question for him?

MR. McCRARY: This business about the proportion of revenue that a newspaper gets from advertising and circulation. That is a popular charge made against newspapers to imply that advertisers control newspapers. Now, Morris, you know the paper, which shall be nameless for the purpose of this debate, that I used to work for. The figures—and you can check them when you get back, Morris—the figures on that paper, and they sell more than a million copies every day now—after I left— you get four times as much revenue from circulation as you do from advertising and the publisher of that paper is very happy about the state of health of his paper.

Incidentally, that is a tabloid newspaper competing against the biggest newspaper in New York City or in the United States and doing very well, thank you.

MR. ERNST: Tex, I'm in entire agreement with you. I think one of the encouraging signs in the American press is the rise in the price of the papers to the readers, so that the reader's responsibility and direct relationship to the publisher is immediate.

But by and large throughout the country, the papers show that 70 per cent of their income comes from advertisers. I make no charge tonight that the advertisers influence the papers. I merely make the charge that it's unwholesome when the public buys a commodity with a concealed price and pays a nickel, allowing a situation to develop that when the public buys its soap or automobiles or something else, it's paying the other ten cents. I don't think that's helpful.

LABOR RELATIONS

STRIKES, WAGES, AND INDUSTRIAL PROFITS [1]

Philip Murray [2]

President Philip Murray gave this opening address at the first session of the Eighth Congress of Industrial Organizations, at Atlantic City, New Jersey, on November 18, 1946.

The convention, in session for four days, was dominated by the issue of communism. At the opening a declaration of policy was adopted which in effect aimed to keep the left wing element under control. Observers, however, were of the opinion that the Convention adjourned with the Communist element still powerful. No important changes were made in the key positions. The United Electrical Workers, the mine, mill and smelter workers, the National Maritime Union, the longshoremen, fur workers, and public workers were all alleged to be dominated by Communist leadership. Communists were said to control a dozen of the forty C.I.O. unions, including some of the strongest. Of the 305 delegates, the Communists were said to count on some 90.

Aside from this major internal issue of control, the delegates were chiefly concerned with their problems of strikes, wages, and the future of their union. Murray's address clearly summarized, from labor's point of view, the results of strikes and wage negotiations. The Murray charges of large industrial profits in 1946 and of rising costs of living that offset wage increases were hardly to be disputed. The speaker, however, did not attempt to outline a specific program for organized labor to follow in 1947.

At the closing session Murray was reelected president. His closing statement to the convention was, "So do you, my good friends, take a parting note from me, organize in the course of the coming year, organize as you have never organized before, not only in the South, but all over our jurisdiction wherever our organizations are either located or such locations as they might be interested in. So let us close this convention with the oft repeated slogan of the C.I.O., 'Organize, Organize, Organize.'"

The deliberations of the C.I.O. at Atlantic City were overshadowed by John L. Lewis and his United Mine Workers' strike (the U.M.W.

---

[1] *Daily Proceedings of the Eighth Constitutional Convention of the Congress of Industrial Organizations*. Monday, November 18, 1946. Permission to reprint through the courtesy of President Murray.

[2] For biographical note see Appendix.

was a branch of the American Federation of Labor). Lewis denounced the contract with the government covering 400,000 miners working in coal mines in twenty-eight states. The government ordered him to reinstate the contract and threatened him with a jail sentence. The miners left the pits, and the Federal court cited Lewis for contempt of court. Thus, as the C.I.O. was holding its sessions and adjourning, steel mills were banking their furnaces, railroads were curtailing schedules, millions were becoming idle, and industrial activity in general was threatened. The C.I.O., much as it disliked Lewis, who had withdrawn from the organization, passed a resolution: "We condemn the action taken by the Federal Government in obtaining a sweeping injunction against the United Mine Workers of America."

The fine against Lewis and his United Mine Workers by the Supreme Court, the affirmation of the Federal Court decision, Lewis' cancellation of the strike, and the continued negotiations between Lewis and the mine owners in April, May, and June 1947, for a new contract when the mines were to be turned back to their owners—these events all helped to develop public opinion against the unionist cause.

The Eightieth Congress, first session, enacted legislation seriously curbing the power of unions, as did the legislatures of a number of states.

Thus the address of Murray in November 1946, hardly anticipated the tremendous strain to which organized labor would be put during the ensuing year. By June 1947, negotiations were under way to merge the A. F. of L. and the C.I.O.; 13,000,000 members presenting a single solid front might be much more effective against both Congress and American industry.

Mr. Murray is a speaker with much power. Accustomed to battle his way through turbulent sessions of his workers, he has physical aggressiveness, vocal intensity, dynamic energy. He can be by turns quiet, soft spoken (with a Scotch accent), conciliatory, and strongly denunciatory. He lacks the eloquence of a Samuel Gompers, but excels in forthright rebuttal skill. He is one of the half-dozen superior speakers among present day labor leaders.

Chairman Holderman, Father Zeger, Distinguished Guests, Fellow Delegates and Friends: I can't but give expression of heartfelt appreciation to the delegates attending this convention for the warmth of your greeting here this morning. This, to my mind, will undoubtedly prove to be one of the most important conventions ever had in the history of this great movement and it will prove to be a unified convention of representatives of all organizations affiliated with the Congress of Industrial Organizations.

The convention will no doubt, as it has in the past, give statesmanlike and constructive consideration to the manifold problems which will undoubtedly be presented to it in the course of its deliberations.

I regard a convention of the Congress of Industrial Organizations as the greatest parliamentary body of workers anywhere in the entire universe. The record of our organization, together with its constructive consideration to the many questions which have presented themselves to it in the course of its career, demonstrates the fitness of our organization to arise to the needs of any occasion. And of course this Eighth Constitutional Convention of the Congress of Industrial Organizations, like preceding conventions, will necessarily concentrate its considerations upon matters of outstanding importance.

In that regard it may not be amiss for me at this juncture to state to the convention that without doubt the most important consideration to be presented to the convention will be the economic or wage aspects of collective bargaining deliberations that are bound to ensue in conferences by many of our international organizations following the adjournment of this convention.

I might point out in that regard a brief resume of an historical nature of certain things that come to my mind at the moment. And in so doing I must refresh the memories of those who are privileged to represent our organizations in this convention about the history of the C.I.O. wage struggle in the latter part of 1945 and the early part of 1946.

Following the ending of Japanese hostilities in August of 1945, industry in the United States, for the most at least, was required to meet its peacetime reconversion needs, to lay off multitudes of men and women that had, during the course of the war been gainfully employed in mines, mills, factories, shops, offices, and in the fields.

During the early part of reconversion, industry assumed direct responsibility for all of the programs incident to the expeditious reconversion of our manufacturing enterprises from wartime to peacetime needs. In so doing the American work week was shortened from something approximating 54 to 60 hours to something less than 40 hours. The shortening of the work week eliminated overtime payments and cast a rather heavy economic shadow over the homes of millions of workers throughout the United States, because the shortening of the work week and the discontinuance of overtime payments resulted in substantial losses in the weekly earnings of American wage earners.

Hence to meet the economic needs of the people this mighty organization undertook the direct responsibility of formulating the wage programs designed to furnish enough money to the wage earners in this nation of ours, first, to provide them with the essentials of life, and, secondly, to provide the necessary purchasing power essential to the acceleration of speedy reconversion and full employment.

In the course of our wage considerations during the latter part of 1945 and the early part of 1946 this organization contended that the profit-making aspects of the industrial picture were such that American industry could absorb the payment of a substantial wage increase without necessarily increasing prices. When argument was adduced by representatives of C.I.O. organizations to that effect, the employers of labor in making answer observed that they would have to secure price increases. Hence for a period of approximately four to five months, beginning with the latter part of 1945 and continuing through to the early spring of 1946, this wage struggle continued, the wage earners on one side contending that they needed the money, they needed the bread, they needed the butter, they needed the shelter, they needed the clothing, they needed the medicine. However, the Office of Price Administration, which was in existence during those days, saw fit to break down completely the barriers of price control, and they in extraordinary if not altogether humiliating fashion, acceded to the demands of the employers in elevating the prices of their particular commodities until they reached almost unbelievable inflationary trends.

Well, it is not for me to recall the history of the strikes that took place in the early part of 1946. That is history. But it might be advisable under the circumstances again to refresh the minds of the delegates as to the attitude assumed by this organization in the course of those wage deliberations before

strikes even took place. And I do so to again pointedly bring
to the attention of the American people through the medium
of this convention one extremely important and incontrovertible
fact, and that is this, that no organization affiliated with the
Congress of Industrial Organizations in the early part of 1946,
whilst the nation was undergoing the rigors of its wage struggles,
precipitated a strike—not a single solitary organization affiliated
with this C.I.O. movement in the early part of 1946, of its own
volition precipitated a strike. And I have but to point to the
record, and that record speaks for itself.

The mighty steel industry, which, by the way, is regarded
as a barometer for matters affecting trade and wages, and so
forth, shall be used at this juncture as an example, because it
was out of that industry's period of collective bargaining, if one
should call it such, that the original 18½-cent-per-hour pattern
was evolved and applied to most of major basic industry in the
United States of America. A record therefore, of some of the
things that transpired in the course of those collective bargaining
deliberations might be of some interest even at this moment.

The United Steelworkers of America endeavored earnestly,
sincerely, and with all of the sincerity, I should say, at its command, to effectuate a peaceable collective bargaining agreement
with the major companies in the steel industry.

Our collective bargaining efforts broke down. Conferences
ensued with Mr. Benjamin Fairless and myself over in the city
of New York some time during the early part of January 1946,
and in the course of those conferences the President of the
United Steelworkers of America, recognizing his responsibilities
not only to his membership but to his country, virtually entreated
the President of the United States Steel Corporation to effectuate
a peaceable working agreement without resort to stoppage. We
failed in that effort, and when failure in that stage of the proceedings became known the President of the United States of
America asked for a conference with Mr. Fairless and me at the
White House.

In the course of that conference the President of the United
States asked me, as the agent of the United Steelworkers of
America, if I would delay the calling of a strike in the steel

industry for one week whilst he was provided the opportunity to look into the matter and see what it was that he could do, as the representative of the American people, to bring about agreement between the conflicting parties. We responded to the President's appeal. We called our strike off, and then the President assumed the role of mediator, counciliator and arbitrator. He heard all of the pertinent testimony from both the representatives of the United Steelworkers of America and the representatives of the steel industry, and in the course of that week he rendered a decision—he, the President of the United States, rendered a decision. Speaking for the people, representing all of the people, he rendered a decision. The Union accepted the decision of the President of the United States and the steel industry politely told the government, through the President, that they were not going to accept his recommendation.

A strike took place, a strike that lasted for a period of approximately three weeks. Who—who was to blame for that strike? I ask those who may be either in this hall or the multitude of people who are not members of labor organizations outside this hall who, under those conditions, should be held responsible for the steel strike. The steel industry had definitely and very arrogantly said to the President of the United States, we will not accept your decision. A strike took place that lasted for a period of approximately three weeks. Who were striking? Who were striking against their government at that time? Was it labor? Was it the steelworkers? Who was it? It was the heart and the core of Big Business striking against its government, striking against a decision made by the President of the United States of America, and the steel industry continued its strike against this government of ours for a period of three weeks, until it defeated the will of the people and it defeated the Government of the United States.

Wage increases amounted to a figure approximating $165,-000,000 for all of the employees in the basic manufacturing steel industry, but when the steel industry eventually perfected an agreement with the United Steel Workers of America it was only after the Office of Price Administration and the Director of Economic Stabilization had acceded to their demands and accorded them price increases approximating $300,000,000 for a $165,000,000 wage increase.

That, my friends, is a record; it is a fact, an uncontrovertible fact; it is the kind of fact that no one here in this country of ours can successfully deny, because the record is there.

I take you now to the automobile industry, where experiences were undergone due to strikes. In that situation the Government of the United States appointed a Fact-Finding Board, a board to ascertain all of the pertinent facts involved in the issue which presented itself at that time to both the union and the industry. In the automobile situation the Fact-Finding Board found for a wage increase approximately 18½ cents. The union accepted. The industry refused.

A protracted strike ensued. And who was responsible for the continuation of that strike? Again a C.I.O. Union had accepted a government verdict. The industry had refused to accept it, hence the public had to be discommoded and the people had to suffer, strikers had to go without bread and butter and other necessaries of life because the automobile industry, in its arrogance had said no, no to another government agency.

Another all-important fact that might be pertinent to this particular wage issue and which might be refreshing in this instance also, in that you will refresh your memories, was the experience which another C.I.O. organization had to undergo. I speak now with particular reference to an investigating committee of impartial conciliators, mediators, fact-finders or arbitrators, composed of Arthur Meyer and William H. Davis, to look into the situation affecting the strike of the United Electrical Workers at the properties of the Westinghouse Manufacturing Company. And what happened there? After some extended hearings before this investigating board the Westinghouse Manufacturing Company walked out of the meetings. It refused to accept governmental mediation and it struck against the Union, it struck against its employees and it defied the Government of the United States, that had selected a fact-finding board, to make certain recommendations affecting that situation.

Why was the oil strike a protracted one? It is true the oil strike was called before any fact-finding board was appointed, but it is nevertheless a fact that the Government of the United States did appoint a fact-finding board that found and made recommendations, and the oil industry, for all practical purposes, refused to accept the findings of that board, necessitating an extended strike.

What happened with reference to the packinghouse dispute? There again another fact-finding board, and there again an evident unwillingness on the part of the major packers of this country to accept a decision from a governmental agency.

I suppose I could continue here enumerating other specific situations where strikes occurred in the early part of 1946, but I do believe it should become evident to any fair-minded man or woman that insofar as the C.I.O. was concerned, in the early part of 1946 and the latter part of 1945, it displayed the keenest interest in the protection of not only the interests of its own members, but the interests of our country, and also the acceleration of the very necessary reconversion needs of the people of the United States.

I point these facts up for the purpose of making one assertion,—one assertion, and that is this, that the public prints in too many instances who have resorted to the use of diabolical slander and misrepresentation, should now, if not in the early part of 1946, take occasion to tell the truth, nothing but the pure unadulterated truth.

Well, since our experiences of last spring and last winter other things have transpired. When our original 18½ cents was accorded us in the early part of the present year, American labor had a presidential understanding,—everybody was aware of it, and that presidential understanding emanated from our government's economists who prepared an exhaustive study for the consideration of the President of the United States as early as a year ago last August. In that report prepared by White House economists there was submitted to the President of the United States through the Director of Economic Stabilization and by the Office of War Mobilization and Reconversion, a report, a factual report, which suggested as early as September, I should say, of 1945, that American business, by and large, perhaps not in all instances, but major business in the United States could afford to make possible the payment of 24 per cent in wage increases without necessarily disturbing or agitating any inflationary spirals here in this country. That was not a C.I.O. report, that was not a biased report emanating from research organizations attached to C.I.O.; that was a government report submitted to the President of the United States by his own employees, employees of the Government of the United States. That is a matter of record.

All right. Out of that record came the conviction on the part of the President of the United States of America that these substantial wage increases which later were to be accorded to American labor could be conceded by American industry without necessarily either agitating or disturbing the inflationary spiral here in the United States of America; and the President so stated. The President of the United States of America so stated.

But what has happened since that time? What has happened? What has happened to this economy? It might be interesting to reveal some of the almost startling revelations that have occurred in the course of the past five or six months. Certainly the 18½-cent wage increase has been completely wiped out. Certainly it is true that a steelworker's wage, which amounted to $54.32 in March of 1946, that wage to the steelworker in the United States today, based upon the value of his earning power is $43.28. So that his status in life as a potential consumer, as a worker, a man obligated to raise and protect a family under our American system, his earning status in life is $13.20 less today than it was in March of last year.

Rather startling,—rather startling, but nevertheless true. That happens to be the status of the American wage earner today.

What has happened to the employer in the meantime? What has happened to the employer interests in the United States in this period of which I make reference? Very interesting—very interesting.

In the year 1939, the year prior to the war—and that was accepted as sort of a year that should be used for the purpose of balancing things during the period of the war—in the year 1939, corporate profits after taxes—I merely refer now to corporate profits after taxes—were five billions of dollars here in the United States. The peak profits of corporate interests in the United States during the year 1944—that was the peak year during the war—their peak profits for that year were ten billions of dollars, after taxes,—after taxes.

Shall we follow through from 1944 until now? What is it now? What sort of a financial status do they occupy now compared to the peak period during the war? Is it less than it was in the peace period of 1939? Is it less than it was during the peak period of 1944? No; no. To the contrary, evidence adduced, facts reported, emanating from governmental sources, indicate that profits for the last quarter of 1946 can reap for American corporate interests a fifteen billion dollar profit predicated upon that rate for the last quarter of 1946,—an unprecedented profit, a higher profit than ever experienced at any time in the history of American business.

Will you take time to contrast that profit picture of American corporate business, as against that of the American wage earner today? The American wage earner, whose living status—and I should correct my former figure of $13.23 per week—is now $13.04 per week less than it was in February and March of 1946.

Who is paying this bill? Why are there so many rumors emanating from so many sources about the dangerous aspects of a predicted recession or depression some time during the year 1947? What could be more dangerous to our national economy, what might constitute a greater threat to full employment and full production in the United States than this distorted, wholly inequitable distribution of our national wealth?

I say that a fifteen billion dollar profit for American industry constitutes a threat, a threat to our national economy, and constitutes a graver threat to the maintenance of our sysem of free enterprise in the United States of America.

These people who propagate false notions about American labor attribute many of the economic ills of the nation to American labor, but in their distortion of the facts they never attempt to present to the American people the simple, pure unadulterated truth.

It is asserted that certain interests here in the United States threaten our institutions and threaten our form of government —and I speak now with particular reference to allegations made concerning the Communist Party—but what could constitute a graver threat to the perpetuity of our free existence in the United States of America, our democratic way of life in America, than this fiscal picture that I have taken the privilege of presenting to you here in this forenoon session of this convention—a far greater threat than anything which ever presented itself to the people of the United States.

My mind's eye goes back to those old days when we went through our last depression, that boom and bust period. The boom is on in the fourth quarter of 1946, and if there is a continuation of these staggering profits at the expense of the American people and the American wage earner, the bust is bound to follow; no one can stop it excepting the exploiters, the exploiters of our system, and the exploiters of our people.

Our convention must necessarily direct its attention to a solution of some of these very vexing problems as they are presented to it in the course of your present deliberations.

There are other aspects of this situation to which I must necessarily direct your attention before the convention is called to order. Some people here in our country have the peculiar notion that as a result of the Republican landslide in the elections of November 5th, that the Republican Party has been given a mandate to do certain things to labor—to do certain things to American labor. Is there anyone in this convention hall, or any sincere thinking individual anywhere in the United States of America, that could believe in the innermost recesses of their heart, their conscience, their mind, that the voters of the United States of America gave to the Republican Party a mandate to put a cross on the back of labor, march it to Capitol Hill, and there in public gaze, witness the actual crucifixion of

American labor? Can anybody believe that? Does the Republican Party believe that? Do the leaders of that party believe that? If they do they are making a grave mistake. No, they can't do that to the American people?

I witness with awe sometimes the reaction of certain elements of our society to things that are transpiring in our midst, and I oftentimes wonder why it is that people in many other lands now, following the recent election, view with a degree of suspicion the motives of certain people here in the United States of America—the belief in many quarters that our money is being utilized for the purpose of changing the thinking of people in many countries, in the distribution of relief, in the lending of money and in other ways. It would indeed be regrettable and most unfortunate if the lending, gift-giving propensities of the American Government should be utilized for the purpose of forcing our way of thinking down the throats of many people all over this world. I make that assertion because that kind of thinking is going on throughout the world in many places, that kind of thinking about our people over here, and it is the business, it is the duty of the Congress of Industrial Organizations to direct the attention of the American people to the dangers which might very well beset us as a result of the promotion of such foolhardy policies.

I am proud, yes, very proud of the record that this great organization of ours has made for itself, the many contributions that this mighty organization has made toward the well-being of America, to all of her people.

War has passed and days of peace, we hope, are to come, and we pray God, through the medium of this convention, that the representatives of the powers now meeting in the city of New York will effectuate for the peoples of the universe a permanent peace, according the utmost degree of security for all people against the ravages of war in the years to come. And it shall be the business of this mighty Union to lend whatever constructive support it may be able to render toward the attainment of these lofty goals. I know they will, I know these Unions will.

We are meeting here today, the 18th day of November 1946, stronger than ever before—numerically stronger, stronger in heart, stronger in mind. In the course of our deliberations we will undoubtedly assess our responsibilities and our obligations to the people whom we are privileged to represent and also to our great and beloved country, the United States of America.

I thank you for your indulgence in the course of this opening address and ask for your cooperation, while the convention is in session, while I am presiding over your destinies as the President of this organization in the course of this meeting.

Thank you.

SHOULD THE TAFT-HARTLEY LABOR BILL BECOME LAW? [3]

HARRY S. TRUMAN AND ROBERT A. TAFT [4]

On June 20, 1947, President Truman sent a message to Congress accompanying his veto of the Taft-Hartley labor bill. On that evening over the radio he attempted to justify his position to the nation. Senator Taft immediately replied, also over the network. A clear-cut debate was thus presented.

For three months Congress had been working on labor legislation. The Senate Labor and Public Welfare Committee, for example, had held twenty-seven hearings. On April 17 the House, 308 to 107, passed a bill that would sharply restrict labor unions. On April 23 the debate opened in the Senate. Senators Taft, Ball, Barkley, Bricker, Ferguson, Hawkes, Ives, Revercomb, Murray, Ellender, Hatch, Morse, O'Mahoney, and Pepper were leaders in what was recognized as the outstanding debate on domestic affairs in the Eightieth Congress.

When the Senate debate opened on May 12, it was conceded that the Taft bill, as amended, would pass by a large majority. Nevertheless, Senator Pepper again spoke against the omnibus bill; Ball and others replied. Then Senator Wagner, author of the twelve-year-old labor bill that bore his name, addressed about a dozen of his colleagues. His appearance was apparently unexpected. It was the Senator's first floor speech during the present session. He had long been ill. Senator George D. Aiken, of Vermont, closed the day's debate by declaring that "We have been subjected to the most intensive, expensive, and vicious propaganda campaign that any Congress has been subjected to."

On May 13 the Senate, after further remarks by Morse, Barkley and others, voted 62 to 24 to pass the bill.

On June 4 the House voted 320 to 79 for the compromise Taft-Hartley bill, worked out by the Conferees named to harmonize the differences of the two versions.

On June 6 the Senate passed the compromise bill 54 to 17.

On June 20, the House voted 331 to 83 to override the President's veto.

On June 23, after a thirty-hour filibuster led by Senators Wayne Morse and Glen Taylor on June 20 and 21, the Senate overrode the veto 68 to 25 and the bill became law.

---

[3] The text of President Truman's radio address is from the *New York Times*, June 20, 1947; that of Senator Taft is from the *Des Moines Register*, June 20, 1947.

[4] For biographical note see Appendix.

The legislation (1) outlaws the closed shop; (2) provides for government injunctions to run for eighty days against so-called public interest strikes; (3) transfers the Conciliation Service from the Labor Department to the National Labor Relations Board; (4) sets up a list of "unfair practices" of unions; (5) guarantees "free speech" for employers; (6) bans certain types of boycotts; (7) permits court suits against unions that break contracts; (8) enlarges the National Labor Relations Board from three to five members and revises its procedure; (8) specifies that unions will lose their rights under the Wagner Act if any officer is a Communist or active sympathizer.

The issues and respective positions of the debaters are clearly brought out in the addresses printed below.

HARRY S. TRUMAN

My Fellow Countrymen: At noon today I sent the Congress a message vetoing the Taft-Hartley Labor Bill. I vetoed this bill because I am convinced it is a bad bill. It is bad for labor, bad for management, bad for the country.

I had hoped that the Congress would send me a labor bill I could sign.

I have said before, and I say now that we need legislation to correct abuses in the field of labor relations.

Last January I made specific recommendations to the Congress as to the kind of labor legislation we should have immediately.

I also urged that the Congress provide for a commission to be made up of representatives of the Congress, the public, labor and management, to study the entire field of labor-management relations and to suggest what additional laws we should have.

I believe that my proposals were accepted by the great majority of our people as fair and just.

If the Congress had accepted those recommendations, we would have today the basis for improved labor-management relations. I would gladly have signed a labor bill if it had taken us in the right direction of stable, peaceful labor relations—even though it might not have been drawn up exactly as I wished.

I would have signed a bill with some doubtful features if, taken as a whole, it had been a good bill.

But the Taft-Hartley bill is a shocking piece of legislation.

It is unfair to the working people of this country. It clearly abuses the right, which millions of our citizens now enjoy, to join together and bargain with their employers for fair wages and fair working conditions.

Under no circumstances could I have signed this bill!

The restrictions that this bill places on our workers go far beyond what our people have been led to believe. This is no innocent bill.

It is interesting to note that on June 4, Congressman Hartley, on the floor of the House of Representatives, made the following statement:

"You are going to find there is more in this bill than may meet the eye."

That is a revealing description of this bill by one of its authors.

There is so much more in it than the people have been led to believe, that I am sure that very few understand what the Taft-Hartley bill would do if it should become law.

That is why I am speaking to you tonight. I want you to know the real meaning of this bill.

We have all been told, by its proponents, that this is a "moderate" bill. We have been told that the bill was "harsh" and "drastic" when it was first passed by the House of Representatives, but that the Senate had persuaded the House to drop out the harsh provisions and that the final bill—the bill sent to me—was "mild" and "moderate."

But I found no truth in the claims that the bill sent to me was mild or moderate. I found that the basic purpose and much of the language of the original House of Representatives bill were still in the final bill. In fact, the final bill follows the provisions of the original House bill in at least thirty-six separate places.

We have all been told that the Taft-Hartley bill is favorable to the wage-earners of this country. It has been claimed that workers need to be saved from their own folly and that this bill would provide the means of salvation. Some people have called this bill the "workers' bill of rights."

Let us see what this bill really would do to our working men.

The bill is deliberately designed to weaken labor unions. When the sponsors of the bill claim that by weakening unions, they are giving rights back to individual working men, they ignore the basic reason why unions are important in our democracy. Unions exist so that laboring men can bargain with their employers on a basis of equality. Because of unions, the living standards of our working people have increased steadily until they are today the highest in the world.

A bill which would weaken unions would undermine our national policy of collective bargaining. The Taft-Hartley bill would do just that. It would take us back in the direction of the old evils of individual bargaining. It would take bargaining power away from workers and give more power to management.

This bill would even take away from our working men some bargaining rights which they enjoyed before the Wagner Act was passed twelve years ago.

If we weaken our system of collective bargaining, we weaken the position of every working man in the country.

This bill would again expose workers to the abuses of labor injunctions.

It would make unions liable for damage suits for actions which have long been considered lawful.

This bill would treat all unions alike. Unions which have fine records, with long years of peaceful relations with management, would be hurt by this bill just as much as the few troublemakers.

The country needs legislation which will get rid of abuses. We do not need—and we do not want—legislation which will take fundamental rights away from our working people.

We have been told that the Taft-Hartley bill is a means by which the country can be protected from the nation-wide strikes in vital industries. The terms of the bill do not support this claim.

Many people are under the impression that this bill would prevent or settle a strike in the coal industry. I sincerely trust that the coal operators and the miners will soon come to an agreement on the terms of a contract and that there will be no interruption of coal mining.

But if the miners and the operators do not reach agreement, and if this bill should become law, it is likely that the most that could be accomplished under the complicated procedures of the bill would be the postponement of a strike from July until October.

Under this bill a work stoppage in the coal mines might be prevented for eighty days and then, if agreement had not been reached, the miners would be free to strike, and it would be mandatory for the President to refer the whole matter to the Congress, even if it were not in session.

Postponing a strike in the coal industry until the approach of winter, when our need for coal is acute, is certainly not the way to protect the nation against the dangers of a shortage of coal.

The bill would not aid fair and early settlements of disputes in vital industries.

We have been told, by the supporters of the Taft-Hartley Bill, that it would reduce industrial strife.

On the contrary, I am convinced that it would increase industrial strife.

The bill would soon upset security clauses in thousands of existing agreements between labor and management. These agreements were mutually arrived at and furnish a satisfactory basis for relations between worker and employer. They provide stability in industry. With their present types of agreements outlawed by this bill, the parties would have to find a new basis for agreement. The restrictions in this bill would make the process of reaching new agreements a long and bitter one.

The bill would increase industrial strife because a number of its provisions deprive workers of legal protection of fundamental rights. They would then have no means of protecting these rights except by striking.

The bill would open up opportunities for endless law suits by employers against unions and by unions against employers. For example, it would make employers vulnerable to an immense number of law suits, since grievances, however minor, could be taken into court by dissatisfied workers.

In so far as employers are concerned, I predict that if this bill should become law they would regret the day that it was conceived. It is loaded with provisions that would plague and hamper management. It is filled with hidden legal traps that would take labor relations out of the plant, where they belong, and place them in the courts.

Another defect is that in trying to correct labor abuses the Taft-Hartley bill goes so far that it would threaten fundamental democratic freedoms.

One provision undertakes to prevent political contributions and expenditures by labor organizations and corporations. This provision would forbid a union newspaper from commenting on candidates in national elections. It might well prevent an incorporated radio network from spending any money in connection with the national convention of a political party. It might even prevent the League of Women Voters—which is incorporated—from using its funds to inform its members about the record of a political candidate.

I regard this provision of the Taft-Hartley Bill as a dangerous challenge to free speech and our free press.

One of the basic errors of this bill is that it ignores the fact that over the years we have been making real progress in labor-management relations. We have been achieving slow but steady improvement in cooperation between employers and workers.

We must always remember that under our free economic system management and labor are associates. They work together for their own benefit and for the benefit of the public.

The Taft-Hartley Bill fails to recognize these fundamental facts. Many provisions of the bill would have the result of changing employers and workers from members of the same team to opponents on contending teams.

I feel deep concern about what this would do to the steady progress we have made through the years.

I fear that this type of legislation would cause the people of our country to divide into opposing groups. If conflict is created, as this bill would create it—if seeds of discord are sown, as this bill would sow them—our unity will suffer and our strength will be impaired.

This bill does not resemble the labor legislation which I have recommended to the Congress. The whole purpose of this bill is contrary to the sound growth of our national labor policy.

There is still time to enact progressive, constructive legislation during the present session. We need such legislation to correct abuses and to further our advance in labor-management relations.

We seek in this country today a formula which will treat all men fairly and justly, and which will give our people security in the necessities of life.

As our generous American spirit prompts us to aid the world to rebuild, we must, at the same time, construct a better America in which all can share equitably in the blessings of democracy.

The Taft-Hartley bill threatens the attainment of this goal.

For the sake of the future of this nation, I hope that this bill will not become law.

ROBERT A. TAFT

The president's message vetoing the labor bill was a complete misrepresentation of both the general character of the bill and of most of its detailed provisions.

Remember that this bill was considered in detail by both houses of Congress for five months. Every provision was worked over and debated, first in the committee, several times on the floor of the Senate, and then in Congress.

Now the President, in ten days, including the three or four days spent in Canada, put his judgment of the meaning and effect of a hundred detailed provisions over that of the great majority of those who have carefully drafted and analyzed these provisions.

It is not surprising, therefore, that the President's veto message shows that he knows practically nothing about the bill itself.

The President ignored the opinion and studied conclusion of the Democrats in the House of Representatives, who voted 106 to 71 this afternoon to override his veto.

On the contrary, the President has apparently adopted in large part the prejudiced arguments of the union labor leaders who from the beginning have opposed any legislation whatever and refused to cooperate with Congress or make any constructive suggestions.

The President's message follows in many details the analysis of the bill prepared by Lee Pressman, general counsel of the C.I.O., inserted in the Congressional Record on June 3 by Congressman Vito Marcantonio [American-Labor, N. Y.] and another memorandum inserted in the Congressional Record of June 6 by Senator [James E.] Murray [Dem., Mont.].

President Truman wholly ignores the detailed arguments to these, which I presented on the floor of the United States Senate. Following the lead of union labor leaders, the President does not find a single good provision in the entire bill.

He ignores every abuse by labor unions which filled the record of evidence before the committee while he gives lip service to the idea of labor reform by saying that he heartily condems abuses on the part of unions and employers.

He nowhere recognizes the existence of any specific abuse. He wants a commission to study the matter carefully studied by committees of Congress for months with the best expert advice. This is the standard plan of those who wish to delay action.

He says that every power given to the union labor leaders is for the benefit of labor, and utterly ignores that these members and their wives and their families are the real sufferers of arbitrary strikes.

No workman is deprived of any fundamental right as the President stated this evening. Only the arbitrary power of labor bosses is curbed.

If there is one subject on which every unprejudiced person is agreed, it is that unions must be made responsible for their acts; that collective bargaining cannot continue to be an important factor in our labor relations unless both parties are bound by their contracts.

The President criticizes every provision designed to make unions responsible. He criticizes the requirement that they file financial and other reports with the department of labor.

Corporations have long been required to file reports both with state and local authorities. Why not unions?

He attacks the provisions that unions may be sued for breach of collective bargaining agreements, on the ground that they should not be bothered with having to defend lawsuits regardless of what they do.

He says they might be harassed by suits by an employer. Everybody else in the United States is subject to harassment by lawsuits. Why not unions?

In any event, the purpose of this provision is to induce them to live up to their contracts, and if they do, few suits if any will ever be filed.

The President attacks the section permitting an injunction against the nationwide strike affecting the national health and safety. It was through such a procedure he secured an injunction against John L. Lewis last fall.

Last year when faced by a nation-wide strike, it was the President himself who recommended government seizure and the drafting of all the strikers into the United States Army.

Because Congress now gives him a carefully considered authority to allay such a strike, to attempt mediation, and finally to conduct a strike vote when other remedies have been exhausted, he says the procedure will do more harm than good.

He refers to letting the Smith-Connally Act expire on June 30 without any protection whatever to the people against nationwide strikes.

He claims that this bill would breed too much intervention in our economic life, and imposes government control over free, collective bargaining.

The bill in no way interferes with the rights of the parties to bargain, in no way limits the right to strike if they fail to agree, except in the case of a nation-wide strike for a period of 90 days until an election can be held.

There might be something in the argument if the government had not intervened in every collective bargaining on the side of labor. Every collective bargaining contract has been subject to the terms of the Wagner Act, the Norris-La Guardia

Act, the Clayton Act, the Fair Labor Standards Act the Walsh-Healy Act; and the intervention of government conciliators.

All this bill does is to say when the government does intervene, it shall be as an impartial public service.

The administration of the Wagner Act by the National Labor Relations Board made it so one-sided as to produce a general public demand that the law operate both ways.

This is the effect of the new bill. The only new limitation on collective bargaining relates to the closed and union shops.

The closed and union shops have developed to such an extent as to make it almost impossible for men to get a job unless they join the union, and impossible to hold a job if they offend the union leaders.

Our regulation of welfare funds requires only that every employee have a legal and enforcible right in the fund so it is not in the arbitrary discretion of the labor union leaders to give or not to give.

These huge funds should of course be subject to government regulations, just as insurance companies are subject to government regulations, to be certain that they remain sound and unimpaired.

I can in a brief time deal with only a few of the direct misrepresentations of the details of the bill.

The President says that a union will be liable for any of its members engaged in an unauthorized wildcat strike. This is simply not so.

The President says the bill would force unions to strike if they wished to have a jurisdictional dispute settlement by the National Labor Relations Board.

This is not so. All the union has to do is to file a petition under the representation section. How could this provision increase strikes when it is not effective at all until there is already a jurisdictional strike or secondary boycott, in effect?

Here are two union abuses which every witness recognizes as abuses. Yet the President criticizes the provision making them illegal and subjecting them to correction by the N.L.R.B. or the courts. The President talks against them. He says that he doesn't want anything to be done about them.

In various places the President asserts that the bill requires election after election, and that the number of them has been multiplied.

He completely ignores the fact that the bill limits elections by specifically permitting only one a year, both with reference to representation and the union shop.

The only elections added to those required by existing law are to find out whether the men really want a union shop. The President objects to an employer having the right to ask for an election when someone claims to be a representative of his men.

Surely an employer ought to have a right to find out whether the union leader really has organized his men or hasn't organized them.

The President says that the provisions regarding the arbitration of grievance disputes are left to be determined by lawsuits. He repeated this statement tonight on the radio. It is not so.

Arbitration provisions are entirely legal and remain effective under our law. As long as either party abides by the arbitration decisions he is of course not subject to suit.

The President says an employer can discharge a man on the pretext of a slight infraction, even though his real motive is to discriminate against the employee for union activities. This is not so.

The board decides, under the new law as under the former law, whether the man was really discharged for union activity or for good cause.

The President says the law will expose unions to suits for acts of violence, wildcat strikes and other actions, none of which were authorized or ratified by them. This is not so.

We have simply provided that unions are subject to the same general laws as any other corporation or agency or citizen in determining their liability for the acts of the agents.

The President attacks the provision giving freedom of speech to employers. The need for such a provision was the one thing admitted even by the labor union leaders.

The bill simply provides that views, arguments or opinion shall not be evidence of an unfair labor practice unless they contain in themselves the threat of coercion or a promise of benefit.

Without such a provision there would be no freedom of speech on the part of employers any more than there has been for the last ten years.

The President criticizes the provisions of state laws permitting union shops to remain in effect. He does not tell you that this is the provision of the Wagner Act which has never undertaken to authorize closed shop agreement if the state law prohibits them.

It is astonishing to find the President objecting to the section which prevents Communists from being officers of labor unions. We have merely required that every officer of a labor union seeking certification must file an affidavit that he is not a member of the Communist party and does not favor the forcible overthrow of the government.

The same affidavit is required to be filed by federal employees. This does not hold up certification of the union, but any Communist who makes a false affidavit can be sent to jail.

The President says:

The mere refusal by a single individual to sign the required affidavit would prevent an entire national labor union from being certified for purposes of collective bargaining.

Why should an individual officer refuse to sign such an affidavit if he is not a Communist? If he is a Communist, why should the union be certified? Why shouldn't every labor union make Communists ineligible for election as officers?

The President's statement simply echoes the argument made by Mr. Lee Pressman in his June 3 memorandum, ignoring the fact that a union could take immediate steps to remove itself from any Communist tie.

There is hardly a sentence in the President's message which is not open to direct challenge, and there are many others besides those I have cited which misrepresent the meaning of the new bill.

The committees of Congress which wrote this bill had no anti-union prejudice. They have tried to restore equality in collective bargaining and correct only those abuses against employers, union members and third parties which were clearly shown to exist by bona fide evidence.

The campaign carried on against the bill by the labor unions has been a complete tissue of falsification to support their contention of the last ten years that the unions are above criticism and above the law—that there must be no legislation on pain of political execution.

It is discouraging to find the President of the United States yielding to their pressure, adopting their arguments and blocking the efforts of the great majority of the people's representatives, including a large majority of the Democrats in the House of Representatives, to secure a reasonable reform.

EDUCATION

AMERICAN EDUCATION AND THE WORLD'S NEEDS [1]

MILDRED MCAFEE HORTON [2]

President Mildred McAfee Horton (Mrs. Douglas Horton), of Wellesley College, gave this address on January 9 at Cleveland, Ohio, at the twenty-first Annual Institute on World Affairs, conducted under the auspices of the Cleveland Council on World Affairs, with the magazine *Time* as co-sponsor. The institute continued for three days and included twenty-three speakers. Some twenty thousand Clevelanders attended the five sessions. Newspapers and radio chains carried the speeches to millions. Cleveland high school students in their forums discussed the questions raised by the speakers.

Conference leaders included James F. Byrnes, retiring as Secretary of State; Senator Arthur Vandenberg; Wellington Koo, Chinese Ambassador to the United States; Carlos Romulo, Philippine delegate to the United Nations; Ezequiel Padilla, Mexico's former Foreign Minister; Sumner Welles; and Francis Cardinal Spellman. Topics for the speeches included the following: What does the rest of the world expect of the United States? What is the United States going to do about it? [3]

President Horton, a graduate of Vassar (1920), was a graduate student at the University of Chicago, Dean of Women and Professor of Sociology at Centre College, and Dean of Women at Oberlin College. In 1936, at the age of thirty-six she became President of Wellesley. In 1942 she was appointed Lieutenant Commander in charge of the newly organized WAVES. In 1945 she married and returned to Wellesley.

Mrs. Horton, although she has had no formal speech training, seems, so she says, to have been talking all her life. She was a member of the Vassar debate team that defeated Wellesley. The speech printed below has considerable humor, personal anecdote, and other factors of audience appeal. The credo at the close of the address has been widely quoted.

Mr. Chairman, Distinguished Guests, and Friends of Cleveland: For the last thirty-six hours my sentiment about this forum

[1] The address is here reprinted through the courtesy of *Time* and of President Mildred McAfee Horton.

[2] For biographical note see Appendix.

[3] For details of the Institute on World Affairs see *Time*. 49:53-60. January 20, 1947.

has been: "Having a wonderful time." As I now face this cozy audience, half of which could leave without my knowledge, I am tempted to add the rest: "Wish you were here."

One of the very great satisfactions of getting out of uniform is that as a civilian I can now differ in public with superior officers.

Last night, General Bradley, who definitely ranks me, simply ruined my speech. He said America in its international relations has achieved maturity, and the whole point of my speech is that I think we are quite adolescent.

I suppose this reflects the difference in opinion of two people, each of whom loves his country, and one deals with veterans, and the other with college students.

I submit that the very fact of having a forum like this reminds me of the title of William Carleton's article in the current *American Scholar*, "Are We Politically Adolescent?" The serious contemplation of the part one plays in the life of his own family is a normal activity of adolescence. But I submit that mature adults, well integrated in their life, don't spend much time wondering what their role in that life is.

But Americans in the family of nations do seem to me to have many of the features of Henry Aldrich, who is entirely willing to accept the destiny of the world or of his own family as his chief responsibility. And what would Judy do in those hours of the radio when she isn't getting dates, if she weren't saving the family?

I do recognize this forum, of course, as a symptom of the fact that America too wants to grow up. We have, indeed, got past the stage through which so many youngsters go of looking at their parents and wondering how they could have such intelligent children.

In the twenties all the world knew that we were blood brothers, sons, and daughters of Europe and the Orient, but we made every effort to deny it, as rapidly growing, somewhat poorly adjusted children often do. But we are over that now. In the forties it is more characteristic of us to admit that we are part of the family of nations, not perhaps by choice, but by obvious relationship. By this time we have grown to full physical strength and we have periods of keen adult insight. I shall call this forum one of those periods. But we have blank spots of juvenile self-righteousness. We love our relatives in the family of nations, when they take us seriously, give us hard jobs to do, which are fitted to our strength, and commend us for doing them better than they could have done them. But we distrust our relatives when, having performed our active, ingenious, technical task we blunderingly volunteer to take on the management of the entire family and find the other members of the family a little hesitant about turning it over to us.

All this is natural with adolescence but means that neither we nor the other members of the family of nations will be at ease until we get over this phase and finish this well-started process of growing up.

One difference between adolescence and maturity is the difference in the size of the world in which the adolescent lives from that of the adult. A mature person—as I would choose to describe maturity—has moved out of self-centeredness into a recognized relationship with a large group. He assumes responsibility because it is inherent in his relationship with people who expect certain things of him. He is not self-conscious in his participation in communal activities. He is identified with them so that he is not doing something *for* his neighbors in their common effort; but he is doing something *with* them for their joint satisfaction.

My favorite WAVE story, and I might say there were many of them, is of the fresh-caught recruit who was enjoying a new-found maturity. She was asked by a former teacher how she endured Navy regimentation. And she replied: "Endure it? I like it. Everybody knows what is expected of her and what will happen if she doesn't do it, but it is all impersonal. And while there is a lot of discipline, none of it is for my own good."

I submit that even partial adults like to have attention directed at something bigger than their own self-interest.

Now, one of the newly strong trends in American education is the recognition of the fact that Americans must learn to live in relation to a world instead of in relation to one section or one region or one continent of it.   And that is a fairly new point of view.

Some forty years ago or thereabouts, I spent a few months in England at an age which I choose to consider tender. It was very hard on a little patriot to discover that the point of view of my English schoolmates was that the only reason America was there and an independent nation was that the British were too busy about important matters in the 18th century to bother with our Revolutionary War.

For such heresy in those days, my only retaliation was to join an equally uninformed and patriotic sister in singing as loudly and as rudely as possible, and with no premonition of my later relationship to Britannia's subjects:

> "Rule, Britannia, Britannia rules the waves,
> "And Britons ever, ever, ever, shall be slaves."

But it is out of just such juvenile behavior that international friendships must be merged when teaching on either side of the Atlantic or Pacific is so provincial—and you know we really are provincial.   How often have you heard the statement made that American children don't really need to learn foreign languages?   Anything worth reading will be translated, and anywhere you go there will be people who can speak English.   And so what?   Who but an adolescent would expect all the rest of the family to adapt its ways to his?

Do you recall that stage of personal growth at which you learned a new fact at school and were simply amazed to find your adult relatives had known it for a long time?   As war-awakened Americans I wonder if we seem a bit like that to some of the peoples of whom we have become conscious since our armies and navies were stationed in various parts of the world. We discovered the Burma Road, West China, Siam, India, the Balkans, North Africa, the islands of the Pacific.   Our sudden interest has been keen and I hope intelligent.   But, in all, a few people—Christian missionaries, business men, explorers— have known for quite a long time that the world was full of interesting places and interesting people, and other lands have dealt for some centuries with problems about which we have just become aware.

I hope we will spare ourselves the embarrassment of claiming priority of discovery just because we only now hit upon the facts.

Now a mature person, as compared with an immature adolescent, has a self-control which makes him effective in accomplishing his purposes. He knows what his purposes are and he knows how to accomplish them.

Americans are not distinguished for the clarity of their convictions; for their strength, yes; for their clarity, no. By and large, we have not done much thinking about the things which matter most to us as Americans. We have many catch words which we like to use—freedom, liberty, individuality, free enterprise, the American way—but we have not done much to study the implications of these words. One reason for this is probably that our form of government is now one of the oldest in the modern world. Our Civil War which tested "whether that nation, or any nation so conceived and so dedicated, can long endure" was eighty-three years ago, and all of us have grown up in a society whose basic tenets could be taken for granted. They have been challenged in two world wars but we have been far enough away from the impact of that challenge that we could and did rise in self-defense without having to do much analytical thinking about what we were defending.

One of the things we used to deplore about German youth was the fact that it was so well indoctrinated in Nazi theory that it was invulnerable to argument. Young Communists, I am told, are apparently trained now not only to know what they believe and why they believe it, but what other people don't believe about it and what the answer is as to what the other person does not believe.

American educators are loath to indoctrinate young Americans, but in our zeal to avoid indoctrination I sometimes think we have deprived young citizens of a foundation for the faith that is in them. They believe in democracy enough to die for it, but they don't always recognize it when they see it nor distinguish it from its enemies when it is attacked.

A great many American young people have had almost no experience in thinking out their personal or national philosophy. Meanwhile, our fellow citizens in the world community are very articulate, explicit, and definite in their plan of action. We don't like the way they have achieved that definiteness by indoctrination from the top of a totalitarian government, but we owe it to our fellow citizens and to our convictions to use our free method of education to accomplish a result which can match the well, though dictatorially, formulated opposition. If we really have the truth we ought to be able to express it.

To the extent that other philosophies threaten to endanger the world, we need to be able to deal with them. That means understanding them so that we can know what there is to fear and not waste fear on what is merely strange. That is the main reason for my honest hope that Russian young people will be permitted soon to come to study in the United States, and that American youth may have the chance to see Russians live behind that curtain that we talk about so much.

I had occasion to look up the word "iron" in the dictionary recently. It can mean "hard, rude, or unyielding," but, you know, another definition is that it is "the most important of the metallic elements; very tenacious but malleable, ductile, and strongly magnetic." To Americans that mysterious iron curtain is "strongly magnetic."

As we try to understand philosophies different from our own, we certainly need to know our own and to understand it so that we can defend it as to the crucial points and modify the unimportant points. No amount of ranting against communism, fascism, naziism, totalitarianism or Bilboism will cure the advocate of those theories. The only cure for bigotry or falsehood is potent truth, and truth is not potent when it is fuzzy, poorly formulated, and diffuse. Nor is truth potent when it is concerned only with words and not with deeds. The adolescent has a high standard for himself and an exorbitant one for his relatives. He insists that they should do what he *says* and not what he *does*. The mature man judges himself on the basis of his own ideals and knows that his actions speak louder than his words.

The December *Harper's* magazine carries a translation of Ilya Ehrenburg's report on his trip to America as prepared for Russian readers. It ought to be required reading for those of us who share with the rest of mankind the difficulty of seeing ourselves as others see us. To the visitor the facts of racial segregation, deprivation of voting privileges, economic inequalities are as significant and characteristic of American life as our magnificent technology. I hope I shall not be accused of being a victim of Russian propaganda if I quote an observation which seems to me important. Mr. Ehrenburg said:

> It would seem that in this country of diverse races united by patriotism, national equality would prevail. However, America, which never knew feudalism, has established a racial hierarchy. The aristocracy are the English, Scotch, and Irish.
>
> At the bottom of the scale are the Negroes.
>
> In the war against Hitlerism America played a prominent part; yet racialism here has a legal standing. . . . I met a lawyer in Nashville who spent a long time trying to persuade me that there are "inferior and superior races." He reiterated the theories of Rosenberg and other ideologists of the Third Reich. Then he showed me the portrait of his brother, who was killed on the Rhine; he was proud of his brother, who had perished in the struggle against racialists.

I wish a visitor from a country we need to know had not had the experiences which would lead Ehrenburg to write this:

> When an American friend asked me what should be done to improve our mutual relations, I replied: "Set up a single standard." . . . Too frequently I saw two standards here: one for the virtuous Anglo-Saxons and another for the dishonorable "Reds."

Americans need communicable and demonstrable convictions, and a plea for convictions instead of prejudices is really a plea for intellectual discipline. A young and growing nation can substitute vigor and strength for trained minds and is still impressed in its accomplishment, but we can't do that as we approach maturity.

America has a phenomenal educational system. We have cultivated individuality, ingenuity, and versatility but, you know, we have been less successful in cultivating trained minds. I suppose brains are not too popular in any society. Here we nominally like brains but actually no brainy people are very popular. We are observing widespread popular support for scientists because they are so practical. Thinkers aren't so popular. It is really no wonder there is a dearth of teachers because teachers represent intellectual activity. The minute that we really want disciplined minds for ourselves and our children we will begin to pay teachers money and prestige to provide those disciplined minds.

Of course, there are always a few enthusiasts who would rather teach than eat. Those are the ones who are living on their salaries.

But, as a matter of fact, we really are growing into a very much more mature status than we used to have. We are trying to learn to recognize the interests of other adult citizens of our own world. The extent to which we know our neighbors is limited, but it is so much more than we ever used to know that it is encouraging. Witness this Council. Witness the kind of mature statesmanship demonstrated by the speakers this evening in the persons of Secretary Byrnes and Senator Vandenberg.

Witness the reestablishment of study arrangements for students in foreign lands, the flow of students from all around the world who are welcomed with genuine enthusiasm on every campus of this country. Witness the Fulbright Bill to finance study of Americans abroad. Witness the zealous participation of the United States in UNESCO, in the World Council of Churches, in the International Federation of University Women, in the World Student Christian Movement, the International Student Congress, International Labor Organization, the YMCA, the YWCA, the United Service to the Near East and China, and all those other projects for which you raise money and for which you wish I would put in a plug.

We are moving now into a world-wide relationship which we do find fascinating.

Our distinguished guests from overseas have done us the honor to come to this gathering to discuss what the world expects of us. May I ask of them the patience to give us the time to grow up to that responsibility which we genuinely do want to assume.

We have the strength of a privileged population. There are those among us who fear that our standard can be maintained only at the cost of a lower standard for the rest of the world. Many of us know that in the long run the whole family must rise or fall together. We offer our people to the world relationship with their growing sense of their responsibility for it.

We have the vigor of a wealthy country. There are some of us who think that those who have must keep that which they have in order to have it in the future. There are many more of us who know that shared wealth is infinitely more productive than hoarded wealth, and we offer our material assets as our part in the world community.

We have within limits the adventurous spirit of a relatively secure country. We dare to experiment, to run risks, to "try anything once." We are bold to undertake the solution of anybody's problem. Now, that may make us a menace or a boon in our world relationships. But we urge you, our foreign friends, to take advantage of our inexperience to let us try some things which need doing but which are impractical. Youth is always impractical but if age dampens its zeal too zealously we lose some dramatic accomplishments.

America can be counted upon to provide plans, personnel. The way in which students would like to go anywhere in the world to be of help is stimulating and a little appalling for those to whom they would go.

But we can provide plans, personnel, equipment, money, all the necessary enthusiasm for a conglomerate mass of experiments. That is wasteful and confusing and perhaps unnecessary, undoubtedly adolescent, but it is the way that we will learn; and we need the understanding of the Old World as we struggle into our mature partnership.

As a people we have some articles of faith which, although they need clarification, amplification, and implementation, are values we are eager to share with the world.

We believe in people; we believe in truth; we believe in justice; we believe in mercy; we believe in kindness; we believe in the power of love and the essential weakness of hate. We don't always practice what we believe. We vary widely in our reasons for believing it, but we believe that such belief is a contribution to a world—and a world in which we want to belong fully and freely and acceptably.

No adolescent grows to maturity expeditiously through his own unaided efforts. We, too, hope for help in achieving mature status, however much we seem to repudiate it, once you believe that we basically welcome it from our older friends. If they are scared of us we will probably take an adolescent's pleasure in making them jump.

If they are angered by us, we will probably resent their wrath and do little to avoid it. If they are sentimental about us, pampering and indulging us fatuously, we will hold them in contempt. But if they believe in us surely we will respond to that belief.

I thank you.

WE MUST RECAPTURE VALOUR [4]

BYRON PRICE [5]

Mr. Byron Price delivered this Phi Beta Kappa address in Sanders Theatre at the Commencement Exercises at Harvard University, Cambridge, Massachusetts, on June 3, 1946. This speaker received an honorary M. A. degree at the graduation ceremonies on June 6. Others also honored at that time included General Dwight D. Eisenhower, Admiral Chester W. Nimitz, Generals H. H. Arnold and A. A. Vandergrift. A prominent commencement speaker was President Frank P. Graham, of North Carolina University.

In the award Mr. Price was cited for his war contribution as Director of Censorship, to which office he was appointed on December 16, 1941. Critics generally agreed that the difficult assignment was conducted with splendid judgment and with minimum curtailment of free speech and press.

As an undergraduate at Wabash College, Price was prominent in public speaking and was winner of the Indiana State Intercollegiate Oratorical Contest of 1911. Immediately upon graduation he began working for the Associated Press. In the First World War he participated in the Meuse-Argonne offensive. In 1919 he was assigned to the Washington Bureau of the Associated Press and later became Executive News Editor. At the conclusion of World War II he became vice president of the Motion Picture Producers and Distributors of America. In 1947 he was appointed Assistant Secretary General for Administrative and Financial Affairs of the United Nations.

Mr. Price has been a frequent speaker before both face-to-face and radio audiences. On January 18, 1942, for example, he appeared on the University of Chicago Round Table on "Censorship," and on March 8, 1942, on the American Forum of the Air discussion "Free Speech and Censorship in Wartime."

A year ago these exercises felt the electric touch of great expectations. After the long night, we sensed the warm approach of a new day.

Had Mr. Emerson returned in 1945 to speak again to this Society, he might aptly have repeated the appellation of 1837: "An anniversary of hope, and, perhaps, not enough of labor."

[4] Text furnished through the courtesy of Mr. Byron Price.
[5] For biographical note see Appendix.

We know now that the mood of 1945 was an empty mood of faith without works. In time of war American valour had become the marvel and salvation of the modern world. Must we ask today whether American neglect and impotence are destined to become equally the marvel and tragic disappointment of the world in the days of peace?

You may say we still live in hope; but that hope becomes now a hope long deferred, without luster, spoken of wistfully and even in sorrow. We shall not feel again the buoyancy of security and self-respect until we recapture valour.

A year ago we thought we saw the old dream of world understanding approaching reality. We thought we saw the irons of intellectual and political serfdom melting finally in the rekindled fires of a vast, universal yearning. We thought we saw a generation of humanity emerging chastened from the sacrifices of war, spurred onward by reborn courage, breathless to put its feet upon the pathway of high achievement. We thought we saw the radiant vision of a risen world.

A year ago a new President at Washington put before the nation a blueprint for redesigning national life, for converting wartime momentum to the uses of peace. The arsenal of democracy was to become a factory for plowshares. From our rich granaries and mills, under the touch of new techniques, would flow the bounties of a new prosperity, healing the broken peoples of the world and lifting our own standards of life to levels heretofore beyond our comprehension.

In the realm of letters, too, arose a new vision. Out of the refinements of human suffering, out of mass experience with the degradations of the bloodiest of all wars, a new and higher concept of man was to appear. We should turn our backs on the old formulas and the old vulgarities. It might be that we should attain at last a literature of confidence, of dignity and of realistic promise.

Were these dreams too bright, too lofty? After the lapse of a year we do not know; for the heralded task of realization has not been undertaken. The blueprints remain blueprints. A few of the beams have been raised, but the bricks have not been ordered. The carpenters and the plasterers are otherwise engaged.

The full sum of these derelictions can be struck off only if the items are examined in detail.

In spite of all our good intentions, in spite of pledges and protestations of unselfish purpose, the great ideal of world unity still is beyond our grasp. Even as in all the days since the world's wars began, the winds of international suspicion and resentment are abroad, rustling fitfully the clustered flags of the new world order. At the gateway of every powerful nation, including our own, the barriers of isolation are rebuilding. Selfishness, inspired fear, and international rudeness continue to shriek in the daily headlines. The childish concept that civilized peoples can live unto themselves alone still circulates among the credulous of all lands, and alarms and rumors of war circle the globe.

Let us not disparage what has been accomplished; but let us not ignore the manifest fact that what has been accomplished is not enough. World unity and even world understanding are goals yet to be attained.

Of all the nations, our own was best equipped in 1945 to point the way for the aspiring world. How shall we characterize the state of the union today: Can we in good conscience hold aloft as an example a national scene of confusion, hesitation and reviving bigotry; of legislative lethargy, timidity and neglect; of economic strangulation at the ruthless hands of marplots; of furtive operations in the black market; of increasing juvenile delinquency; of padded relief rolls, while work waits for millions; and of waste and profligacy in a world in dire need? To this we have come in so short a time since the valorous days of 1945.

And what shall we say of the present state of the man of letters? The bright dream of renaissance in the creative arts also has eluded us. The scholar pursues his appointed ways, but his mighty yearning remains unsatisfied. "Man Thinking" continues earthbound, greatly as he aspires to loftier things. Bewilderment seizes upon our philosophies, and the sweet music still defies transcription.

Of the making of books it may be said that no age has exceeded this, provided we speak only in terms of press runs and dollar sales. But how often shall the seeker find between these myriad covers an ounce of literary beauty, or a thimblefull of spiritual elevation? In even greater measure than heretofore, we are served a fare of dissoluteness and destruction. We are asked to sneer at man and regard him as no better than the worm. We are invited to improve our minds by studying the endless sagas of criminals and harlots, moving in sordid surroundings, and worshipping only the flesh.

So runs the uneasy chronicle of these times. We have lost valour at the very moment of our greatest need. Twelve months ago the tools were sharp and the blueprint fresh and intriguing. Now we have come to the end of a year of hope, and not enough of labor.

How shall we isolate the source and cause of these manifold infirmities? It would be easy for every American to point an accusing finger at his neighbor, and exhort him to reform; but we have tried that already, and it has achieved measurably less than nothing. It would be easy (and to some degree plausible) to put the blame on politicians afraid of their shadows; or the perversity of foreign peoples; or a weakening of the churches; or a breakdown of our schools; or the blindness of book publishers, or the press, or the radio, or the theater. That way we have explored also, and it has returned us precisely to the starting point.

The truth is that in our thoughtless haste to accuse one another, we have rendered complicated a really simple matter. The one great human force left in the world is the force of public opinion. If our affairs are out of joint, the great mass of our citizens cannot escape the blame. We need not look afield; the fault is yours and mine.

Let us face it. Timid and procrastinating political leadership can endure only as the voters give permission. Selfish magnates of labor and management can keep their power only so long as mass opinion tolerates their excesses. Shorn of popular patronage, bad books, bad newspapers, bad motion pictures, bad radio would disappear with the day's sunset. Black markets prosper in exact proportion to the dereliction of normally respectable citizens. Church and school do not fail except as the people fail.

The measure of the failure is rendered plainer by specific illustration. A year ago this nation assumed, without audible dissent from any quarter, unprecedented obligations growing out of an unprecedented war. We contracted to police effectively large areas of conquered territory in Europe and Asia. We covenanted with other nations to help enforce the peace. We pledged ourselves, in short, to remain a strong world power, not alone in our own interest, but to serve a great ideal of world security.

How well have the American people met the payments due on the promissory note? We began by raising a loud demand that the boys be brought home. If by such a policy our occupying armies were denuded of experience, stripped of special skills, and reduced to ineffective strength, no matter. Let the generals worry. Next we looked supinely on while Congress sabotaged a presidential program to consolidate the remnants of our military and naval strength into a single fighting force. Now we have compounded our default by an overpowering popular pressure to nullify the selective draft, and thus make certain finally that our solemn promises cannot be kept.

The valour that was ours a year since was the valour of millions. So now the shortcomings are the shortcomings of millions. We shall not find the way again, unless, as in other decisive hours long ago "we, the people" set our course resolute again toward national greatness.

If we appear to dwell overlong upon this painful theme, it is only because diagnosis comes before treatment. It is for the purpose of arriving, not at a counsel of despair, but at a sound counsel of regeneration. For there is yet time to mend. The same Providence which so many times before has given this nation another chance of salvation still keeps the door ajar. Our rich endowment of resources and resourcefulness still waits upon us. If we have grown heedless today, we shall still have eyes to see tomorrow. The very universality of our failing is cause for hope; for we are the self-same individuals we were a year ago, and it is beyond reason that the spark of so great a nobility does not still burn behind the facade of our indifference. It is not too late to come to ourselves. There is yet time for valour.

There is yet time, but no one should assess lightly the difficulties of regaining ground once held, and lost. Half-hearted leaders and half-baked thinking will never be equal to the challenge. If the prize is great, so must the effort be. None but the best we have will be good enough.

For the work now to be done, therefore, the special responsibility of the disciplined mind is manifest. Whether we call him by the name of scholar, or humanitarian, or plain seeker-after-truth, it is the thoughtful man to whom the thoughtless must turn to save them from their folly. Such a call ought never to remain unanswered.

Many wise men have spoken on this theme in times past, often with little effect. No person of education seriously disputes the conclusion of Huxley that "the great aim of life is not knowledge but action." Yet how often does practice betray conviction! Whether from overmodesty, or disillusionment at the ingratitude of the people, or sheer timidity, it still is too much the normal inclination of the scholar to remain merely a scholar, recoiling at every brush of shoulders on the busy street. The notion still prevails that seclusion can mean security from a harsh world—a notion as false from man as for the snail within its fragile temple.

That the cloister pattern of behavior is neither necessary nor profitable for the thinking man was established with dramatic finality during the war years, particularly by our great men of science. In the direction of destruction, their services proved more influential than we or they really expected, because they had the will to try. Will enough of them have the will to try in equal measure now that construction replaces destruction at the head of the list of human priorities? Or will they return to the shelter of private laboratories, shunning the larger challenges of public thinking, and leaving on the scrap heap of war the laurels so valourously won by selfless devotion and cooperation?

Nor is the challenge less significant in any other field of intellectual endeavor. In these strange days we have begun carelessly to speak of scientific progress as a sort of panacea. Yet we know well enough that science can never fabricate a complete man; and it is a sign of our confusion that we need remind ourselves of a truth so elemental.

For the mind and soul of man, also, new concepts must be fashioned. Upon all who teach rests the obligation to clarify thought, to cast out the devils of frustration, to reawaken the will to try. In war our young manhood and womanhood was not afraid of dying, but strangely now it shrinks from living. The highest mission of our schools and colleges has become the restoration of self-respect and confidence to a generation woefully bewildered. Before this practical task the old theories and the old curricula become inconsequential. For so long as every day's news is greeted with foreboding, so long as young Americans live in fear of themselves and of life, all our teaching will be in vain. No process of cramming, even if it encompasses the learning of the ages, will suffice.

The dimensions of the task are, of course, far broader than the classroom. Tomorrow may be in the keeping of youth, but today is the responsibility of maturity. Youth has the right to expect, moreover, that the heaviest burdens of reconstruction will be borne by the generation which brought matters to their present unhappy state. That will require adult thinking, courageous enough to embrace new policies and seek far horizons. It will require that the individual American regain his famed capacity for bold adventure, and cease to live introspectively, fearful that he will encounter some mishap, or will not get his share.

It would be possible to subdivide the responsibility of the thoughtful man, in these circumstances, almost indefinitely. By such a process we would confront every specialist with the record of his own peculiar obligation in the assignment book of our destiny. It will be sufficient, however, to illustrate the whole by examining one or two of the specific items. Let us look at the challenge written opposite the name of the philosopher, and opposite the name of the writer of fiction.

Surely it is time every adult philosopher conceded that brooding will accomplish nothing. To take note of gloomy surroundings is one thing, but awareness alone does not fulfill the mission of Man Thinking. Viewing all time in perspective, the philosopher should be the last to surrender to the apprehensions of the moment and, like the drowsy-minded floor painter, imprison himself in a corner. If he really aspires to be of service he must find exits for his genius, and preach a doctrine of construction and accomplishment. He must have valour to press out beyond the old conceptions and the old limitations.

In this particular sector of intellectual yearning, encouraging signs already are appearing. Writing recently in the *Saturday Review of Literature*, Dr. Ralph Barton Perry counseled his fellow philosophers to rid themselves of defeatism, and to be "honest and careful, but not timid."

> The substance of the matter [said Dr. Perry] is that philosophy has today a supreme opportunity if philosophers will be true to their calling. It is still, as it always has been, the mission of philosophy to take the most inclusive possible view of things, at the risk of overextending itself, at the risk of overstepping the bounds of assured fact, at the risk of logical uncertainty, at the risk of ill repute among men of affairs and exponents of common sense.

Similarly, the times challenge the writer of fiction to break the bonds of custom which have reduced so many current novels to stereotype. No thoughtful man should be intimidated by the momentary success of helter-skelter narrative retailing only the baser instincts of man, thrown together in stark and discordant phrase, and exploited under the false label of realism. Unfortunately, the peddler of the pornographic always finds his market. But in that circumstance the true artist discovers no cause for despair.

We need a revival of courage in the writing of books and of plays. Let us hear something of the dignity of man. Let us speak of humankind, not with contempt, but with a new appreciation and a new respect, no longer as a horde of little animals indulging their appetites in the mire, but as the noblest work of the universe, capable of standing upright in the image of

God. Let us give belated thought to a new beauty and charm of expression, which is the hallmark of literature.

If in this matter we have the valour of our convictions, the best seller lists need not worry us. It is no excuse to say that such novels have been written, and have stood unsold upon the bookshop shelf. The answer is that they have not been written well enough. Man is inately proud of his place of preeminence among living things. He is inmately religious, and flattered to see the soul that is within him linked up with cosmos. He will respond willingly and even eagerly, as he has from the beginning of time, to words which speak with real inspiration of his nobility and his eternal worth.

It would be profitless to become involved in a hen-and-egg speculation as to the relative influence of literary environment on the people, and of the people on literary standards. It is enough to know that, in any case, much can be done from the side of the literary man, and that today much needs to be done. In this, as in all things intellectual or temporal, let us take to ourselves and to our times the sage advice of Jefferson:

Cherish the spirit of our people and keep alive their attention. Do not be too severe upon their errors, but reclaim them by enlightenment.

It is only from such faith in the ultimate that true valour springs. The thinking man sacrifices his birthright whenever he measures his capabilities against the whims of a particular hour. He must hold the vision before him, even in the dark of night. Only thus shall we realize the prophecy made here by Emerson, who saw what he was constrained to call "the sluggard intellect of this continent" awakening to new achievement. Only thus shall we attain the Golden Age of American culture.

Nor need such a day be long postponed. The bright constellations we beheld so briefly but a year hence still shine somewhere above us. The lessons learned dearly in the greatest of human experiences, the spiritual awareness born of bitter trial, a well-tested capacity for selfless cooperation, in short, the priceless know-how of courageous living still is ours if we are willing to embrace it. It is not opportunity which has failed us; it is ourselves.

The sign still is in the heavens, if only we have strength to look upward.

TAKE YOUR COLLEGE IN STRIDE [4]

WILLIAM G. CARLETON [5]

Professor William G. Carleton delivered this address at a meeting of first year students, mostly veterans, at the University of Florida, Gainesville, Florida, on November 25, 1946.

This speech is in almost every sense a model for school and college speechmakers. It is brief; original in concept and expression; personal and direct in audience appeal; well organized; filled with suggestions of humor and appreciation of campus associations, including faculty, students and library. It does not lack motivative elements that supplement the logical propositions stated or implied. The speech is based upon a mature social and educational philosophy and is couched in the moving language of public address, as illustrated by the parallelism and balanced structure. It is attention-getting in the first sentence and impressive in the final understatement.

Professor Carleton was a high school debater at Evansville, Indiana, a varsity debater at the University of Indiana, and a member of Tau Kappa Alpha, honorary debating society. He speaks frequently before civic and professional organizations. During World War II he addressed many army camps and civilian defense groups.[6]

College offers you five great opportunities—professors, contact with fellow students ~~who themselves are the products of a winnowing process~~, laboratories, a library filled with books, and leisure time. And the greatest of these is leisure time.

Is it not strange that the greatest good provided by a university is something intangible—something that cannot be seen, something that cannot be written down in catalogues or reduced to clock hours, credits, degrees? But the leisure time offered you during your university days is the priceless boon. Never again in your life will you have so much time—time to browse, to think, to dream, to discuss, to argue, to question, to create, to construct. Even if you should become a college professor you

[4] Permission to reprint through the courtesy of William G. Carleton and the City News Publishing Company. The text is from *Vital Speeches of the Day.* 13:3-20. March 1, 1947.

[5] For biographical note see Appendix.

[6] For further comment on Professor Carleton as a Speaker and for an example of his speaking, see *Representative American Speeches: 1943-1944.* p. 209-29.

will never again have so much precious leisure. Beware of those educators who want to put you in a straight jacket and make you account for every minute of your waking hours. Those educators do not want a university; they want an army.

What any professor can give you in any subject is limited —limited by the inability of any man, however great his sense of the vicarious, to impart but a small fraction of his knowledge and experience; limited by the necessarily formal nature of the student-teacher relationship; limited by the professor's own talents and background; limited by cultural and traditional restraints. Even the greatest of teachers are limited, limited by the very clarity of the point of view which brings them to prominence and makes them "great."

Your professor, to be sure, will be able to suggest, to encourage, to help tie up loose ends, to put things together, to point out connections where none seemed to exist before. If he is the sort of person who can do this in an interesting and exciting way, so much the better. If he has developed enough maturity in his own subject to have come to a definite point of view and to have made some original contributions, then you are blessed. And if he can impart his ideas without pomposity and with humor and sparkle, then you are twice blessed.

However, even the most gifted professors can give you little real insight, understanding, ripeness of judgment, wisdom. These are the results of living, countless contacts with men and events, wide experience, travel, observation, the reading of great books, the doing of great deeds, thinking and acting in real life situations.

The library, even in this scientific age, is the student's chief source of knowledge. A university library is a truly wonderful place. There you can find almost all the ideas that men in all times and places have thought—the ugly and the beautiful, the foolish and the wise, the grotesque and the sensible, the curious and the useful. There you can relive the life experience of the race—the story, still unfinished, of man's slow groping for civilization.

As sources of ideas, professors simply cannot compete with books. Books can be found to fit almost every need, temper, or interest. Books can be read when you are in the mood; they do not have to be taken in periodic doses. Books are both more personal and more impersonal than professors. Books have an inner confidence which individuals seldom show; they rarely have to be on the defensive. Books can afford to be bold and courageous and exploratory; they do not have to be so careful of boards of trustees, colleagues, and community opinion. Books are infinitely diverse; they run the gamut of human activity. Books can be found to express every point of view; if you want a different point of view you can read a different book. (Incidentally, this is the closest approximation to objectivity you are likely ever to get in humanistic and social studies.) Even your professor is at his best when he writes books and articles; the teaching performance rarely equals the written effort.

Students who come to the university merely to learn a trade will not understand what I have had to say. Neither will those who come merely to earn high grades or deliberately to make Phi Beta Kappa. But the others—those who have come to learn of life in this puzzling and complicated world of ours—will, I think, understand.

1946: YEAR OF DECISION [7]

W. NORWOOD BRIGANCE [8]

Dr. W. Norwood Brigance, President of the Speech Association of America in 1946, gave this address at the opening session of the annual convention of that organization, at the Hotel Sherman, Chicago, on December 30, 1946. On the opening program also were James A. Winans, Professor Emeritus, Dartmouth College; Clarence T. Simon of Northwestern University, a member of the American Speech Correction Association; and Valentine Windt of the University of Michigan, President of the American Educational Theatre Association. The audience of more than one thousand consisted mainly of college, university, and secondary school teachers of general speech, dramatic art, or speech correction.

The address here included is an excellent example of speech composition. The educational philosophy is clearly set forth and defended; the refutative elements are boldly but persuasively presented; the style is alert and personal; the general structure and the sectional organization are carefully developed. The delivery was dominating.

Dr. Brigance has been in constant demand as a speaker before both professional and general audiences. He has been editor of the *Quarterly Journal of Speech* and is the author of many popular texts in speech. *The History and Criticism of American Public Address*, prepared under his editorship and under the sponsorship of the Speech Association of America, is a notable contribution in this field. His students at Wabash College have had unusual success in intercollegiate debate and oratory.

This speaker seldom writes a speech. Usually he prepares a full outline with the facts in mind. His speaking is, therefore, extempore, "without notes or preparation of any kind" before him.

Of the December, 1946 address Dr. Brigance stated "This is the first speech I have delivered from a manuscript in exactly twenty-five years, excepting only the papers, which really were not speeches at all, that I have presented from time to time at our conventions." This address he wrote in full and read because, as he states, his convention duties kept him "going full tilt without opportunity for assimilating the material." Furthermore, he preferred to have an exact copy of what was said in case the speech happened to be quoted widely.[9]

[7] Reprinted through the courtesy of the author. Text furnished by Dr. Brigance. See also *Congressional Record*. 80th Congress, 1st session. 93:570-2. January 14, 1947; *Quarterly Journal of Speech*. 33:127-33. April, 1947.

[8] For biographical note see Appendix.

[9] Letter to the editor of this volume, February 17, 1947. For further comment on Professor Brigance as a speaker and for his address, "The Backwash of War," see *Representative American Speeches: 1945-1946*. p. 75-94.

That iconoclastic historian, Bernard De Voto, wrote a significant book three years ago entitled *The Year of Decision: 1846.* It was a history of America in that one year, 1846, and it was De Voto's contention that the course of American history and the pattern of American life for the half century following were determined by events and decisions that took place in the year 1846.

It is a paradox that the year 1946, even more than 1846, is likely to be significant as a Year of Decision: 1946 is Year One of the atomic bomb; 1946 is Year One of the United Nations organization; 1946 is Year One of a power struggle between two political philosophies, communism and democracy —or what passes for communism and democracy—that is likely to test both our ability to handle atomic weapons without explosion and to live under a united nations organization.   As a discerning wit remarked, "From now on, we know it is One World, all right; but we don't know yet whether it is to be This World or the Next World."

Robert M. Hutchins said last May to the American Council on Education: "The great problems before us are first, can we survive? and second, what kind of life are we going to lead if we do?"   Then he added that the world must try to arrive at a destination where survival is possible within "not more than five years."

If Hutchins is right, then 1946 is Year One of our five years of grace.   If he is wrong it is still a Year of Decision, because what we have done in this year, and shall do during the first half of 1947, is likely to determine for a long time to come the course of history, not for America alone but for the world.

Now this Year of Decision in international affairs is also a Year of Decision in American education, for the obvious reason that the repercussions in the political and military world have set off seismic tremors in the academic world: 1946 is Year One of the Harvard report on *General Education in a Free Society*; 1946 is the year of the Columbia University report on *A College Program in Action*; 1946 is a year in which more than one hundred colleges and universities, including what we may call the eminent institutions, have either announced or instituted a revised curriculum; 1946 is a year in which Mr. Hutchins' pronunciamentos on the fall of man have been accelerated in tempo.

In brief, 1946 is a year in which American education is attempting to fix a new pattern of education. It is the most widespread curriculum revision since the day of Charles W. Eliot, and it is likely to determine the direction of education for at least the next generation.

Therefore, I want to look at two of these recommendations for curriculum change, two that are widely known and that reflect the thinking of a large area of traditionalism in education, and I want to estimate their implications.

The first is that proposed by Mr. Hutchins. Mr. Hutchins, of course, is a curious cross between Peck's Bad Boy in education and a lonely, austere Savonarola who thunders, "Repent ye, or be doomed!" His tenets are these:

1. The human race is either about to destroy itself, or to survive under a "peace more horrible than war"—unless we change our present system of education, drastically and at once.

2. To save the human race from this ill-fated alternative, we must abandon vocational education in the schools, and make all education a liberal education "for the common vocation of citizenship."

3. The core of this liberal education is not to be found in a study of modern science or social science, or in focusing on the contemporary problems that beset man. It is to be had in the study of Great Books of the past—let us say, Homer and Thucydides, Virgil and Augustine. Somewhere along the line I either read or heard a speech of Mr. Hutchins in which he said that the curriculum he proposed would not be essentially altered over the period of one hundred years, or even one thousand years. Pure knowledge, because it was pure, was not defiled by time. I believe I am not doing Mr. Hutchins an injustice by saying that this is an inherent part of his plan of education.

Now Mr. Hutchins' faith is appealing. He is so earnest and so unashamed that you cannot help but admire him. In the midst of a modern world, created for the most part by the educators who rebelled against the ascetic pattern of education—I assume it is understood by persons in this room that the scientific and economic foundations of modern society were laid by educators who broke away from the classical tradition—Mr. Hutchins repeats without apology an old refrain:

> Faith of our fathers, living still,
> In spite of dungeon, fire, and sword: . . .
> We will be true to thee til death!

He stirs in us old memories. We want to believe him. Perhaps we want to believe him because he calls to us with a childlike faith. Perhaps also we want to believe him because his is a *simple* faith, and we are hungry for simplicity. So many of our problems are complex. We want to get back to the days when life was simple, or we thought it was simple.

But we cannot quite give our intellectual assent to Mr. Hutchins. If it were wholly an act of faith, we might go along; but reason compels us to pause. Perhaps too we remember that warning spoken by Dr. Donald B. Tresidder, once an eminent physician and now president of Stanford University. Said Dr. Tresidder to a group of educators last May at which Mr. Hutchins was present: "I have long been interested in Robert Hutchins—from a *medical* point of view!"

Essentially, Mr. Hutchins' grand scheme of education breaks down at that point which Ortega y Gassett calls "historic reason." Gassett has pointed out that when a people think effectively, they think in terms of their historic past, and they use "historic reason." Mr. Hutchins, in calling upon the faith of his fathers, denies historic reason.

He would take us back to the educational concept of the early Middle Ages, to a pattern of education that closed the Platonic schools, and rested *its* learning on the Sacred Book of the Past —with the result that the intellectual world was frozen for one thousand years. It was not inevitable that we have the Middle Ages. Part of the responsibility for it rests on those educators who closed the Platonic schools and anticipated Mr. Hutchins by fifteen hundred years. They were the original worshipers of great books.

Mr. Hutchins is seemingly unaware that the educational gospel he preaches was also the dominant theme of education in the oldest of all civilizations—that of China—and that its effect was to still the spirit of inquiry in the Chinese mind, or at least to prevent its ever arising, and that this pattern of education was perhaps the single most influential factor in the slow withering of what otherwise might have become a great civilization. Again, it was not inevitable that China should be as it is today. Part of that responsibility rests on those educators of China twenty-five hundred years ago who fixed on China the pattern of education that Mr. Hutchins would fix on us.

Thomas Jefferson warned us against Mr. Hutchins' doctrine a century and a quarter ago. At the age of seventy-three, when many minds look backward instead of forward, Jefferson wrote urgently that ". . . institutions must go hand in hand with the progress of the human mind . . . . as new discoveries are made . . . institutions must advance also, and keep pace with the times"; and he warned against any society remaining "ever under the regimen of their ancestors."

Ralph Waldo Emerson repeated that warning 109 years ago. Speaking before the Phi Beta Kappa Society of Harvard, he said bluntly:

> Each age, it is found, must write its own books. . . . Meek young men grow up in libraries, believing it their duty to accept the views which Cicero, which Locke, which Bacon, have given; forgetful that Cicero, Locke, and Bacon were only young men in libraries when they wrote these books.
>
> Hence, instead of Man Thinking, we have the bookworm.

Mr. Hutchins' plan of bookworm education fails in the test of historic reason.

Next, I would like to look at the Harvard Report on *General Education in a Free Society*. I began reading that Report before the printer's ink on it was decently dry. I had been waiting for its appearance for almost a year. I think I can truthfully say I started reading it with excitement. I expected something of the institution that had produced Charles W. Eliot, who touched off the educational changes of the late nineteenth century.

Well, one is not wholly disappointed in the Harvard Report. In many respects it is what one would expect from Harvard: scholarly, thorough, and at times brilliant. *But it is characterized by the limitations of the Harvard institutional mind*, limitations from which Charles Eliot had been wholly free (and from which the Harvard scientists are free today). I do not mean to imply that the institutional mind of Harvard is a separate and distinct species. It is rather a particularized pattern of the academic institutional mind, but it *is* characterized by its own particular limitations. These limitations, for example, are seen in the historical writings of those Harvard historians, Albert Bushnell Hart and Edward Channing, as contrasted with their Harvard successor, A. M. Schlesinger, who was educated at Ohio State and Columbia. It was the pattern of mind dealt with by Vernon L. Parrington, himself a Harvard man, in his *Main Currents in American Thought*.

But if you want to meet the Harvard institutional mind at its best, you will find it in John P. Marquand's delightful satire, the Pulitzer Prize-winning novel of 1938, *The Late George Apley*. Marquand understood the type of mind that produced the Harvard Report, and he satirized it in a wicked and delightful manner. To anyone who plans to read that Report, I recommend first reading *The Late George Apley*. Having done that, you can read more discerningly between the lines of the Report:

Dear John: [wrote the late George Apley to his son] When I come I want you to take me to some of the new plays, and please don't feel that I shall be shocked by them. Your father can stand a good deal.

And again:

Dear John: . . . Yesterday I found that your mother had actually taken this [Sigmund] Freud book out of the Athenaeum. She was embarrassed when I found her reading it . . . , and gave as her reason that she wished to know what [your sister] Eleanor was doing. I am now reading it for the same reason.

Throughout the Harvard Report there is this shocked acceptance of the *present*, a resentment that we are living today instead of yesterday. In the allied Harvard Report made in 1942 on *The Training of Secondary School Teachers Especially with Reference to English*, this resentment against having to live today produces the following incredibly delightful statement:

> *Unfortunately* [italics mine], however, there is another element . . . —and this is the mass-communication of the newspapers, magazines, movies, and (especially) the radio. The tendency of all of them . . . is to cajole and lull readers, onlookers or listeners into a permanent state of unquestioning receptivity; to prevent their becoming reasoning, critical beings.

The late George Apley said exactly the same thing in the same overtones:

> Dear John: I wish there weren't quite so many new ideas. Where do they come from? . . . I try to think what is in back of them and speculation often disturbs my sleep.

This attempt to deny the existence of the present, or at least a resentment against having to deal with it, is the underlying philosophy of the latter half of the Harvard Report. It states and adheres to the premise that one of the purposes of education is to free the student from the tyranny of the present. We all agree with that, of course. I want to make that very clear. There is no understanding the present without knowing a significant part of the past. That is precisely what I had in mind in quoting Ortega y Gassett that we think effectively only when we think in terms of the historic past and use "historic reason." I believe that. But the effect of the Harvard Report is to free the student from the tyranny of the present by fixing on him the tyranny of the past. To some of us, tyranny in any form is bad.

It was against this tyranny of the past in education that Thomas Jefferson struck when he turned his back on his own alma mater, William and Mary, and established the new University of Virginia—to break the grip of the dead hand of the past that smothered living learning.

It was against this tyranny of the past that Charles Francis Adams II protested to Harvard University itself in a year when he was a member of the Harvard Board of Overseers. Of the education he had received at Harvard he said:

> No matter how long I may live, I shall never be able . . . to overcome some of the great disadvantages which the . . . wrong theories and

worse practices of my *alma mater* inflicted upon me. And not on me alone. . . . We were college graduates; and yet how many of us could follow out a line of sustained, close thought, expressing ourselves in clear concise terms?

It is one thing to study the past. It is another to be smothered by it.

I want to make it clear that much of the Harvard Report is good—is in fact very good. Especially, it seems to me, that its statement of the traits of mind that constitute education are the best I have ever read. These abilities are, the Report states:

> . . . *to think effectively, to communicate thought, to make relevant judgments, to discriminate among values.* They are not in practice separable and are not to be developed in isolation.

Its exposition of these abilities is profound and penetrating. For example, it recognizes three aspects of effective thinking: (1) Logical thinking, or "the capacity to extract universal truths from particular cases and, in turn, to infer particulars from general laws." (2) Relational thinking, or the "understanding of complex and fluid situations, in dealing with which logical methods are inadequate . . . thinking in a context." (3) The element of imagination in thinking, which is "distinctive in the thinking of the poet" and may be described as neither straight thinking, nor crooked thinking, but as "curved thinking." This part of the Report states explicitly that "education is not merely the imparting of knowledge but the cultivation of certain aptitudes and attitudes."

If the Report adhered to this throughout, it would be the greatest document on education of the twentieth century. Its failure is that it does not. Having set this as the qualities of mind to be developed by education, the Report then—curiously and without explanation—settles back on the orthodox curriculum divisions of the natural sciences, the social sciences, and the humanities. From that point it ceases to offer any further original or profound contribution.

One is at loss to explain the inconsistency, or shall we say the failure to follow through. Was it because the two parts of the Report were developed by two subcommittees which, being unable to reconcile their differences, simply let them stand unreconciled? Or was the committee a victim of structural monism, seeking for a unified simplicity? At any rate it settled back on a structural unity, simple but adequate, of natural sciences, social sciences, and humanities.

Basically the weakness of Mr. Hutchins' grand scheme and of the latter part of Harvard Report is that they rest tacitly on the assumption that knowledge is power. "Give students knowledge," they say in effect, "and they will be able to think effectively, to communicate thought, to make relevant judgments, and to discriminate among values." No one questions this need for knowledge, not in the least, but knowledge alone does not enable people to think effectively, to communicate thought, or make relevant judgments, or discriminate among values. Having the knowledge is not enough. There must be added ability to *use* that knowledge.

In every crisis of the twentieth century there has existed enough knowledge in the world to solve it. But it was not in the right place at the right time. That is another way of saying that it could not be *communicated* to the point needed at the time needed.

Twice before I have referred to Ortega y Gassett's insistence on the importance of "historic reason." Let me use it now in specific instance. In his *A Short History of the British Commonwealth* Ramsey Muir, one of the most competent of English historians, at the close of his discussion of the English Civil War, set forth one of the issues of modern education. He had just finished the account of this conflict which rent the English people three hundred years ago. It was a conflict between two political forces that rejected compromise. The Royalists had lost, their king had been executed, their leaders had been proscribed, and Cromwell had been made dictator. The Puritans had won a victory as complete as any victory by force can ever be won. Yet at Cromwell's death five years later, the fruits of victory were lost and the Stuart kings were restored to the throne. It was a conflict in which the Puritans lost in the end *because* they had won the war. After describing this, Muir came to his momentous statement:

The war had taught the English people "that even the noblest and the most enlightened aims are vitiated and will eventually be frustrated if those who advocate them try to secure their victory by force, and not by discussion and persuasion. These [discussion and persuasion] were to be henceforth the characteristic notes of the growth of free institutions in the British Commonwealth."

The British people learned that in the seventeenth century, not through their educational system, but through war and dictatorship. What it thus learned is what every democracy must teach to every successive generation: *That democracy rests on discussion and persuasion, that its people shall discuss their problems and reach an intelligent consensus, that they shall not goose-step to military commands, nor yield to mob law.*

There are two kinds of nations in the world today, only two: those who in crises want to *shoot* it out, and those who have learned how to *talk* it out. There are these two kinds, no more. They are the democratic nations, and the totalitarian nations. That is the essence of what Macaulay meant when he made the famous statement that "Parliamentary government is government by speaking."

Now the education of each successive generation in this process, always essential to democracy, has now become essential to the survival in its present form of what we choose to call civilization. Uranium 235—and its derivative, plutonium—have brought us exactly to that point. Either we accept it, or accept the alternative given by Reuben Gustavson: "I believe in one uranium atom, divisible, with oblivion for all."

The England described by Muir could develop this by methods not to be relied on today. To paraphrase Disraeli, it was a government, "by the few, and the very few.' Only one man in ten had the right to vote, and none of the women. But the gentlemen of England who ran that government had been trained in the home, trained also by tutors, and trained, finally, in college—not only to communicate their ideas effectively, but also to *settle their differences by talk*. That was the core of their democracy.

Today, in contrast, we have universal suffrage. This is simply another way of saying that *the nine men in ten who did not vote three hundred years ago now control the government.* Yet we have not developed any system comparable to the home-tutor-college training among the gentlemen of England for educating the whole electorate of today in the use of discussion as an instrument for making group decisions. The Hutchins scheme and the Harvard Report fail entirely to provide in any way for this inherent feature on which democracy now rests and has always rested.

These educators are irked by the present. They want to escape from it by living in the past. But the relentless pressure of the present cannot be escaped by ignoring it. Consider one aspect of this pressure of the present. The radio and talking picture now carry the human voice around the world. They have become the most powerful instruments in existence for mass education and mass thought-stimulation, for people today hear and are influenced by the voices from Hollywood, Washington, London, Rome, and Moscow. The sheer existence of the radio determines to a large degree our choice of national rulers. It exerts a constant influence on the operation of democratic government. Is it asking too much that educators in this Year of Decision face the fact frankly that these inventions compel a reappraisal of some of the older methods of education that were based on the primacy of the printed page?

What do Hutchins and the Harvard committee say should be done about these forces of mass education and mass thought-stimulation? Nothing. Nothing at all. They not only fail to recognize the new form of an old force. They failed to recognize the old force itself. The only reference I can find to the radio or moving pictures appears in the 1942 Harvard Report on the training of English teachers. I quote: "The recommended program contains no element of special training . . . in such instruments of education as the radio and the moving pictures."

I don't want to be facetious, but the general impression I get from the Harvard Report is that the teaching, let us say, of Beowulf is highly acceptable in a modern curriculum, and that one may devote a substantial part of time in college to pursuing the pronunciation of the phoneme [i] in Wessex during the late twelfth century—or indeed anything that comes out of the past, just so long as it can be examined in terms of course content. The fact that "much of yesterday's wisdom is today's banality and tomorrow's baloney" does not trouble the framers of this Report.

But I submit that an inherent part of education is to be able to *do* something, as well as to *know* something. I submit further that every educated person ought to know when a thing is proved and when it is not proved, should know how to investigate and to analyze a proposition that confronts him, and how to search for a solution, how to talk about it effectively before others, and how to contribute to a discussion on problems of joint interest.

Above all, I submit that any educational system should produce an understanding in the next generation—and here I am quoting Eric Hodgins, vice president of Time, Inc.—

. . . that clear and understandable communication between man and man is the most important necessity in the material world; that wars, plagues, pestilences, and famines are eventually to be done away with only through this means. Here indeed is a proposition on which free and Christian mankind can unite as upon almost nothing else.

Mr. Hutchins' grand scheme and the Harvard Report stop short of this vital aspect of education. They fall short, therefore, of offering a full philosophy of general education in a free society.

It is our duty in this Year of Decision to see that this omission shall not go unnoticed and unchallenged.

Here perhaps I ought to stop. But there is one thing more I want to say, a reference to a fact that ought to make every educator uneasy in conscience, namely, the grave indictment against education that *those great political and social upheavals which have marked the history of man have been too largely caused by men of education. The French Revolution, the American Revolution, the Jeffersonian Revolution, the Jacksonian Revolution— and I forbear to mention political disturbances of the past twenty years—represent upheavals in which the underprivileged and undereducated were compelled to overthrow the dominion of the privileged and educated.* I grant that leadership in these movements came from a few, a very few, of the educated class. I remind you that the majority of the so-called educated people stood against change, until much of the violence of these upheavals came from delayed pressure which the educated people had helped to create.

To what extent was this due to the kind of education given them in school—that study of the dead past *as* a dead past, the curriculum criticized by Jefferson as "the regimen of their ancestors," the educational practices branded by Charles Francis Adams as the "wrong theories and worse practices . . . inflicted upon me. And not on me alone"?

The concept of Greek education was, "Know thyself." The concept of some of educational planners today is, "Know the Greeks," or "Know the novelists of the nineteenth century, including the obscure ones."

I heard a man who calls himself an educator say the other day, "All right, we can make an atomic bomb. So what? That has nothing to do with the college curriculum." That our educational system could produce such a man is an indictment of that system.

RELIGION

THE GLORY AND TRAGEDY OF MAN [1]

JOHN SUTHERLAND BONNELL [2]

Dr. John Sutherland Bonnell gave this radio sermon on Sunday, February 2, 1947, over the American Broadcasting Company network. The address was the first in the 1947 series to be given by this Presbyterian clergyman.

Dr. Bonnell has been pastor of the Fifth Avenue Presbyterian Church since 1935. He has attracted large audiences and much favorable note by his pulpit eloquence and sermonizing ability. He has also established a reputation as a radio speaker.

His sermon method is conservative. He usually uses a text, quotes extensively from the Bible, grounds many of his illustrations on the Bible or literature, and constructs his sermon in a typical homiletic pattern.

Although he constantly reflects the problems of the hour, he does not absorb himself in political or social issues. Neither is he evangelical. He commands wide influence by his pulpit intelligence, his persuasive personality and his efficiency (force, clear-cut enunciation, good voice quality) in delivery.

I am deeply grateful to the American Broadcasting Company for the privilege of addressing you on National Vespers each Sunday until the end of May. It is a distinct honor to be given a place on this program, which has become almost inseparably associated with the name of Dr. Harry Emerson Fosdick. My immediate predecessor with whom I am privileged to share this program, Bishop G. Bromley Oxnam, has served with distinction, and I in common with many others have been benefited by his deeply spiritual messages.

In dealing today with the subject "The Glory and Tragedy of Man" I am reminded of a conference I had recently with a

[1] Issued by the Department of Religious Radio of the National Broadcasting Company. Reprinted through the courtesy of Dr. Bonnell and of the National Broadcasting Company.

[2] For biographical note see Appendix.

group of young, eager, intelligent high school students. In the course of the discussion a sixteen-year-old girl turned to me suddenly and asked: "Honestly, do you believe that in twenty years' time there will be any world at all?"

The average adult has little understanding of how heavily the burden of this grim question bears upon the minds of thoughtful young people to-day.

One recalls the observation of a prominent writer: "The atomic age is here to stay, but are we?"

Nearly every week there comes to my desk a magazine or a news-letter with the prediction that World War III has now become inevitable.

I sometimes wonder if the people who make these statements have any adequate realization of what they are saying. In effect, they declare that a new cycle of devastative wars will shortly begin.

We are lost if we settle down into a mood of hopeless fatalism or accept the collective insanity of war as the only solution of international problems. Shall we tell the young men who have come back to America from battle fronts all over the world that a new war is inevitable? Was it for this that our sons fought in the cold and mud of the Italian mountainsides or flung their bodies against the concrete and steel defenses of Normandy? Was it for this that they battled on the islands of the Pacific or languished in the prison camps of Japan? Shall we say to them: "All your sacrifice, all your magnificent services to your country, all your valor has been expended in vain; we must begin to prepare a new generation for the next global war"? That would be a betrayal of the living and the dead.

Listen to these prophetic words from a letter written by Lieut. Gordon R. De Blois eight days before he was killed in action in Italy:

This is what I am afraid of, Mother and Dad. I am afraid that the day peace is declared, people are going to return to their own narrow aspirations and lives and forget all those swell lads that didn't come back, by refusing to sacrifice and work for a better world. All that I pray for is that we who are here shall not be forgotten when the war is over. I pray that our sacrifice will not have been in vain, and that in another few years the world will not be drowned in blood again.

Each and every one of these prophecies of inevitable war is conditioning the minds of men and women to accept this ghastly alternative to understanding and peace.

We need not look far to find the reason for the almost universal pessimism. Millions of people are discouraged today because the peace has not been fashioned more quickly.

Any one who thinks realistically at all might know that we cannot convulse the world in a universal struggle for almost six years and then expect a rapid and easy peace.

There is another reason why gloom has settled on men's hearts. We had come to believe that man is capable of achieving anything to which he puts his hand; that he has become as powerful as God. It is a bitter and humiliating experience to find that the resources of human wisdom and human ingenuity are not sufficient to perform the colossal tasks confronting us. False hopes have been encouraged by a deceptive belief in human self-sufficiency by a philosophy which affirms that we don't need God any longer.

This attitude has penetrated into every area of thought in our Western civilization.

You may recall that a spokesman for this viewpoint who is a professor of an American university told us some time ago that we ought to have a moratorium on God for about thirty years so that men could build the brave new world of their dreams. We must all believe in the potentialities latent in every man, but we have blundered into deifying him.

Faith in man rather than faith in God has been further promoted by the phenomenal advance of science. Has it ever occurred to you that in George Washington's day the wheel moved no faster than it did in the time of the Roman Emperors? The most startling advances of science have come within the last one hundred and fifty years. The minds of men have been bewildered and dazzled by the splendors of scientific advance. Consequently, for many science has become a god and millions bow down at its shrine.

A group of religious leaders expressed their boundless faith in man in these words:

Man is at last becoming aware that he alone is responsible for the realization of the world of his dreams, and that he has within himself the power for its achievement. He must set intelligence and will to the task.

Then they sang Swinburne's "Hymn to Man":

Glory to man in the highest, for man is the master of things.

Well, what has happened to him now? Where is man's vaunted mastery? During the lifetime of most of us man has demonstrated his mastery in ruin and death. His wisdom today is baffled; his resources of good will are depleted, and the glowing hopes of fifteen years ago have vanished.

If human wisdom and understanding were all that we possess the future would be dark indeed.

John Flavel, in the seventeenth century, said: "Man's extremity is God's opportunity." That statement is true of our time. We are in extremity now; we are baffled, frustrated, defeated, desperately afraid of what the next ten years will bring.

Yes, this is God's opportunity, and some men and women who have given little thought to God in the last twenty years are turning to Him now. Hundreds of thousands have taken the trouble to send a postcard to one Christian Laymen's Organization pledging themselves to pray every day for leaders of our own and other nations. But we still have a long way to go before God is given His rightful place in the hearts of men.

In the eighth Psalm light is shed upon man's present predicament. The author of this spiritual poem doubtless caught his inspiration as he stood on the heights of Mount Zion looking up into the Syrian night. The sun had gone to rest behind the western hills as he watched the stars stepping forth one by one into the canopy of space as the army of heaven marshaled its hosts.

Marveling at the wonder of it, and the greatness of the Creator who had fashioned it all, he chanced to look down far below him and saw the twinkling lights of Jerusalem, man's lights as contrasted with God's.

He thought of man with his prejudices and passions, his loves and his hates, his failures and his sins, and said:

When I consider Thy heavens, the work of Thy fingers, the moon and the stars, which Thou hast ordained; what is man, that Thou art mindful of him or the son of man that Thou visiteth him?

But despite man's insignificance in comparison with the universe around him, the Psalmist knew that the Creator had endowed him with God-like powers.

Thou hast made him [continued the Psalmist] a little lower than the angels [or, as the Revised Version puts it, "a little lower than God"] and crowned him with glory and honor. Thou madest him to have dominion over the works of Thy hands; Thou hast put all things under his feet.

In other words, God has invested man with some of His own glory and power. He has made him king on earth with dominion over the whole of creation. The spirit of man is akin to the Eternal Creative Spirit. He bears the likeness of God. If that kinship were not a fact there could be no such thing as science. Man possesses in his own mind the key that unlocks the mysteries of the universe, and so he harnesses the forces of nature to do his bidding.

Again, without this kinship there could be no such thing as revelation, for God could not then manifest Himself to man and man could not enter into fellowship with God.

These facts are man's glory; his tragedy lies in his inability to see or his refusal to acknowledge what the Psalmist emphasizes: that man's greatness and power is all derived from God.

Just as surely as he proclaims his creed of self-sufficiency and his independence of his Creator, man's disintegration and destruction begins.

Make no mistake about it, the moral disease that afflicts mankind today is not confined to international relations as many people think. It has affected every area of human life.

One hears people ask: "Why cannot France, and Britain, and the United States, and Russia come to terms? Why can't they reach an harmonious understanding? What is the matter with them anyway?"

But there are other questions to be asked: "Why can't labor and management come to some understanding instead of repeatedly dislocating the entire life of this nation? Why are so many homes breaking up? Why has the divorce rate increased to a volume that imperils the foundations of our national life? Why are clinics of psychiatrists and studies of ministers crowded with men and women seeking a solution to their unsolved personal problems? What is the matter with us?"

The trouble exists not only in the international field; it is in the human heart. Basically, it arises from selfishness, greed, the determination to have our own way at whatever the cost. In every area we seek to be a law unto ourselves. We have left God out of our lives, and we are now paying the penalty for it.

In the second Psalm the revolt against God is depicted:

The kings of the earth set themselves, and the rulers take counsel together, against the Lord, and against his anointed, saying: Let us break their bands asunder, and cast away their cords from us.

A seldom-quoted poem which was written more than half a century ago depicts with no little faithfulness present-day life.

> Our life is like a narrow raft,
> Afloat upon the hungry sea,
> Whereon is but a little space,
> And each man eager for a place,
> Doth thrust his brother in the sea,
> And so the sea is salt with tears,
> And so our life is worn with fears.

What we see in the modern world is not the rule of God, but the rule of self, with all the tragedy that this involves for mankind.

During the fall of 1927, almost twenty years ago, I heard Sir Oliver Lodge, a noted British physicist, deliver a lecture on the atom. Little did I dream then what startling developments the next two decades would bring.

"The time is coming," said Oliver Lodge, "when science will be able to release the incalculable forces bound up in the heart of atom." Then he stooped and picked up a small object from the table beside him, and, holding it in his hands, he said: "There is more energy in this bit of matter if it could be released than can be produced today by all the coal mines in Britain."

The great scientist paused, and in solemn tones continued: "Please God, the discovery will not be made in our time, because humanity is not ready for it."

Well, for good or ill, the discovery has been made in our time. Man can now turn the whole world into a wilderness or he can make the desert rejoice and blossom as the rose. He can accomplish his own destruction or he can use these mighty forces to drive back the frontiers of disease and death, and lift the burden from the backs of toilers everywhere.

In this fateful hour the teachings of Jesus are triumphantly vindicated. The nations of the world must either live by the golden rule or perish from the earth. We must love our neighbors as ourselves, or succumb to mutual destruction.

There is but one Personality on the world's horizon great enough to unite all classes, races, and nations of men into one family of God. The words of Jesus Christ come sounding down the centuries in accents of warning and of hope:

Whosoever heareth these sayings of mine and doeth them, I will liken him unto a wise man, which built his house upon a rock.

SIGNS OF OUR TIMES [3]

FULTON J. SHEEN [4]

The Right Rev. Monsignor Fulton J. Sheen, of the Catholic University of America, gave this sermon, the first in a series of seventeen, on the Catholic Hour on January 26, 1947. The Catholic Hour was initiated in 1930 by the National Council of Catholic Men. Father Sheen was the first speaker on this program and continues to give a considerable number of the sermons each year.

The program is given each Sunday throughout the year over the National Broadcasting network and has an outlet through more than one hundred stations. The preachers are invariably leaders in the pulpit, and the sacred music is provided by a unit of the Paulist choir. Reports the National Council of Catholic Men: "A current average of 41,000 audience letters a month, about twenty per cent of which come from listeners of other faiths, gives some indication of its popularity and influence."

Father Sheen has established himself as perhaps the leading Catholic preacher of present-day America. His voice is rich, flexible, now calm and conversational, now deeply emotional. He is an orator, but he uses his voice to full advantage over the radio.

His sermons are well constructed and expressed. They are often polemical as he analyzes the current national and international political and social scenes. His religious philosophy is logically organized and expressed. He accompanies it with strong personal appeal. [5]

God Love You!

I want those to be my first words of greeting to you as they will be the concluding words of each broadcast. They embody three ideas: God is Love; God loves you; and since love is reciprocal may you love God in return.

This is the seventeenth year I have had the privilege of addressing you on the Catholic Hour and it is probably safe to say that at no time in those years—not even during the war when we saw victory ahead—have the souls of men been more in the dark about the future, less insecure about the present. We are

[3] Permission to reprint this sermon through the courtesy of Rt. Rev. Msgr. Fulton J. Sheen, The National Council of Catholic Men, the Catholic Hour, and the National Broadcasting Company.

[4] For biographical note see Appendix.

[5] See also *Representative American Speeches: 1938-1939*. p. 245-52; *1942-1943*. p. 299-304.

living in the twilight of a civilization, and for that reason, we have entitled this series *Light Your Lamps*. Under this title we will discuss in eleven broadcasts a subject which we were unable to discuss the last few years, and it will be that which is contained in the Papal Encyclical *Divini Redemptoris*: the all important subject of Communism.

It is very difficult to do justice to any phase of this encyclical in the sixteen minutes allotted to me, so this year I shall write a much fuller treatment of each broadcast which will be put into pamphlet form and which the National Council of Catholic Men will send to you free each week if you make your request known to them.

Why is it that so few realize the seriousness of our present crisis? Partly because men do not want to believe their own times are wicked, partly because it involves too much self-accusation and principally because they have no standards outside of themselves by which to measure their times. If there is no fixed concept of justice how shall men know it is violated? Only those who live by faith really know what is happening in the world. The great masses without faith are unconscious of the destructive processes going on. The tragedy is not that the hairs of our civilization are gray; it is rather our failure to see that they are. The very day Sodom was destroyed, Scripture describes the sun as bright; Balthasar's realm came to an end in darkness; people saw Noah preparing for the flood one hundred and twenty years before it came, but men would not believe. In the midst of seeming prosperity, world-unity, the decree to the angels goes forth but the masses go on their sordid routines. As Our Lord said:

For as in the days before the flood, they were eating and drinking, marrying and giving in marriage, even till that day in which Noe entered into the ark, and they knew not till the flood came, and took them all away; so also shall the the coming of the Son of man be. (*Matthew* 24:38, 39)

Well may Our Saviour say to us what He said to the Saducees and Pharisees in His time:

When it is evening, you say: It will be fair weather, for the sky is red. And in the morning: Today there will be a storm, for the sky is red and lowering. You know then how to discern the face of the sky: and can you not know the signs of the times? (*Matthew* 16:2, 3)

Do we know the signs of these appointed times? Most of us are afraid to face the unpalatable fact that not a single *positive* major objective for which we fought this war has been achieved. Few realize that barbarism is not only outside us, but beneath us, that science by making us spectators of reality has blinded us to the necessity of being actors, while the atomic bomb by putting human power in our hands has hidden the weakness of our hearts.

The signs of our times point to two inescapable truths, the first of which is that we have come to the end of the post-Renaissance Chapter of history which made man the measure of all things. More particularly the three basic dogmas of the modern world are dissolving before our very eyes. We are witnessing: (1) The liquidation of the economic man, or the assumption that man who is a highly developed animal has no other function in life than to produce and acquire wealth, and then like the cattle in the pastures, be filled with years and die. (2) The liquidation of the idea of the natural goodness of man who has no need of a God to give him rights, or a Redeemer to salvage him from guilt, because progress is automatic thanks to science—education and evolution, which will one day make man a kind of a god as H. G. Wells said, with his feet on the earth and his hands among the stars. (3) The liquidation of rationalism, or the idea that the purpose of human reason is not to discover the meaning and the goal of life, namely the salvation of the soul, but merely to devise new technical advances to make on this earth a city of man to displace the city of God.

We are witnessing the death of Historical Liberalism (and I shall in these broadcasts always understand Liberalism as such) which like a sundial is unable to tell the time in the dark and which can function only in a society whose basis is moral and when the flotsam and jetsam of Christianity is still drifting about the world. Historical Liberalism is a parasite on a Christian Civilization and once that body upon which it clings ceases to be the leaven of society, then Liberalism itself must perish. The individual liberties which Liberalism emphasizes are secure only when the community is moral and can give an ethical foundation to these liberties. It may very well be that Historical Liberalism is only a transitional era in history between a civilization which was Christian and one which will be definitely anti-Christian.

The second great truth to which the signs of the times portend is that we are definitely at the end of a non-religious era of civilization, which regarded religion as an addendum to life, a pious extra, a morale-builder for the individual but of no social relevance, an ambulance that took care of the wrecks of the social order until science reached a point where there would be no more wrecks; which called on God only as a defender of national ideals, or as a silent partner whose name was used by the firm to give respectability but who had nothing to say about how the business should be run.

The new era into which we are entering is what might be called the religious phase of human history. But do not misunderstand; by religious we do not mean that men will turn to God, but rather that the indifference to the absolute which characterized the liberal phase of civilization will be succeeded by a passion for an absolute. From now on the struggle will be not for the colonies and national rights, but for the souls of men. There will be no more half-drawn swords, no divided loyalties, no broad strokes of sophomoric tolerance; there will not even be any more great heresies, for they are based on a partial acceptance of truth. The battle lines are already being clearly drawn and the basic issues are no longer in doubt. From now on men will divide themselves into two religions—understood again as surrender to an absolute. The conflict of the future is between the absolute who is the God-man and the absolute which is the man God; the God Who became man and the man who make himself God; brothers in Christ and comrades in anti-Christ.

The anti-Christ will not be so called; otherwise he would have no followers. He will wear no red tights, nor vomit sulphur, nor carry a trident nor wave an arrow tail as the Mephistopheles in Faust. This masquerade has helped the devil convince men that he does not exist, for he knows that he is never so strong as when men believe that he does not exist.

When no man recognizes, the more power he exercises. God has defined Himself as "I am Who am" and the Devil as "I am who am not."

Nowhere in Sacred Scripture do we find warrant for the popular myth of the devil as a buffoon who is dressed like the first "red." Rather is he described as an angel fallen from heaven, and as "the Prince of this world" whose business it is to tell us that there is no other world. His logic is simple: if there is no heaven there is no hell; if there is no hell, then there is no sin; if there is no sin, then there is no judge, and if there is no judgment then evil is good and good is evil.

But above all these descriptions, Our Lord tells us that He will be so much like Himself, that he would deceive even the elect—and certainly no devil we have ever seen in picture books could deceive even the elect. How will he come in this new age to win followers to his religion? He will come disguised as the Great Humanitarian; he will talk peace, prosperity and plenty not as means to lead us to God, but as ends in themselves. He will write books on the new idea of God to suit the way people live; induce faith in astrology so as to make not the will but the stars responsible for sins; he will explain Guilt away psychologically as inhibited eroticism, make men shrink in shame if their fellowmen say they are not broad-minded and liberal; he will be so broadminded as to identify tolerance with indifference to right and wrong, truth and error; he will spread the lie that men will never be better until they make society better and thus have selfishness to provide fuel for the next revolution; he will foster science but only to have armament makers use one marvel of science to destroy another; he will foster more divorces under the disguise that another partner is "vital"; he will increase love for love and decrease love for person; he will invoke religion to destroy religion; he will even speak of Christ and say that he was the greatest *man* who ever lived; his mission he will say will be to liberate men from the servitudes of superstition and Fascism, which he will never define; he will organize children's games, tell people who they should and should not marry and unmarry, who should bear children and who should not; he will benevolently draw chocolate bars from his pockets for the little ones and bottles of milk for the Hottentots; he will tempt Christians with the same three temptations with which he tempted Christ: The temptation to turn stones into bread as an earthly Messias will become the temptation to sell freedom for security, as bread became a political weapon, and only those who think his way may eat; the temptation to work a miracle by recklessly throwing Himself from a steeple will become a plea to desert the lofty pinnacles of truth where faith and reason reign, for those lower depths where the masses live on slogans and propaganda. He wants no proclamation of immutable principles from the lofty heights of a Church, but mass organization through propaganda where only a common man directs the idiosyncrasies of common men. Opinions, not truths; commentators, not teachers; Gallop polls, not principles; nature, not grace—and to these golden calves will men toss themselves from their Christ.

The third temptation, in which Satan asked Christ to adore him and all the Kingdoms of the world would be his, will become the temptation to have a new religion without a Cross, a liturgy without a world to come, a city of man without a city of God, a religion to invoke a religion, or a politics which is a religion—one that renders unto Caesar even the things that are God's.

In the midst of all his seeming love for humanity and his glib talk of freedom and equality, he will have one great secret which he will tell to no one; he will not believe in God. Because his religion will be brotherhood without the fatherhood of God, he will deceive even the elect.

He will set up a counterchurch which will be the ape of the Church because he, the devil, is the ape of God. It will have all the notes and characteristics of the Church, but in reverse and emptied of its divine content. It will be a mystical body of the anti-Christ that will in all externals resemble the mystical body of Christ. In desperate need for God, whom he nevertheless refuses to adore, modern man in his loneliness and frustration will hunger more and more for membership in a community that will give him enlargement of purpose, but at the cost of losing himself in some vague collectivity. There will be verified the paradox, that the very objections with which men in the last century rejected the Church will be the reasons why they will now accept the counter-Church.

The last century rejected the Church because it was infallible; it refused to believe that any so-called Vicar of Christ could be immune from error when he spoke on matters of faith and morals as chief shepherd of Christendom. But the twentieth century will join the counter-Church because it claims to be infallible when its visible head speaks *ex cathedra* from Moscow on the subject of economics and politics, and as chief shepherd of world Communism.

The Church was critically spurned in the last few centuries because it claimed that it was Catholic and universal, uniting all men on the basis of one Lord, one faith and one Baptism. No man, the nineteenth century claimed, could be a good American, a good Frenchman or a good German if he accepted shepherding, albeit spiritual, from a spiritual head. But in the new era, what the modern lost soul will take particularly about the counter-Church, is that it is catholic or international. It breaks down all national boundaries, laughs down patriotism, dispenses men from piety to country which the Christ enjoined, makes men proud that they are not Americans, French, or British, but members of a revolutionary class under the rule of its Vicar who rules not from the Vatican, but the Kremlin.

The nineteenth century rejected the Church on the ground that it was intolerant, excommunicating heretics who did not accept the apostolic traditions, teaching as it did that Christ founded only one Church, that Truth is one, that its dogmas were like living things, and that like a babe, one had to accept the whole child or nothing. But in this evil hour, the sons and grandsons of those who so objected are embracing the counter-Church simply because it is intolerant, because it purges its heretics, liquidates its Trotskyites, and excommunicates all those who do not accept the party line that there may be not one fold and one shepherd, but one anthill and one ant-eater.

The Liberal world rejected the Church because it was too dogmatic with its exact definitions of Hypostatic Union and Immaculate Conception; too hierarchical with its bishops who derived their authority from the Apostles, and claimed to be guardians of the faith and morals of the people. But lo and behold, millions today are embracing the counter-Church for these reasons; they love its infallibly defined dogmas of Dialectical Materialism, Economic Determination and its Labor Theory of Value; they like its hierarchy or approved party leaders who as bishops of the new counter-Church derive authority from the Apostles, Marx and Lenin, and who in their role of secret police keep the errant in the party line, even indeed to the consummation of the world.

Because the signs of our times point to a struggle between absolutes we may expect the future to be a time of trials for two reasons: Firstly, to stop disintegration. Godlessness would go on and on if there were no catastrophes. What death is to a sinful person, that catastrophe is to an evil civilization: the interruption of its Godlessness. Why did God station an angel with a flaming sword at the Garden of Paradise after the Fall, if it were not to prevent our first parents from entering the garden and eating of the tree of life, which, if they ate they would have immortalized their evil. God will not allow unrighteousness to become eternal. Revolution, disintegration, chaos, must be reminders that our thinking has been wrong, our dreams have been unholy. Moral truth is vindicated by the ruin that follows when it has been repudiated. The chaos of our times is the strongest negative argument that could ever be advanced for Christianity. Catastrophe becomes a testimony to God's power in a meaningless world for by it God brings a meaningless existence to nought. The disintegration following an abandonment of God thus becomes a triumph of meaning, a reaffirmation of purpose. Adversity is the expression of God's condemnation of evil, the registering of Divine Judgment. As hell is not sin, but the effect of sin, so these disordered times are not sin, but the wages of sin. Catastrophe reveals that evil is self-defeating; we cannot turn from God without hurting ourselves.

The second reason why a crisis must come is in order to prevent a false identification of the Church and the world. Our

Lord intended that those who are His followers should be different in spirit from those who were not.

> I have taken you out of the world, therefore the world hateth you. (*John* 15:19)

Though this is the Divine intent it is unfortunately true that the line of demarcation between the followers of Christ and those who are not is often blotted out. Instead of black and white, there is only a blur. Mediocrity and compromise characterize the lives of many Christians. Many read the same novels as modern pagans, educate their children in the same godless way, listen to the same commentators who have no other standard than judging today by yesterday, and tomorrow by today, allow pagan practices such as divorce and remarriage to creep into the family; there are not wanting, so-called Catholic labor leaders recommending Communists for Congress, or Catholic writers who accept presidencies in Communist front organizations to instill totalitarian ideas in movies. There is no longer the conflict and opposition which is supposed to characterize us. We are influencing the world less than the world influences us. There is no apartness. Well indeed might St. Paul say to us what he said to the Corinthians (2 *Corinthians* 6:14, 15).

> What has innocence to do with lawlessness? What is there in common between light and darkness? What harmony between Christ and Belial?

St. Paul is here asserting that those who were sent out to establish a center of health had caught the disease; therefore, they lost the power to heal. Since the amalgamation of the Christian and the pagan spirit has set in, since the gold is married with an alloy, the entirety must be thrust into the furnace that the dross may be burned away. The value of the trial will be to set us apart. Evil must come to reject us, to despise us, to hate us, to persecute us, and then shall we define our loyalties, affirm our fidelities and state on whose side we stand. How shall the strong and weak trees be manifested unless the wind blows? Our quantity indeed will decrease, but our quality will increase. They shall be verified the words of Our Master:

> He that gathereth not with me, scattereth. (*Matthew* 12:30)

There are Times of Troubles and it is not so much a Third World War that is to be feared, as the re-birth of Leviathan, the coming of the Day of the Beast, when there will be no buying or selling unless men have been signed with the sign of the Beast who would devour the child of the Mother of Mothers. All great minds, non-Christian and Christian see these days as perilous. Spengler believed we are at the winter of civilization; Unamuno, at the end of a Christian culture; Fisher, at the death-rattle of European civilization; Sorokin, at the end of sensate culture; Berdyaev, at the end of the days of reason illumined by faith; Marx at, the collapse of capitalism; Lippmann, at an hour when men feel it is no longer wise, necessary, or useful to pass on to succeeding generations the good Christian heritage of the past; Toynbee, at the third stage of crisis in the Greek drama, the first which (Hybris) was pride that came from material prosperity showing itself in power; the second of which (Nemesis) was arrogance or contention against God, in which man arrogates to himself the attributes of Deity, and finally (Ate) disaster where Divine Justice will humble the vain pretension of man. Going back further, Lord Gray at the close of the First World War said that the lights were being put out of Europe and they would not be lighted again in our generation. Before that a great German poet and a Russian novelist warned people of the signs of the times. Writing in 1834 in *Religion and Philosophy in Germany*, Heine warned, look out for Germany when the Cross of Christ no longer casts its spell over His people.

Christianity has—and that is its fairest merit—somewhat mitigated that brutal German lust for battle. But it could not destroy it; and once the taming talisman, the Cross, is broken, the savagery of the old battlers will flare up again, the insane rage of which Nordic bards have so much to say and sing. That talisman is brittle. The day will come when it will pitiably collapse. Then the old stone gods will rise from forgotten rubble and rub the dust of a thousand years from their eyes; and Thor will leap up and with his giant hammer start smashing Gothic cathedrals . . . and when you hear a crash as nothing ever crashed in world history, you'll know that the German thunder has hit the mark. At that sound the eagles will fall dead from the sky and the lions in the farthest desert of Africa will pull in their tails and slink away into their royal caves. A play will be performed that will make the French Revolution seem like a harmless idyll in comparison. . . .

In 1842 Heine, this friend of Karl Marx the founder of Communism, saw the evil effects of his philosophy and warned:

Communism is the secret name of the dread antagonist setting proletarian rule with all its consequences against the present bourgeois regime. It will be a frightful duel. How will it end? No one knows but gods and goddesses acquainted with the future. We only know this much: Communism, though little discussed now and loitering in hidden garrets on miserable straw pallets, is the dark hero destined for a great, if temporary, role in the modern tragedy. . . .

It would be war, the ghastliest war of destruction—which would unfortunately call the two noblest nations of civilization into the arena, to the ruin of both: France and Germany. England, the great sea serpent always able to crawl back into its vast watery lair, and Russia, which also has the safest hiding places in its vast fir forests, steppes, and icy wastes—those two, in a normal political war, cannot be annihilated even by the most crushing defeats. . . That, however, would only be the first act of the great melodrama, the prologue, as it were. The second act is the European and the World Revolution. . . Will the religious doctrines of the past rise in all countries, in desperate resistance —and will perhaps this attempt constitute the third act? . . . How could that drama end? . . .

I do not know; but I think that eventually the great sea serpent will have its head crushed, and the skin of the Northern bear will be pulled over his ears. There may be only one flock then and one shepherd—one free shepherd with an iron staff, and a shorn-alike, bleating-alike human herd!

Wild, gloomy times are roaring toward us, and a prophet wishing to write a new apocalypse would have to invent entirely new beasts— beasts so terrible that St. John's older animal symbols would be like gentle doves and cupids in comparison. The gods are veiling their faces in pity on the children of man, their long-time charges, and perhaps over their own fate. The future smells of Russian leather, blood, god-lessness, and many whippings. I should advise our grandchildren to be born with very thick skins on their backs. [Heinrich Heine, *Works of Prose*, ed. by Hermann Kesten, p. 51-3].

And Dostoievsky:

Every member of society spies on the others, and it is his duty to inform against them . . . all are slaves, and equal in their slavery. Cicero will have his tongue cut out, Copernicus will have his eyes put out, Shakespeare will be stoned . . . slaves are bound to be equal. . . . A teacher who laughs with children at their God, and at their cradle is on our side; the lawyer who defends an educated murderer because he is more cultured than his victims and could not help murdering them to get money is one of us; the school boys who murder a peasant for the sake of sensation are ours; the juries who acquit every criminal are ours; the prosecutor who trembles at a trial and fears he shall not be advanced enough is ours; among officials and literary men we have lots, and they don't know it themselves. . . . We will proclaim destruction, we will set fires going, we will set legends going, every scurvy group will be of use. Well there will be an upheaval; there's going to be such an upset as the world has never seen before. Russia will be overwhelmed with darkness, and the earth will weep for its gods.

The Holy Father says that we are at the return of the early centuries of the Church, while many others believe we are saved from utter chaos only by habits of thinking, rules of the road and conventions which depend for their validity on beliefs which have long been abandoned. With the family disintegrating with one divorce for every two marriages in thirty-five major cities in the United States, with five divorces for every six marriages in Los Angeles—there is no denying that something has snapped. Beyond all these and other tragic facts, such as the attempt to ground peace on compromises between powers, rather than on justice and pledges such as the Atlantic Charter, the startling fact stands out that our times—and our times alone—have witnessed for the first time in human history, the persecution of the Old Testament by the Nazis and the persecution of the New Testament by the Communists. Anyone who has had anything to do with God is hated today, whether his vocation was to announce His Divine Son, Jesus Christ, as did the Jew, or to follow Him as the Christian.

And those of us who have followed the systematic and organized world campaign for atheism, which insinuates itself ever into government bureaucracies, and are familiar with the anti-God attacks, are compelled to say to one's adversaries: "You have not convinced us that there is no God, but you have convinced us that there is a devil!"

Every now and then in history the devil is given a long rope, for we must never forget that our Lord said to Judas and his band: "This is your hour." God has His day, but evil has its hour when the shepherd shall be struck and the sheep dispersed. Has the Church made the preparations for just such a dark night in the decree of the Holy Father outlining the conditions on which a Papal Election may be held outside of Rome?

Though we speak of the emergence of the anti-Christ against Christ, think not that it is because we fear for the Church. We do not; it is for the world we fear. It is not infallibility we are worried about, but the world's lapse into fallibility; we tremble not that God may be dethroned, but that barbarism may reign; it is not Transubstantiation that may perish, but the home; not the sacraments that may fade away, but the moral law. The Church can have no different words for the weeping woman than those of Christ on the way to Calvary:

Weep not over me; but weep for yourselves and for your children. (*Luke* 23:28)

The Church has survived other great crises in her nineteen centuries of existence and she will live to sing a requiem over the evils of the present. The Church may have its Good Fridays but these are only preludes to its Easter Sundays, for the Divine Promise shall never be made void:

. . . and the gates of hell shall not prevail against it. (*Matthew* 16:18)

Behold I am with you all days, even to the consummation of the world. (*Matthew* 28:20)

Whosoever shall fall upon that stone, shall be bruised. (*Luke* 20:18)

Never before in history has there been such a strong argument for the need of Christianity, for men are now discovering that their misery and their woes, their wars and their revolutions increase in direct ratio and proportion to the neglect of Christianity. Evil is self defeating; good alone is self-preserving.

These three practical recommendations in conclusion: (1) As Christians we must realize that a moment of crisis is not a time of despair, but of opportunity. The more we can anticipate the doom, the more we can avoid it. Once we recognize we are under Divine Wrath, we become eligible for Divine Mercy. It was because of famine the prodigal said: "I will arise, and will go to my father. . . " (*Luke* 15:18) The very disciplines of God create hope. The thief on the right came to God by a crucifixion. The Christian finds a basis for optimism in the most thorough-going pessimism, for his Easter is within three days of Good Friday.

As we look about the world and see the new barbarism move whole populations into slavery, we may ask: "Why do so many innocent people suffer? God should have pity on them." God does. One of the surprises of heaven will be to see how many saints were made in the midst of chaos and war and revolution. When John saw a

> . . . great multitude, which no man could number, of all nations and tribes, and peoples, and tongues, standing before the throne, and in sight of the Lamb, clothed with white robes, and palms in their hands: And they cried with a loud voice saying: Salvation to our God, who sitteth upon the throne, and to the Lamb. And all the angels stood round about the throne, and the ancients, and the four living creatures: and they fell down before the throne upon their faces, and adored God. (*Apocalypse* 7:9-11)
>
> And one of the ancients answered and said to me: These that are clothed in white robes, who are they? and whence came they? And I said to him: My lord thou knowest. And he said to me: These are they who are come out of great tribulation, and have washed their robes, and have made them white in the blood of the Lamb. (*Apocalypse* 7: 13, 14)

After Our Divine Lord had pictured the catastrophes that would fall upon a morally disordered civilization, after He foretold how the military would take it, and their holy places be abominated. He did not say "Fear," but

> When these things begin to come to pass, look up, and lift up your heads, because your redemption is at hand. (*Luke* 21:28)

(2) Jews, Protestants, and Catholics alike, and all men of good will, must realize that the world is serving your souls with an awful summons—the summons to heroic efforts at spiritualization. Catholics ought to stir up their faith, hang a crucifix in their homes to remind them that we too have to carry a cross, gather the family together every night to recite the rosary that through corporate prayer there might be intercession for the world; go to daily Mass that the spirit of love and sacrifice might be sprinkled in our business, our social life, and our duties. More

heroic souls might undertake the Holy Hour daily, particularly in parishes conscious of the needs of prayers of reparation as well as petition, conducting such devotions in their churches. As for Jews, Protestants, and Catholics alike an alliance is necessary not to fight against an external enemy, for our

> . . . wrestling is not against flesh and blood; but against principalities and powers, against the rulers of the world of this darkness, against the spirits of wickedness in the high places. (*Ephesians* 6:12)

but rather a unity on the basis of men of good will, who believe in the moral law, the family, God, and the Divinity of Christ. It is not a unity of religion we plead for that is impossible when purchased at the cost of the unity of truth, but a unity of religious peoples, wherein each marches separately according to the light of his conscience, but strikes together for the moral betterment of the world, through prayer, not hate. In a word, if anti-Christ has his fellow-travelers then why should not God and His Divine Son? The Roman sergeant who built a temple for the Jews was a fellow traveler with them in their belief in God. The woman at Tyre and Sidon became a fellow traveler of Christ. The forces of evil are united; the forces of good are divided. We may not be able to meet in the same pew—would to God we did—but we can meet on our *knees*.

You may be sure that no sordid compromises nor carrying of waters on both shoulders will see you through. Those who have the faith had better keep in the state of grace and those who have neither had better find out what they mean, for in the coming age there will be only one way to stop your trembling knees, and that will be to get down on them and pray. The most important problem in the world today is your soul, for that is what the struggle is about. As St. Peter told the Romans in days of delirium:

> Seeing then that all these things are to be dissolved, what manner of people ought you to be in holy conversation and godliness? (2 *Peter* 3:11)

The only way out of this crisis is spiritual, because the trouble is not in the way we keep our books, but in the way we keep our souls. The time is nearer than you think. In 1917 Lenin, addressing a group of students in Switzerland, said: "This revolution may not come in my lifetime." Within three months he was leading it. The struggle is so basically spiritual, so much concerned with the forces of Christ and anti-Christ, that there is a definite planned policy put into practice by the Communists in Korea. They go to the Christian homes converted by missionaries and ask: "Do you believe in Christ?" If the householder answers in the affirmative, the Communist says he will be back next week. If then he answers: "I believe in Stalin" he keeps his house and his land. Otherwise it is confiscated and he is liquidated. And you think the struggle is between individualism and collectivism!

Because the struggle is between the Kingdom of mass-atheism and the Kingdom of God there are two especially whose intercession we much invoke because they both are conquerors of evil. To the first, St. Michael, we pray: "O Michael, Prince of the Morning, Who didst once conquer Lucifer who wouldst make himself God, save us from our world of little gods. When the world once cracked because of a sneer in heaven, thou didst rise up and drag down from the seven heavens the pride that would look down on the most high. So now:

> Michael, Michael of the mastering,
> Michael of the marching on the mountains of the Lord,
> Marshal the world and purge of rot and riot
> Rule through the world till all the world be quiet:
> Only establish when the world is broken
> What is unbroken is the Word. [Chesterson]

To the second, Our Lady, pray:

"It was to Thee as the Woman that was given the power to crush the head of the serpent who lied to men that they would be as gods. May thou who didst find Christ when He was lost for three days, find Him again for our world has lost Him. Give to the senile incontinence of our verbiage the Word. As Thou didst form the Word made flesh in Thy womb, form Him in our hearts. Be in our midst as tongues of fire descend upon our cold hearts and if this be night, then come, O Lady of the Blue of Heaven, show us once again the Light of the World in the heart of a day."

God love you!

FIFTY YEARS OF ZIONISM [6]

STEPHEN S. WISE [7]

Dr. Stephen S. Wise, Rabbi of the Free Synagogue, New York, delivered this address on the opening day of the Twenty-second World Zionist Congress at Basle, Switzerland, on December 9, 1946.

Rabbi Wise, born in Budapest and the descendant of a long line of rabbis, was educated in New York City, and received his doctor's degree from Columbia. He founded the Free Synagogue, New York City, foremost in influence among American synagogues, and since that time has been its Rabbi.

Dr. Wise was one of the founders of the Zionist movement and was president in 1936 of the Zionist Organization of America. He was also a founder of the American Jewish Congress and of the World Jewish Congress. He was a leader of the Jewish People in militant self-defense against the war of Hitlerism upon the Jews of the world.

He has been active in religious, educational, and civic work in the city of New York and throughout the country, and has had a wide reputation as a platform orator. At Cooper Union lectures and before similar cosmopolitan audiences he has repeatedly impressed his listeners by his combined logic, emotional and imaginative force, voice, posture, gesture, and platform personality.

Dr. Wise states that "there can be no doubt about the importance of public speaking as a force in democracy. Democracy rests on public opinion. Public opinion is influenced by every manner of public communication. Public speaking still remains one of the chief media of public communication." [8]

To dwell in this hour upon the great Day of Herzl is not to ignore the significant men and movements that went before, nor yet the equally significant developments of the cause and movement within the half century that has passed since we first met within this to us little less than sacred city of Basle, Switzerland.

Herzl's predecessors were unknown to him: his successors are not unknown to us. Before him stood some historic Jewish figures though he knew them not: Moses Hess, author of *Rome and Jerusalem,* which despite its obvious limitations and defects

---

[6] *Opinion.* 17:6-8. February, 1947. By permission of Rabbi Stephen S. Wise.
[7] For biographical note see Appendix.
[8] Letter to the editor, March 2, 1947.

remains one of the classical operas of our immortal enterprise, and Leo Pinsker, author of *Auto-Emancipation,* a title which reveals the deepest meaning of the Zionist purpose. Not only books and their authors went before Herzl, but a number of in-deflectibly faithful groups, the earliest pre-Herzlian groups, in-cluding Chibath Zion, that admirable company of for a time ineffective Zionist dreamers, the memorable *Bilu,* and other Rus-sian, Rumanian, Hungarian companies of men and women. With prescience these foresaw and with prophecy they foretold, chiefly to themselves, that as it was later to be expressed in the formula of the great Achad Haam, there was no other way, that despite a thousand years of residence in Eastern and South Eastern Europe, it could not and never would be their home, their permanent and inalienable home, that their home was and must for ever be *elsewhere,* and that elsewhere was Erez Israel.

They were not impatient in reaching this conclusion. A thousand years during which dispersed Israel had tested itself and the mood of its hosts had in its own sight throughout been a watch in the little relieved darkness of the night. Never in his-tory had a people been so long alienated from its own land and retained its unaltered and unlessened love for the land, nor sus-tained its hope for the restoration of its nationhood. These trends of discontent, these tendencies to abandon at last an unen-durable way of life, found understanding and voice in the person and Jewish genius of him whom history has come to know as Dr. Theodor Herzl. His little more than one-hundred-page brochure, *Der Judenstaat,* marks one of the turning points of Jewish history. In order to appraise and evaluate it, it is neces-sary to say no more than that it has changed Jewish history, which, having changed its course, can never be the same again. A new epoch began, not to be without its evil days and its ter-rible years, but these were to come to a people, which under the impact of *Der Judenstaat,* had, without losing faith in human-kind, resolved to be the master of its fate and the captain of its soul.

What did Zionism as propounded by Herzl mean? Much, everything, but one thing supremely! We had lived throughout the centuries on decisions, permissions, or inhibitions by others,—

rulers, governments, nations. The world had too long said to us, you may or you must, you can or you cannot. Herzl at last spoke the magic word—you can, we can. We may fulfill our own prayers and purposes. The answer to our prayers lies with, even within, us. At one and the same time every need of the Jewish people was or was to be fulfilled—faith, people, nation.

It was not quite extraordinary for Herzl to predict the continuance of Jewish oppression, the intensifying of wrong inflicted upon the Jew. But it was more than extraordinary that Herzl should have seen what the world begins to see, namely, that "The Jewish State is essential to the world: it will, therefore, be created." What he could not easily have foreseen was that the last supreme effort to destroy the Jewish people grew out of the understanding by nazism that mankind cannot be enslaved as long as Jews survive, that Jewish survival must forever signify revolt against human enslavement and inhuman injustice.

It may be that the nations slowly begin to comprehend the role of the Jew on the world's stage, as the indestructible servant of eternal faith and freedom. If so, why do not the nations, led by Britain and the United States, offer to the decimated but undestroyed Jewish people, the one supreme reparation which it merits, the creation of the Jewish State of Palestine as healing for the almost immedicable wounds of the "tribe of the wandering foot and weary breast" of which Byron sang "How shall you flee away and be at rest?"

Herzl was a Titan, one of a race of giants, which includes glorious and resounding names in Jewish history: Max Nordau, David Wolfsohn, Otto Warburg, Nahum Sokolow, Menachem Ussischkin, and the one figure, who has functioned as leader throughout two wars, happily before and after both, whose stature has grown with the years, to whom the Institute bearing his name is a scientific tribute, to whose political genius and statesmanship our cause is under deep and uncancellable indebtedness, Dr. Chaim Weizmann.

Unimaginably electric was the effect upon us, upon world Jewry, upon the world, of the publication of *Der Judenstaat*. The day after the opening session of the first Zionist Congress, the then Mr. Brandeis, temporarily staying in San Francisco, said

to a member of his family as he read the opening address of
Dr. Herzl, "Now that is a cause for which I could work and
give my life."

The twenty years before the day of Herzl had not been
wholly unlike these last twenty years of horror. In the then
largest Jewish settlement of the world instead of Nazism there
was Pobiedonostoff. The measure of the effect of Herzl and the
first Zionist Congress it is not wholly impossible to appraise.
After every other calamity in Jewish history, some manner of
escape complete or partial had been come upon—from Jerusalem
to Rome, from Spain and Portugal to Holland, France, and Germany, from Russian-Rumanian pogroms to America, flight, escape, refuge for self-preservation, always Exodus without Palestine. For the first time in twenty centuries, Herzl had dared to
propose that there be no more escape, no more retreat, no more
refuge—but *going home* and thus the end of dependence upon
others, the substitution of our own will for the good or ill will
of other peoples, other nations, other faiths, no further extension
of the boundaries of the Golah. Herzl's discovery and thesis was
that the mission ideal of Israel, as urged for half a century or
more especially among the German-speaking Jewish peoples,
could not be carried out by an Israel which had ceased to be; in
a word, a non-existent Israel was least able to serve and to bless
the world.

It was not as if another way, every other way, had not been
tried, the kindly and the ruthless regimes, the benevolent and
maleficent rulers of States alike, all alike, and the Dreyfus affair
was not more than the final and unanswerable proof of Herzl's
faith, that for a people proud and honourable, a people not made
up of gypsies, the status of permanent guest is not tolerable, least
of all secure. Herzl's was a true mission theory as well. All
that Israel scattered, dispersed, impotent, could not be or do,
Israel in its own land, Israel in its own National Home, could
be and must do.

The terrible persecution of Jews in Eastern Europe in Herzl's
day no more explains Zionism than the shocking surprise of the
Dreyfus affair. There was a combination of causes and circumstances, which together explain Herzl and the Zionist move-

ment—a sense of Jewish life's lack of dignity and adequacy, loneliness, spiritual loneliness, a world arranged for or against us, whether good or bad, instead of being determined by us, a deep nostalgia organizing itself at last the transcendent effect of an unsatisfied yearning and love for Palestine, plus a sense of the urgent need of the substituting for the shadow of perfunctory emancipation by an alien world, the substance and truth of a passionately eager and voluntary self-emancipation.

No story of these fifty epic years dares fail to pay tribute however inadequate to our Jewish youth, verging upon and reborn in Palestine, our Chaluzim and Chaluzoth, pioneers, whose labor, devotion, sacrifice, did more than all else to make their and our precious dream come true.

Many and grievous were the crises which befell the Movement beginning in 1920. There were the first terrible disorders, though the unnumbered political crises antedate and postdate all disorders. Later there ensued the crisis of 1929, resolved only in part by the Ramsay MacDonald dissent from the lamentable and still inexplicable Passfield Document. Happier days came too: the year 1935 with its blessed immigration figure of more than 60,000, followed, alas, by the renewed Arab disorders, and the attitude on the part of the attacked, which was their moral glory but not their complete physical saving, *Havlagah*.

Nothing worse befell us throughout the two generations of resettlement than the White Paper, the failure to reject which out of hand was a terrible blunder on the part of all of us. That evil, the White Paper, has dogged our footsteps since the day it was framed, and, far graver, hardened a line of policy, which by its limiting of immigration to 75,000 over a period of five years, including a narrowly fixed "bonus" of refugees, committed one of the most terrible of crimes against the Jewish people, crime of crimes, for hundreds of thousands of these crushed, slaughtered martyrs might have become the living and creative members of the household of Israel instead of the victims of inexpiable crime.

Herzl was no more the creator of Zionism than Moses was the creator of liberation. Each was, we devoutly believe, a human instrument in the hands of divine purpose, and, above all, equal to that purpose. Herzl focused, expressed, glorified the spirit of his people. The symphony of his people had been writing itself in blood and tears throughout nearly 2000 years. The magic hand of a great conductor was needed. Others before him had essayed to interpret that Jewish symphony of the ages—Moses Hess with deep intuition, withal an inadequate sense of the human drama; Pinsker, it may be, too near to the unfolding tragedy to envisage its majestic outlines. Herzl came at last, deeply troubled albeit unconfused and daring to direct the rendition of the symphony of his people for centuries, to utter the protest of his people's soul, in the terms of heroic and noblest prophecy.

We Jews had throughout the ages been pessimists with respect to ourselves, as if we could not do for ourselves, as if it were unthinkable that we could help to save ourselves; and yet, strange to say, we had always been optimists with regard to the world which least justified our optimism. We could not have lived without acquiring the high habit of forgetting wrongs and forgiving the hurt which we suffered, even when our honor was no less hurt than was the life of the wounded and the slain. To forget and to forgive was easier for us than to plan hopefully and to labor creatively for ourselves. Herzl was the first to see that the roles must be reversed, namely, we were to be meliorists if not pessimists with respect to the world, and optimists with regard to ourselves. History has borne out and abundantly vindicated the revolutionary view, which in a sense merely substituted enriching self-trust for the ancient and impoverishing self-distrust, a view which voiced the renascent faith of a people still equal to greatness of spirit and achievement.

There came the joyous day, November 2, 1917, with its issuance of the Balfour Declaration to which the Jewish people have almost ever since been equal even when and though England was not. Five years later the Jewish Agency was established, the Hebrew University of Jerusalem created some years after that, with its unalterable ideal, students of all peoples, races, and faiths shall be welcomed within its walls. In 1919 the Agency was enlarged, the value of such enlargement yet to be proved, though the non-Zionist leaders of the enlarged Agency met the crisis of 1929 with utmost strength.

Sorrowfully, we recall the Vienna Congress of 1925, when, twenty years after Herzl's death, in his own city, you and I heard thousands of paraders marching to one raucous tune, "Juden Heraus." Only one answer to that cry was possible: "Anybody might have heard it, but God's whisper came to me— 'Juden Herein.'" But most cowardly of all the answers to "Juden Heraus," to the anti-Semitism of Central Europe, and in the end most cruelly punished was the pitiful plea of them that sought not to accuse others but to excuse themselves in the lamentable words, "We are not Semites nor even Jews; we are merely citizens of the Jewish faith."

One needs do no more than contrast these fifty years of Zionism with the fifty years that had gone before, confused, groping, pulseless, with the assault of Chassidim upon the bulwark of Rabbinism not yet wholly spent, with Jews of Central Europe still groping towards a mild and disguised assimilation, little redeemed even by the fruitful creativeness of *Jüdische Wissenschaft*, Reform Judaism, lapsed into the grievous blunder of minimizing the difference between Synagogue and Church, as if there were no other differentiation of Israel from the world than that inherent in religion, with the implication that if we Jews minimize the religious or credal differences, we shall be more and more like the rest of the world, and the last surviving difference will finally have vanished.

I will be forgiven if I dwell for one moment upon the incredible growth of American Jewry and American Zionism in these fifty years, especially throughout the last decade. Best of all, this growth of American Zionism has been the token of American Jewish awakening and of American Jewish understanding of all that Zionism means. Again, I know I will be forgiven if I make mention of the names of two great American Zionists, each of whom made a precious contribution to Zionism, Justice Louis D. Brandeis and Henrietta Szold. Brandeis great as American, as Jew, as Zionist, and Henrietta Szold, who gave nothing to the Zionist cause equal to the purity and nobility, I had almost said holiness, of her own life.

Invited to essay the role of historian, it is not for me to deal with current political situations, and yet the present crisis of crises can hardly be ignored. Certain it is that a situation has been reached which admits of only two ways of dealing therewith. Palestine is not an independent Dominion, nor yet a dependent Colony. Mandate and Mandatory mean one thing, Trustee and Trusteeship. Either England will cancel the White Paper, the blighting White Paper, and resume as genuine Mandatory over Palestine, or it must be assumed that it has resolved to abandon the Mandate.

This brief sketch of Zionism over a period of fifty years can hardly come to a fitting close without a twofold appeal alike to the mandatory power and to the British people. It is barely credible that the British Government should within a generation descend from the heights of the Balfour Declaration to the depths of Yagur and Cyprusism.

Surely the British Government, which long stood as a friend to the Jewish people, will not be satisfied to accept the role of the betrayer of Zionism. After all the infinite woe of the Jewish people—one of every three of whom has been most foully and unnaturally murdered—the Jews returning to Palestine merit a kinder fate than to be transshipped from its shores to Cyprus or to any place on earth outside of Palestine. The hand of Britain that wrote the Balfour Declaration should not now be used to drag war-weary and disinherited refugees away from Palestine instead of facilitating their pilgrimage to the heart of Palestine, which is the heart of their heart.

To our fellow Jews we appeal in another key. Resist, resist, resist the oppression of our brothers but let no deeds of our own soil the blameless record of a long unsullied history. We Zionist dare never forget "What thou wouldst have highly thou must have holily." Zionism was ever a cause of moral and social standards, of ethical and spiritual regeneration. If these moral standards of ideals are foresworn, Zionism will have sunk to the low level of a rabble-rousing chauvinism.

These fifty years of Zionism must fittingly end with the proclamation of the tenth verse of the twenty-fifth chapter of the book of Leviticus:

. . . and ye shall hallow the fiftieth year and proclaim liberty throughout the land unto all the inhabitants hereof: it is to be a Jubilee to you; and ye shall return every man unto his possession and ye shall return every man unto his family.

As if interpretation were necessary, Sifra adds the significance of the word *deror*, liberty, is *cherut*, freedom.

Let mankind unite to make it a year of Jubilee for the Jewish people. We have made and we shall keep Palestine Jewish and free. We call upon the nations of the world to guarantee never to suffer that freedom to be violated, to make Jews free wherever they dwell and to make free all the inhabitants of the earth.

And when this Zionist Congress after celebrating the close of fifty years shall have been ended, let it stand as the reaffirmation of the unwithstandable purpose, the unbreakable unity, the unimpairable faith of the Zionist movement—and with God be the rest.

REDEEMING OUR REGRETS [9]

RALPH W. SOCKMAN [10]

This radio address Dr. Sockman gave on Sunday, January 12, 1947, over WNBC and the network. It was the fifteenth in the regular series of the National Radio Pulpit, a presentation of the National Broadcasting Company.

Dr. Sockman, since 1917 pastor of the Madison Avenue Methodist Church (now Christ Church), New York City, has grown steadily in fame and leadership as one of America's leading pulpit speakers.

For the past eighteen years he has been active as a radio speaker. Since 1937 he has been a preacher with the National Radio Pulpit. During eight months of each year he has ministered to this program. The network includes from Sunday to Sunday a varying number of from forty-six to sixty-seven stations. His ministry has also been extended in recent years through short wave to other continents.

Dr. Sockman is unusually effective in vocal abilities, voice quality, pitch, rate, and intensity control. As a preacher he follows the Methodist tradition. His sermons are usually based on Biblical texts; they are well organized, heavily illustrated from literary, historical, contemporary, and personal sources, and are highly inspirational. His language is brisk, personal, unhackneyed, vivid, and well adapted to radio, as well as to his face-to-face cosmopolitan audiences.[11]

While the year is yet young, may I ask each of you to say silently to God something which the Psalmist said. It is this: "My times are in Thy hand."

At the turn of the year we are especially conscious of time. Of course, we modern Americans seem always to be time-conscious. Our eyes are ever on the clock. We strive strenuously to figure out time-saving devices. Whatever our hand findeth to do, we keep looking at our wrists to see how long it takes to do it.

Yet fussily conscious as we are of time-schedules, we are not all so aware of time-sequence. We count the minutes and the

[9] Issued by the Department of National Religious Radio, 297 Fourth Avenue, New York 10, New York, and here reprinted through the courtesy of Dr. Ralph Sockman.

[10] For biographical note see Appendix.

[11] For further comment on Dr. Sockman as a speaker see *Representative American Speeches: 1942-1943.* p. 267-8.

hours, but we do not always stop to figure out what they are adding up to.

I do not know how many of you keep a diary. It is one of the good habits which I do not have. But the mere keeping of a diary does not matter so much as the nature of it. It aids the memory to register a daily list of the things we do, the places we visit, the people we see. Do we put down some of our reflections on the things that happen? That is the way to keep a real diary which registers our growth through the years.

Some time ago a man wrote his autobiography. A critic in appraising it said, "He has faithfully rendered his emotions without collecting his thoughts." Just to jump from engagement to engagement without stopping to reflect tends to beget a "busyness" without real effectiveness. The late Glenn Frank once described a futile, flustered busybody in these words: "Like a turnstile, he is in everybody's way, but stops nobody; he talks a great deal, but says little; looks into everything but sees nothing; and has a hundred irons in the fire, but very few of them are hot, and with these few that are, he burns his fingers."

Well, the Psalmist was not harried by our hurried schedules. He carried no wrist watch, and I venture to believe kept no engagement book. He measured the passing of the hours by the shadows on the eternal hills. But he had patience to reflect on what his days and years were adding up to. And he looked up to God with this conclusion: "My times are in Thy hand."

This declaration meant, first of all, "My life as a whole is in the hand of God." The Psalmist could not understand many aspects of his life, but he trusted where he could not see. J. Arthur Thompson, the Scottish scientist, said some years ago that life is like a book in which the first and last pages are missing, some others still uncut, and others stuck together. That is true both of our individual lives and of life in the large sense of history. But however many of the pages may be unreadable to our eyes, the Psalmist and those who share his faith believe that the volume of life is held in the hands of a purposeful God.

Elsewhere the Psalmist said, "We spend our years as a tale that is told." But life is a story with a plot and a purpose and not "a tale told by an idiot, full of sound and fury, signifying nothing." In a sense each of our lives seems a mystery story. Look at what and where you are now and ask yourself whether twenty years ago you could have foreseen such an outcome. Yes, there is mystery in our lives but our life-story is not as mysterious as one of our current thrillers, which was described to me recently as having its plot so well concealed that even the author did not discover until the last page who committed the murder. Not so with the mystery of your life and mine. The Divine Author knows how we are going to turn out, He knows what we shall be doing at the end of 1947. But God's foreknowledge, in my opinion at least, does not foreshorten our freedom. God has to leave us free of will so that we can grow up into manhood.

Winifred Holtby in her novel *South Riding* was taken to task by one critic who complained that there was "no completely praisworthy character in the whole book." Miss Holtby made this reply: "I intended to make them good but they would not be." In a sense can we not reverently see here a parallel to the Divine Author of our being? Back in the Genesis story each act of creation is followed by the refrain, "And God saw that it was good." God intended man to be good, but man had to be left free to make his choices. And each choice together with the pressure of events serves to shape character. Then the psychological unity of the individual must be preserved by acting in character. Thus lives go on, some of them from bad to worse, thwarting God's intention, and some from good to better fulfilling God's purpose.

The development of each individual depends on how well he gears his ongoing actions with God's ongoing life. For remember every day each of us is writing his autobiography and so is God writing his.

Also when at New Year's we say, "I'll turn over a new leaf," it is more than turning a page in a tablet and starting to write our record on a clean sheet. When we turn over a new leaf in time's calendar, it is to read what God is writing as well as to write our own record. I am to fit my biography into God's biography, for as the Psalmist said, "My times are in Thy hand."

Ah, the New Year's season is not a time for making light resolutions as if all depended on our good intentions and will power. We should sit down and reflect on what God is writing as well as on what we are to write. Amiel, the Swiss philosopher, depicts the power of reflection thus:

Reverie, like the rain of night, restores color and force to thoughts which have been blanched and wearied by the heat of the day. With gentle fertilizing power it awakens within us a thousand sleeping forms, and, as though in play, gathers round us materials for the future.

Last Sunday I referred to David Lilienthal's reported utterance, "So help me God," as he opened the first session of the national Atomic Energy Commission. If this report is true and if this spirit should spread through our scientific circles, it augurs immeasurably much for the future. Our physical scientists because of their concrete achievements have attained a prestige in popular thought above that of our statesmen, our generals, or our preachers. A reverent science could help to start a religious revival.

And why should not scientists be sobered into awe? They have unleashed mechanical and atomic power which without God's help will work our destruction. Thank God, intelligent persons today are not lightly mouthing the slogan with which men tried to restore things after World War I—the old slogan, "Back to Normalcy." World War II has tossed us into an atomic age so fraught with new dangers and possibilities that we are no longer so cocksure that we know what normalcy is.

Another hopeful phase in this crucial time of transition is the serious leadership which the women of the world are assuming. They are now coming to take their rightful place in civic, industrial, and social planning. This very day, January 12, is being observed as International Women's Sabbath and women throughout America are dedicating themselves to the great postwar tasks ahead of them. Under the leadership of the Y.W.C.A., womanhood will give to world rebuilding the human touch, the spiritual sensitivity and the pioneering social strategy for which this great organization is so justly noted.

Our times have gotten out of hand with us. But they are still in God's hand. Let us, therefore, at the start of 1947 hum-

bly admit the failure of our own cleverness, but confidently say
with Browning:

> Our times are in his hand,
> Who saith, a whole I planned;
> Youth shows but half; trust God:
> See all, nor be afraid.

Yet it is not enough to sit in our homes this day and say as
our general philosophy of faith, "My times are in thy hand."
The test is, can we continue to say this when the dark days come,
for to most of us 1947 will bring some shadows. Can we say
in the second place, "My bad times are in Thy hand"? That is
the faith the Hebrew singer was revealing in that Twenty-first
Psalm.

If we are to have confidence that our bad times are in God's
hands, we must recognize that death is involved in the daily
process of living. At our burial service we read the scriptural
words, "In life we are in death." There is dying in the act of
growing. We all want our children to grow, yet in the process
of growing the graceful curves of infancy give way to the awk-
ward lengths of adolescence. Some of the charm and grace of
childhood dies. In mental development there must be concentration, and in focusing our mental powers on certain objectives,
we allow other faculties to atrophy through neglect. Yes, we
are ever dying to live.

A radio listener sometime ago wrote to ask my view of his
interpretation of the Twenty-third Psalm. He believes that "the
valley of the shadow of death" is a region we travel through
from infancy on and not just in our last days. And I am inclined to agree with him. But if we travel with the Divine
Shepherd, "life is ever lord of death." Growth involves dying,
but something goes on, for even our bad times are in the hand
of God.

And if our bad times are in God's hands, then we must
cooperate with him in leaving some of them behind us. The
art of leaving is an essential part of the art of living. Jesus made
much of this. He said to a would-be follower, "Let the dead
bury the dead." To another he said, "No man having put his
hand to the plow and looking back is fit for the Kingdom of

God." We must learn the art of letting bygones be bygones, of closing the gate on yesterday's pack of yelping worries so that they do not dog our steps to destroy today's peace of mind. We must practice Saint Paul's principle, "Forgetting those things which are behind, and reaching forth unto those things which are before, I press toward the mark for the prize of the high calling of God in Christ Jesus."

But in forgetting the things that are behind, forgetfulness must be blended with forgiveness. A relationship is never safe when one person says to the other, "I'll try to forget but I can't forgive." Nor is a friendship safe when one says to the other, "I'll forgive but I can't forget." Forgiving must accompany forgetting in our relations with our fellows and with our Heavenly Father. You can never bury a live sin in the grave of forgetfulness. It will kick its way out to torment you tomorrow. Only when we penitently seek God's forgiveness, does he blot out our transgressions and put them as far from us as the east is from the west.

But when we commit our badness and our sorrows to God they fall into proper place. In the play, *Smilin' Through* two blessed spirits in glory are looking down at an old man who cannot forget his hatred for one who has wronged him. One of the saints, Sarah, says: "He looks such a kind old man."

Mary, the other, replies, "He is, at heart. He just hasn't learned to vanquish hate. It takes them so long to learn that. Their little human worries and troubles and sorrows are so real to them."

Sarah, smiling, retorts, "I can remember how real mine seemed to me." Mary: "So do children's sorrows seem real when they lose their marbles or break their toys. If only these poor grown-up children could learn to know that their marbles cannot be lost, nor their toys broken."

No, our lost marbles, our broken toys, our forgiven sins, our loved ones we loved long since and lost awhile, all those "dear dead days beyond recall"—they are in Thy hand, O God.

Can we catch the confidence of Katherine Stevenson in lines which a radio friend sent me?

> The gladdest messengers of all the past
> Have worn disguise of sorrow or of pain;
> And can I doubt Thy love to me doth last,
> Or fear to trust Thy wisdom once again?
> "My times are in Thy hand."

But this new year of 1947 is going to bring us some glad days as well as some bad days. If we are to feel the full force of our text, we should be able to say also, "My good times are in Thy hand."

We mortals are prone to plead for God's help in handling our bad times. But we seem to assume that we can look after our good times without the Lord's help.

But I wonder if we do handle our pleasures very well. Most of us who are of middle age or past are prone to look back upon our youth as the happiest time of life. I noted that the Town Meeting of the Air, which discusses such vital issues, had as its theme recently the question of finding happiness by turning the clock back. My youth was a fairly normal one, and to me from this distance it is filled with happy memories. But when I really try to recover the thoughts of my childhood, I remember how many good times I spoiled by little worries and fears. For instance I would look forward to a Sunday School picnic out there in Green Valley, Ohio; and I would be so eager for the day to arrive that I partly spoiled the preceding days with my impatience. Then the great day came. About three o'clock in the afternoon I began to count the hours remaining and allowed the enjoyment of the occasion to be clouded by the gloom over its shortness. Then I helped to spoil several days afterward by futile regret that it was all over. Thus I ate away the edges of such good times on both ends, fore and aft. No, our youth wasn't as carefree as it now looks to us.

We need God to help us handle our good times. When we really put them in his hands, he makes us so "all there" in our enjoyment that we forget time. That is what eternal life is—it is time so full of living that we forget to think about the beginning or its ending. When we are caught up in some activity body and soul, we forget the clock and the calendar. Then we are living a bit of the life eternal. Eternal life is not measured in terms of time but of states of mind.

> One glorious hour of crowded life
> Is worth an age without a name.

When our times are in His hand, God helps us to handle the past tense by forgetting and forgiving; He helps us to handle the present tense by putting an eternal quality into it; and He helps us to handle the future tense by patience and hope. Often I long for the time when I can sit down leisurely and read what I want to read, without any pressure of engagements or any need of reading for promoting utilitarian purposes. Then the disturbing thought comes to me, would I get a zest from reading if I had no work to look forward to? Would I enjoy reading Dickens on my death bed? Does not what we read interest us because we link it with our experience in the past and other experiences hoped for in the future? By the structure of our bodies, sensation is planned to lead to motion, feeling to effort, vision to action.

Aye, because of this ongoing process within us, life is never satisfying unless our little finite daily experiences are framed in the infinite. When we can say with the confidence of the Psalmist, "My times are in Thy hand," then ours is the assurance that feeling and effort, vision and action have the glory of going on—forever and forever. Then we feel with Oliver Wendell Holmes,

> Leave they low-vaulted past,
> Let each new temple, nobler than the last
> Shut thee from a heaven with a dome more vast
> Till thou at length art free,
> Leaving thine outgrown shell by life's unresting sea.

Now my friends on this second Sunday of 1947 may we not all say together, each in his own place,—yes, say it aloud if you will, "My times are in Thy hand."

APPENDIX

BIOGRAPHICAL NOTES [1]

AUSTIN, WARREN ROBINSON (1877-   ). Born in Highgate, Vermont; Ph.B., University of Vermont, 1899; dr., *honoris causa*, Vermont, 1932, Columbia University, 1944, Norwich University, 1944; studied law, St. Albans, Vermont, 1899-1902; admitted to Vermont bar, 1902; Circuit of United States, 1906; Supreme Court of United States, 1914; Attorney, American International Corporation in China, 1916-17; elected United States Senator (Republican), 1931, reelected 1934, 1940; President, Vermont Bar Association, 1923; studied Palestine conditions, 1936; Puerto Rico judicial system, 1937; American delegate to Chapultepec Conference, 1945; head of the American delegation to the United Nations General Assembly, since 1946. (See also *Current Biography: 1944.*)

BONNELL, JOHN SUTHERLAND (1893-   ). Born in Prince Edward Island, Canada; A.B., Dalhousie University, 1919; B.D., Pine Hill Divinity Hall, Halifax, 1927, D.D. 1934; LL.D., Washington and Jefferson, 1943; Pastor of Canadian churches, 1922-35; pastor of Fifth Avenue Presbyterian Church, New York City, since 1935; lecturer, Theological Seminary, Princeton, since 1938; preacher in England, Scotland, 1941; served in Canadian Army, World War I, 1916-18; member, Sigma Xi; author of *Fifth Avenue Sermons,* 1936; *Pastoral Psychiatry,* 1938; *Britons Under Fire,* 1941; weekly broadcasts over the American Broadcasting Company networks. (See also *Current Biography: 1945.*)

BRIGANCE, WILLIAM NORWOOD (1896-   ). Born in Olive Branch, Mississippi; A.B., University of Nebraska, 1916,

[1] The chief sources of these notes are *Who's Who in America, Current Biography, Religious Leaders in America, International Who's Who, Who's Who in American Education, Directory of American Scholars,* and the *Congressional Directory.*

A.M., 1920; University of Chicago, 1921, University of Wisconsin, 1922; Ph.D., University of Iowa, 1930; secondary school teacher, 1916-17, 1920-22; professor of speech, Wabash College, 1922-36; professor and head of Department of English, University of Hawaii, 1936-38; again professor of speech, Wabash, since 1938; teacher, summer sessions, University of Nebraska, University of Southern California, University of Wisconsin and elsewhere; enlisted in regular army 1917, later 2nd lieutenant, 32nd Division, A.E.F.; president, Speech Association of America, 1946; Lambda Chi Alpha, Tau Kappa Alpha, Phi Beta Kappa, American Legion; author of numerous works including *The Spoken Word*, 1927, *Speech* (with W. G. Hedde) 1935; *Speech Composition*, 1937; editor (for National Association of Teachers of Speech) *A History and Criticism of American Public Address*, 1943; editor *Quarterly Journal of Speech*, 1942-44.

CANHAM, ERWIN DAIN (1904-   ).   Born in Auburn, Maine; A.B., Bates College, 1925; Rhodes Scholar, Oxford (England), B.A., 1936, M.A., 1936; reporter, *Christian Science Monitor,* 1925; covered sessions of League of Nations, 1925-28; reporter, London Naval Conference, 1930; head of Washington Bureau, *Christian Science Monitor,* 1932-39; general news editor, 1939-41; managing editor, 1941-44; editor since 1945; trips as reporter in Far East, 1935, 1946-47; radio commentator, 1938-39, and since 1945; Phi Beta Kappa, Delta Sigma Rho; vice president, American Society of Newspaper Editors, 1947.   (See also *Current Biography: 1945.*)

CARLETON, WILLIAM GRAVES.   Born in 1903, in Evansville, Indiana; A.B., Indiana University, 1926; A.M., 1928; J.D., University of Florida; professor of political science, University of Florida, and Chairman of Social Sciences in the General College; chairman of War Training Course in History for military personnel, University of Florida; speaker for Democratic National Committe, 1928, 1932, 1936; speaker at army camps throughout the United States, 1942; author of various articles on Middle Period in American history; member of Tau Kappa Alpha, honorary intercollegiate forensic society.

DENNY, GEORGE VERNON, JR. (1899-   ). Born in Washington, North Carolina; B.S., University of North Carolina, 1922; LL.D., Temple University, 1940; instructor in dramatic production, University of North Carolina, 1924-26; actor, 1926-27; manager of W. B. Feakins, Inc., 1927-28; director, Institute of Arts and Sciences, Columbia University, 1928-30; associate director, League of Political Education, 1931-37; founder and director, America's Town Meeting of the Air; treasurer, Economic Club of New York; member of executive board, American Association for Adult Education; president, Town Hall, Inc.; served, Students' Army Training Corps, 1918. (See also *Current Biography: 1940.*)

ERNST, MORRIS LEOPOLD (1888-   ). Born in Uniontown, Alabama; A.B., Williams College, 1909; LL.B., New York Law School, 1912; in business, New York City, 1911-15; member of Greenbaum, Wolff, and Ernst law firm, New York, since 1915; attorney for American Newspaper Guild; drafted legislation for Governor Lehman on banking and insurance; special assistant to Attorney-General in election fraud matters; special consultant to War Production Board; author, *America's Primer,* 1931; *Ultimate Power,* 1937; *The Censor Marches On* (with A. Lindey), 1939; other books and magazine articles; popular lecturer before colleges and clubs. (See also *Current Biography: 1940.*)

FRANKFURTER, FELIX (1882-   ). Born in Vienna, Austria; in the United States, 1894; A.B., College of City of New York, 1902; LL.B., Harvard, 1906; DC.L., Oxford, 1939; Assistant United States Attorney, Southern District of New York, 1906-10; professor, Harvard Law School, 1914-39; visiting professor, Oxford University, 1933-34; Major and Judge Advocate, O.R.C., U.S. Army; chairman, War Labor Policies Board, 1918; Associate Justice of Supreme Court of the United States since 1939; author, *The Case of Sacco and Vanzetti,* 1927; *The Business of the Supreme Court* (with J. M. Landis), 1928; *Labor Injunction* (with Nathan Greene), 1930; *Mr. Justice Holmes and the Supreme Court,* 1939; editor of several legal volumes. (See also *Current Biography: 1941.*)

HORTON, MILDRED McAFEE (Mrs. Douglas Horton) (1900-   ). Born in Parkville, Missouri; A.B., Vassar, 1920; M.A., Chicago, 1928; intercollegiate debater (against Wellesley); instructor, Monticello Seminary, 1920-22; professor of economics and sociology, Tusculum College, Greenville, Tennessee, 1923-25; dean of women and professor of sociology, Centre College, 1927-32; dean of women, Oberlin, 1934; president of Wellesley since 1936 (on leave, 1942-45); honorary degrees from Oberlin, Williams, Mt. Holyoke, Bates, Boston University, Wesleyan, and many other institutions; married Rev. Dr. Douglas Horton, 1945; director of Women's Reserve of U.S.N.R., with rank of lieutenant commander (later captain), 1942-45. (See also *Current Biography: 1942.*)

LILIENTHAL, DAVID ELI (1899-   ). Born in Morton, Illinois; A.B., Depauw University, 1920, LL.D., 1945; intercollegiate orator; LL.B., Harvard Law School, 1923; admitted to Illinois Bar, 1923; in practice of law, Chicago, 1923-31; edited Public Utilities and Carriers' Service for the Commerce Clearing House, 1931; director of the Tennessee Valley Authority, 1933-46; appointed chairman of Board of Directors, 1941; appointed Chairman of the Atomic Energy Commission, 1947; Phi Beta Kappa, Delta Sigma Rho; author, *T.V.A.: Democracy on the March*, 1944. (See also *Current Biography: 1944.*)

LIPPMANN, WALTER (1889-   ). Born in New York City; A.B., Harvard, 1910 (degree in 1909), graduate student, 1909-10; associate editor, *New Republic*, and editor, *New York World;* after 1931 special writer for *New York Herald Tribune* and other newspapers; assistant to Secretary of War, 1917; captain, U.S. Army Military Intelligence, A.E.F., 1917-18; member, Board of Overseers, Harvard, 1933-39; his column "Today and Tomorrow" in about 180 papers; member, Phi Beta Kappa; author, *A Preface to Politics*, 1913; *Liberty and the News*, 1920; *The Phantom Public*, 1925; *A Preface to Morals*, 1929; *The United States in World Affairs*, 1931; *Interpretations,* 1933-35; *The Good Society*, 1937; *The United States Foreign Policy*, 1943; and other books. (See also *Current Biography: 1940.*)

MCAFEE, MILDRED HELEN. *See* Horton, M. M.

MCCRARY, JOHN REAGAN, JR. (1910-   ). Born in Calvert, Texas; educated at Phillips Exeter Academy; was graduated at Yale with degree in architecture, 1932; newspaper reporter, editorial staff, *Daily Mirror*, until 1942; executive officer, *American Mercury*; film commentator, radio commentator; lieutenant colonel, U.S.A.A.F. in all theaters of war, World War II; Skull and Bones, Yale; author, *First of Many*.

MARSHALL, GEORGE CATLETT (1880-   ). Born at Uniontown, Pennsylvania; student, Virginia Military Institute, 1897-1901; honorary graduate, United States Infantry-Cavalry School, 1907; graduate, Army Staff College, 1908; honorary degrees at Washington and Jefferson, Pennsylvania Military College, William and Mary, Trinity, and elsewhere; mounted through the grades to major general, 1939; served in the Philippines, 1902-03, 1913-16; with A.E.F., 1917-19; on General Staff, and in Meuse-Argonne operations; in China, 1924-27; chief of staff with rank of general, 1939-1945; awarded the D.S.M. and many other military awards from United States and various other countries; on military mission to China, 1945-46; "One of the principal brains and powers behind the vast military effort of the Allies in World War II"; Secretary of State, 1946; author of *Selected Speeches and Statements of George C. Marshall*, 1946. (See also *Current Biography: 1940; March, 1947.*)

MORSE, WAYNE LYMAN (1900-   ). Born in Madison, Wisconsin; Ph.B., University of Wisconsin, 1923, M.A., 1924; LL.B., University of Minnesota, 1928; J.D., Columbia, 1932; instructor in argumentation, Wisconsin, 1924; assistant professor, Minnesota, 1924-28; faculty of law school, University of Oregon, 1928-30, dean and professor, 1931-44; special assistant to Attorney General of United States, 1936-39; arbitrator for U. S. Department of Labor, 1938-42; chairman, President's Emergency Board, 1941; member, War Labor Board, 1942-44; United States Senator from Oregon (Republican) since 1945; member of several national legal or educational committees or boards; member, Delta Sigma Rho, Order of the Coif; author,

A Survey of the Grand Jury System, 1931; *The Administration of Criminal Justice in Oregon,* 1932; other legal publications. (See also *Current Biography: 1942.*)

MURRAY, PHILIP (1886-   ). Born in Blantyre, Scotland; came to the United States, 1902, naturalized, 1911; member, International Board of United Mine Workers of America, 1912, international vice-president, 1920; president of Congress of Industrial Organizations since 1940; member of numerous governmental commissions related to labor problems. (See also *Current Biography: 1941.*)

PEPPER, CLAUDE DENSON (1900-   ). Born in Dudleyville, Alabama; A.B., University of Alabama, 1921; LL.B., Harvard, 1924; practiced law in Florida after 1925; numerous offices, elective and appointive, in Florida; United States Senator from Florida (Democrat) since 1936. (See also *Current Biography: 1941.*)

PRICE, BYRON (1891-   ). Born in Topeka, Indiana; A.B., Wabash, 1912, LL.D., 1943; had been almost continuously with the Associated Press, 1912-1941; member A.E.F., World War I, in Meuse-Argonne offensive; after 1919 with the Washington, D.C. bureau of the Associated Press; later executive news editor; on December 16, 1941 appointed Director of Censorship; vice-president of the Motion Picture Producers and Distributors of America, 1945-47; Secretary General for Administrative and Financial Affairs of the United Nations, 1947; Phi Beta Kappa. (See also *Current Biography: 1942.*)

SHEEN, FULTON JOHN (1895-   ). Born in El Paso, Illinois; A.B., St. Viatore College, 1917, A.M., 1919; St. Paul Seminary, 1919; S.T.B. and J.C.B., Catholic University of America, 1920; Ph.D., Louvain University, 1923; D.D., Rome, 1924; honorary degrees from Marquette, Loyola, and other colleges and universities; member of faculty, Catholic University of America since 1926; famous preacher on the Catholic Hour radio program since 1930; author, *God and Intelligence,* 1925; *Divine Immanence,* 1931; *The Way of the Cross,* 1932; *The*

Eternal Galilean, 1934; the *Mystical Body of Christ,* 1935; and other publications. (See also *Current Biography: 1941.*)

SOCKMAN, RALPH WASHINGTON (1889-   ). Born in Mount Vernon, Ohio; educated at Ohio Wesleyan University, A.B., 1911, D.D., 1923; Columbia University, A.M., 1913, Ph.D., 1917; Union Theological Seminary, graduate, 1916; numerous honorary degrees; minister, Madison Avenue Methodist Church (now Christ Church), since 1917; preacher, National Radio Pulpit, since 1937; Lyman Beecher lecturer at Yale, 1941; trustee of a number of colleges and universities; member of Phi Beta Kappa, Delta Sigma Rho; author, *Live for Tomorrow,* 1939; *Now To Live,* 1947; and numerous other volumes on religion. (See also *Current Biography: 1946.*)

STRAIGHT, MICHAEL WHITNEY (1916-   ). Born in Southampton, New York; educated at Lincoln School, New York City; Dartington Hall, Totnes, England; London School of Economics, 1932 (under Harold J. Laski); Trinity College, Cambridge, 1933-37 (under John Meynard Keynes); M.A. in economics, "triple-first" honors; first American to be elected president of Cambridge Union, 1936; Department of State, 1939-40, 1940-41; editor of *New Republic,* 1943, and publisher since 1946; U.S. Army Air Forces, 1943-45; author, *Make This the Last War: the Future of the United Nations,* 1943. (See also *Current Biography: 1944.*)

TAFT, ROBERT ALPHONSO (1889-   ). Born in Cincinnati, Ohio; attended public schools of Cincinnati and the Taft School; was graduated from Yale University, A.B., 1910; Harvard University, LL.B., 1913; attorney at law; assistant counsel for the United States Food Administration, 1917-18; counsel for the American Relief Administration, 1919; Republican member of the Ohio House of Representatives, 1921-26, speaker, 1926; Ohio State Senate, 1931-32; United States Senate since 1939. (See also *Current Biography: 1940.*)

TRUMAN, HARRY S. (1894-   ). Born in Lamar, Missouri; student, Kansas City School of Law, 1923-25; captain,

Field Artillery, World War I; judge, Jackson County Court, 1922-24; presiding judge, 1926-34; United States Senator from Missouri, 1935-41, reelected for the term 1941-47; elected Vice President on the Democratic ticket, November 1944; sworn in as President of the United States on the death of President Roosevelt, April, 1945. (See also *Current Biography: 1942; 1945.*)

VANDENBERG, ARTHUR HENDRICK (1884-   ). Born in Grand Rapids, Michigan; studied law at the University of Michigan, 1901-02, honorary A.M., 1925; LL.D., Hope College, 1926; editor of *Grand Rapids Herald,* 1906-28; United States Senator, since 1928; Chairman of Republican Senate Legislative Committee, 1933-34; received 76 votes for Republican presidential nomination, Philadelphia, 1940; American delegate, United Nations Organization Conference, San Francisco, 1945; United States Delegate to United Nations, 1945-47; chairman, Senate Committee on Foreign Affairs, 1947; member, Authors' Club, London, England; author, *Alexander Hamilton, the Greatest American,* 1921; *If Hamilton Were Here Today,* 1923; *The Trail of a Tradition,* 1925. (See also *Current Biography: 1940.*)

WALLACE, HENRY AGARD (1888-   ). Born in Adair County, Iowa; B.S., Iowa State College, 1910, honorary M.S. in agriculture, 1920; editor of Wallaces' Farmer since 1910; Secretary of Agriculture in Cabinet of President Roosevelt, 1933-40; Vice President of the United States, 1941-45; visited Latin America, 1943; defeated for nomination for reelection as Vice President on the Democratic ticket in 1944, but campaigned actively for Roosevelt; appointment as Secretary of Commerce confirmed in March, 1945, after vigorous Senate opposition; resigned, September, 1946; spoke in England, France, and other European countries, April, 1947, in opposition to Truman policies; author of *America Must Choose,* 1934; *Statesmanship and Religion,* 1934; *Whose Constitution?* 1936; *Paths to Plenty,* 1938; and other books and articles on agricultural, political, and religious topics; editor of *New Republic* since 1946. (See also *Current Biography: 1940; January 1947.*)

WISE, STEPHEN SAMUEL (1874-   ). Born in Budapest, Hungary; College of City of New York, 1887-91; A.B., Columbia, 1892; Ph.D., 1901; honorary degrees, Temple, Syracuse, Rollins, Bates, Oregon, Hebrew Union College, and elsewhere; founder and since 1907 Rabbi, Free Synagogue of New York; founder, Federation of American Zionists; founder, Zionist Organization of America; president of delegation of American Jewish Congress at Peace Conference at Paris; officer, World Zionist Organization; president, American Jewish Congress, World Jewish Congress; officer in many other professional, philanthropic, and religious organizations; author of *Free Synagogue Pulpit* (10 volumes); *How to Face Life; As I See It;* and other volumes; editor, *Opinion.* (See also *Current Biography: 1941.*)

CUMULATED AUTHOR INDEX

An author index to the volumes of *Representative American Speeches* for the years 1937-1938 through 1946-1947. The date following the title of each speech indicates the volume in which it appears.

University Debaters' Annuals

E. M. PHELPS, Ed. *Cloth. Price $2.25*

Series of yearbooks, each a collection of representative intercollegiate debates on important questions of the day. Constructive and rebuttal speeches for both sides. Each debate is accompanied by selected bibliography and briefs.

Vol. XXXIII. 1946-1947.

United Nations: A world organization; Statehood for Hawaii; Our national labor policy; War with Russia; Cooperation with Russia; What of our future; Labor legislation; Public health legislation; Atomic energy; Alliance with Great Britain and the United States.

Vol. XXXII. 1945-1946.

Fraternities and sororities; The United States foreign economic policy; Ownership of patents on atomic energy; American college in the postwar world; Compulsory health insurance; British colonial policy in India; Compulsory arbitration of industrial disputes.

Vol. XXXI. 1944-1945.

The Partition of Germany; World Peace Settlement; Admission of All Races to State Universities; Cartels; Compulsory Military Training; Permanent Government Economic Controls; Settling Labor Disputes by Legislation.

Vol. XXX. 1943-1944. o.p.

Vol. XXIX. 1942-1943. o.p.

Vol. XXVIII. 1941-1942.

Federal Incorporation of Labor Unions; A League of Nations; Military Training; Failure of Colleges to Meet Student Needs; A Federation of Democracies Based on the Churchill-Roosevelt Principles; A Federal Sales Tax; Compulsory Saving; Postwar Reconstruction; Western Hemisphere Solidarity; Freedom of Speech in Time of National Emergency.

Vol. XXVII. 1940-1941.

Industry Can Solve the Employment Problem; Conscription of Capital for Defense; Preservation of Democracy Through Decreased Government Control; Interstate Trade Barriers; Japanese Aggression; Union of United States and British Commonwealth of Nations; Regulation of the American Press; Compulsory Military Training; Strikes in Defense Industries; Western Hemisphere Defense.

Vol. XXVI. 1939-1940.

The Basis of a Lasting Peace; Shall the United States Enter the War?; Government Ownership and Operation of Railroads; Neutrality of the United States; Extension of Reciprocal Trade Agreements; The Third Term for President; Should the Roosevelt Administration Be Approved?; The Dies Committee; Civil Liberties; Labor; Foreign Affairs; Government and Business.

Speech and Debating

Anthology of Public Speeches. Mabel Platz, comp. 895p. 1940. $3.75.

Selections from speeches representing all cultures from Pericles and Cicero to Chiang Kai-shek and Neville Chamberlain.

Competitive Debate: Rules and Strategy. By George McCoy Musgrave. 128p. 1945. $1.25.

Debate Coaching. By Carroll P. Lahman. (Handbook Series. Ser IV, Vol. 1) 2d rev. ed. 428p. 1936. $2.40.

A manual for teachers and coaches. Especially helpful to the inexperienced coach.

Discussion Methods: Explained and Illustrated. By J. V. Garland and C. F. Phillips. (Reference Shelf. Vol. XII, No. 2) 2d ed. rev. 378p. 1940. $1.25.

High School Forensics: An Integrated Program. By Arnold E. Melzer. 153p. 1940. 90c.

How to Debate: A Textbook for Beginners. By H. B. Summers and F. L. Whan. 336p. 1940. $1.25. Revised edition in preparation.

Oral Interpretation of Literature in American Colleges and Universities. By Mary Margaret Robb. 242p. 1941. $2.75.

Representative American Speeches. By A. Craig Baird, comp. Published annually in The Reference Shelf. Eight volumes now available from 1937-1938 to 1945-1946 (1938-1939 o.p.) inclusive. Price $1.25 a volume, except 1939-1940 which is $1.50.

Each volume contains representative speeches by eminent men and women on public occasions during the year. Each speech is prefaced by a short sketch of the speaker and the occasion.

Selected Readings in Rhetoric and Public Speaking. By Lester Thonssen, comp. 324p. 1942. $3.